The Which? Guide to Giving and Inheriting

About the author

Jonquil Lowe trained as an economist, worked for several years in the City as an investment analyst, and is a former head of the Money Group at Consumers' Association. She now works as a freelance researcher and journalist. She writes extensively on all areas of personal finance and is author of several other books, including *Be Your Own Financial Adviser, The Which? Guide to Planning Your Pension, Take Control of Your Pension* (an Action Pack), *The Which? Guide to Money in Retirement, The Which? Guide to Shares*, and, with Sara Williams, *The Lloyds-TSB Tax Guide.*

The Which? Guide to Giving and Inheriting

Jonquil Lowe

which

?

Which? Books are commissioned by
Consumers' Association and published by
Which? Ltd, 2 Marylebone Road, London NW1 4DF
Email: books@which.net

Distributed by The Penguin Group:
Penguin Books Ltd, 80 Strand, London WC2R 0RL

First edition October 1992
Seventh edition July 2003
Reprinted October 2003
Reprinted February 2004
Reprinted September 2004

British Library Cataloguing in Publication Data
A catalogue record for this book is available from the British Library

ISBN 0 85202 946 2

For a full list of *Which?* books, please call 0800 252100, access our
website at www.which.net or write to Which Books, PO Box 44
Hertford SG14 1SH. A selection of available titles is listed at the back of
this book

Editorial and Production: Alethea Doran, Caroline Ellerby, Vicky Fisher,
Robert Gray
Original cover concept by Sarah Harmer
Cover photograph by Mark Stevenson, ace photoagency

Typeset by Karran Group, Guildford, Surrey
Printed and bound in England by Clays Ltd, St Ives plc

Contents

Introduction 7
1 Gifts and taxes 11

Part 1 Giving to charity
2 Choosing the charities 21
3 Special schemes for giving to charity 31
4 Other ways of giving to charity 49

Part 2 Lifetime gifts to family and friends
5 Tax-free gifts 65
6 Capital gains tax on lifetime gifts 79
7 Inheritance tax on lifetime gifts 107
8 Income tax and gifts 123
9 Using trusts 131
10 Taxation of trusts 149
11 Lifetime gift planning 167

Part 3 Inheritance
12 Making a will 175
13 Tax at the time of death 195
14 Inheritance planning 215

Part 4 Special situations
15 Your home as a gift 237
16 Giving to children 243

Glossary 259
Addresses* 269
Index 277

*An asterisk next to the name of an organisation in the text indicates that the address can be found in this section.

Introduction

Inheritance tax has been described as a voluntary tax because there are so many opportunities for planning away a tax bill. But this should not lull you into thinking that this tax regime is benign. Fail to plan and the penalty is a hefty 40 per cent bite out of whatever you leave your heirs.

Moreover, inheritance tax is no longer a tax on the rich. This tax and its predecessors were originally designed to catch inherited estates passed on from generation to generation. Now its jaws also snap when wealth that has been built up through hard (and taxed) work is passed on. Many families who would not consider themselves to be wealthy are within the scope of this tax, often because of the value of their homes.

In 2003–4, the first £255,000 of everything you leave is tax-free; everything else is taxed at 40 per cent. Some 69 per cent of households in Britain own their own home outright or are buying with a mortgage. Five years ago, the average UK house price was just over £72,000 which was around a third of the estate value at which inheritance tax kicked in. In 2003, the average house price has risen to £127,000 which is almost half the inheritance tax threshold. And the regional variations are enormous. If you live in London or Southeast England, the value of your home on its own is likely to use up most or all of the tax-free slice, let alone any other possessions you might want to hand on.

Fortunately there are numerous ways to avoid inheritance tax – for example, making lifetime gifts, equalising estates if you are a couple, and changing the way you jointly own possessions. This guide shows you the ins and outs of these and other techniques, and how to minimise the other taxes (capital gains tax and income tax) that could affect your inheritance planning. Part 2 looks in depth at the range of lifetime gifts you can make without incurring a tax bill, while Part 3 deals with making a will and ensuring that your bequests are tax-efficient and your aims are achieved. Part 4 draws together the planning points that apply to two common situations: giving away your home and making gifts to children.

Planning to minimise tax on death is particularly difficult if your major asset is your home or if you can't afford to lose the income generated by assets that you might otherwise have been able to give away. In this edition, an expanded Chapter 13 outlines some of the more complex planning tools that might work for you.

In some cases you may want to arrange gifts but to retain some control over how they are used – for example, if the recipient is as yet too young to handle income or wealth wisely, or if, say, you want to provide income for your widow but ensure your assets eventually pass to your children by an earlier marriage. These are classic situations where using a trust could be the answer. Chapters 9 and 10 describe the different types of trusts available, when using these might be appropriate and the tax implications.

Using trusts and complex planning tools are both areas where you should seek professional help. By giving you a foundation of knowledge of the tools available, this book will help you to explain your wishes to a solicitor or tax adviser and appraise the advice you are given.

It's not just gifts to family and friends that can be wrapped in an unnecessary tax bill. There is now enormous scope for making charitable donations tax-efficiently. Cash donations of any size – small or large; and whether regular or ad hoc – can qualify for tax relief with the minimum of admin on your part, and can give a tax boost both to the charity and you. And gifts of shares or land can be even more tax-efficient. Part 1 of this guide explains how you can take advantage of the various tax schemes for giving to charity, including the new arrangements for 'carrying back' donations to the previous tax year and paying tax refunds direct to a charity of your choice. It also looks at other methods of giving to charity, such as the National Lottery and affinity credit cards, and asks how efficient these are as a way of making your gifts.

Information in this guide applies if you are resident and domiciled in the UK and making gifts to people, trusts, charities and other organisations based in the UK. The tax system applies throughout the UK. However other laws – for example, concerning intestacy and trusts – are sometimes different in Scotland and Northern Ireland from those for England and Wales. (This is particularly so in Scotland, where law has developed from a different tradition than in the rest of the UK.) Where there are variations, the guide makes this clear and outlines the different systems that apply.

This fully revised edition takes account of changes up to and including the April 2003 Budget. However, it should be noted that Budget measures can be changed during the passage of the Finance Bill through Parliament (expected to become law in July 2003) and that the government may make additional announcements in its Pre-Budget Report due in November 2003.

Chapter 1
Gifts and taxes

Gifts to charity

It is a fortunate paradox that people are willing to give to total strangers through the medium of charities. But, while it is not so odd that we care about, and want to help with, such matters as poverty, suffering, the global standard of living, protecting culture, bio-diversity and saving the environment, it is surely very strange that many people ignore the encouragement which the government offers to charitable giving in the form of tax reliefs.

There are numerous ways to give to charity, including street collections, envelopes through the door, telethons, church collections, mailshots and sponsorship. Often giving is spontaneous and unplanned, but with a minimum of fuss many of these gifts can now be made tax-efficiently. And where you have agreed to donate regularly – say, by direct debit – it does not make sense to overlook the tax-efficient schemes open to you. These are designed to encourage charitable giving by either adding tax relief to the amount you give (boosting the amount the charity gets), giving tax relief directly to you (reducing the cost of your donation), or both.

According to the National Council for Voluntary Organisations (NCVO),★ the British public gave a total of £6.76 billion to charity in 2001, with an average monthly donation of £12.12. (This figure excludes legacies left to charity in wills.) Around two-thirds of the population make charitable donations, although a tiny 6 per cent account for nearly 60 per cent of the total given. However, the proportion of the population who give tax-efficiently is small. A joint survey by the NCVO, Charities Aid Foundation (CAF)★ and Inland Revenue★ in March 2001 found that only 7 per cent of the population use gift aid, 3 per cent covenants and 2 per cent payroll giving – see Chapter 3 for details of these schemes. This low take-up means that both charities and individuals are missing out on substantial amounts of tax relief.

Inland Revenue data show that in the 2001–2 tax year just over £2 billion was given to charity using tax-efficient schemes. Charities were able to claim back nearly £450 million of tax relief on these donations and it is estimated that taxpayers received another £90 million or so direct. This suggests that some £4.7 billion of donations that could have been made tax-efficiently were not. So potentially charities lost £1.3 billion of tax relief and individuals paid perhaps £200 million more tax than they needed to by failing to use the tax-efficient schemes.

Part 1 of this book looks at the range of charitable and similar gifts which now qualify for tax reliefs and shows you how to use the special schemes for giving to charity. It also looks at a variety of other ways to give, such as the National Lottery and affinity credit cards, and asks whether these can be a useful way of helping charities.

Gifts to family and friends

Giving to people you know is not so paradoxical. Most people see themselves as part of a social group and care about the well-being of its members. The most intimate circle is the family where there is a natural desire to pass on wealth, particularly from one generation to another.

The distribution of wealth

Left unchecked, inheritance within families would, sooner or later, lead to a concentration of wealth in the hands of relatively few people. However, most advanced societies take the view that wealth should not be distributed too unevenly. The reasons for this are varied – political, economic and humane. For example, a wide gulf between the poorest people and the richest may encourage political unrest; the votes of relatively poorer people can perhaps be 'bought' by redistributing wealth to them. Economic activity may be improved if wealth is spread more evenly as a result of the different spending and saving patterns of the rich and poor.

But there are less pragmatic reasons too. The majority of people want to accumulate enough possessions and wealth to support an enjoyable and sustainable lifestyle but are not comfortable ignoring the relative, or absolute, poverty of others. Our sense of justice demands that others should also have the chance of a reasonable life.

Yet, even in a society as mature as that of the UK, the distribution of wealth across the population is uneven, as Table 1.1 (see page 14) shows. Just one-tenth of the adult population in the UK owns well over half of all the wealth, and a quarter of the population owns nearly three-quarters of all the wealth.

The distribution of wealth is now more even than it was in the early part of the last century (see Table 1.2, page 14) which reflects, in part, the deliberate redistribution policies of successive governments. However, the trend reversed in the early 1990s with the gap between rich and poor widening again.

The main tool which governments use directly to influence the distribution of wealth is the tax system. Taxes can be used to 'take from the rich' in several ways. One obvious way might be to tax people regularly on the amount of wealth they have. Wealth taxes are used in some countries and have been proposed for the UK in the past.[1] At present in the UK, however, there is no tax on simply *owning* wealth. Instead, the emphasis is on taxing wealth as it changes hands.

Taxing wealth and gifts

Originally, taxing the transfer of wealth was confined to a tax at the time of death and can be traced back to the Anglo-Saxon 'heriot' – a feudal tax paid to the local lord on the death of a tenant. But the modern form of this type of taxation started with estate duty, introduced in 1894 with a swingeing top rate of 8 per cent!

Although estate duty was designed mainly to tax the passing on of wealth at the time of death, it also taxed gifts made in the few years before death to close an otherwise obvious loophole: that is, avoiding the tax through last-minute 'death-bed bequests'. Even so, with planning, it was possible to avoid the worst ravages of the estate duty, particularly by giving away wealth during one's lifetime.

In 1975, Harold Wilson's government scrapped estate duty in favour of capital transfer tax (CTT). This was a fully fledged gifts tax and estate duty rolled into one. The aim was to tax all transfers of

[1] *Wealth Tax*, Labour government green paper, London, HMSO, 1974.

Table 1.1 Who owns what in the UK (2000)

Percentage of population[1]	Percentage of wealth owned[2]
1	22
5	42
10	54
25	74
50	94

Notes: [1] Percentage of the most wealthy of the UK adult population.
[2] Percentage of all UK wealth excluding pension rights.
Source: Inland Revenue, 2003.

Table 1.2 Changing fortunes

Year	Percentage of wealth[1] owned by the wealthiest 1%[2]	Percentage of wealth[1] owned by the wealthiest 10%[2]
1911–13	69	92
1924–30	62	91
1936–8	56	88
1954	43	79
1960	38	77
1966	32	72
1972	30	72
1976	21	50
1980	19	50
1985	18	49
1990	18	47
1995	19	50
1998	23	56
2000	22	54

Notes: [1] Percentage of all UK wealth.
[2] Percentage of the most wealthy of the UK adult population.
Sources: *Diamond Commission Initial Report on the Distribution of Income and Wealth*, HMSO, 1975; *Inland Revenue Statistics 2000*, London, TSO; Inland Revenue, 2003.

wealth whether made in life or at death – with a few exceptions, such as gifts between husband and wife, small gifts to other people and up to £2,000 a year (in the 1975–6 tax year) of otherwise taxable transfers. And there were special reliefs to help farmers and businesses. Taxable gifts were added together and the first slice of this total was tax-free. Tax, at progressively higher rates, was levied on subsequent slices until it reached a top rate of 75 per cent. Although this appeared to be a serious tax that would affect even people of relatively modest means, in the event CTT lasted only 11 years.

The Conservative government came to power in 1979 determined to reduce the role of the state and encourage individual initiative. Reform of the tax system was an important part of its strategy and CTT was on the agenda. In 1986, CTT was replaced by inheritance tax (IHT). In many respects the two taxes are similar but a major difference is that under the IHT regime most lifetime gifts between people are free from tax, apart from gifts made in the last seven years before the death of the giver. This means that the majority of gifts you make in the course of your day-to-day affairs are not caught up in the IHT net. When the Labour party came to power in 1997, its manifesto included a commitment to '*fair taxation*' designed to '*benefit the many, not the few*'. It was widely thought that a tightening of IHT was on the cards, in particular the possibility that the taxation of most lifetime gifts might be reintroduced. But, at the time of writing, Labour is into its second term and no substantial reforms have so far been made.

The switch from CTT to IHT has not been so benign in other ways. Until 1987, IHT, like CTT and estate duty before it, was levied according to a scale at progressively higher rates. From 14 March 1988 onwards, a single, hefty rate of tax (40 per cent on death, 20 per cent during life) is charged whatever the scale of the giving. The threshold at which tax starts has been raised substantially but, with house prices rising by more than 40 per cent over the two years to end-2002, many people who consider themselves to have relatively modest means worry that they may now find themselves within the inheritance tax net. And government statistics do show a steady upward creep in the number of estates caught by inheritance tax (see Table 1.3, page 16).

You may need to watch out for other taxes too. When you give away something (other than cash) during your lifetime, you have 'disposed' of it – just as if you had sold it. If the value of the thing has risen since you first acquired it, you will be judged to have made a profit from owning it and there may be capital gains tax (CGT) to

Table 1.3 More estates falling within the inheritance tax net

	1998	2000	2003
Proportion of estates paying inheritance tax on death	3%	4%	5%
Number of estates paying inheritance tax on death	19,000	23,000	29,500
Average house price	£72,196	£85,005	£127,040
Inheritance tax threshold	£223,000	£234,000	£255,000
Average house price as a proportion of inheritance tax threshold	32.4%	36.3%	49.8%

Sources: Inland Revenue statistics, Budget 2003 announcement, HBOS house price index.

pay – even though you did not actually receive the profit yourself. And income which you give away can sometimes be like a boomerang which keeps coming back to haunt your tax assessments.

Part 2 examines the various taxes you need to watch out for when making gifts in your lifetime and looks at how to arrange your gifts tax-efficiently. Chapter 11 pulls together key tips for planning your lifetime giving. In addition, Part 2 discusses using 'trusts' (special legal arrangements), which can be a way of giving something but retaining some control over how the gift is used. Contrary to popular opinion, trusts are not just for the very wealthy; they can be useful even if you have fairly small sums to give.

As with charitable giving, the pitfalls of the taxes on gifts to family and friends can often be avoided if you plan ahead. Nowhere is this more crucial than in the area of inheritance planning. The first step is, of course, to make a will – though seven out of ten people do not even do this.[2] Yet, without a will, your possessions may not reach the people you want to leave them to and you lose a chance to plan away a possible tax bill.

Part 3 considers the problems of estates where no will is made, explains how gifts made at the time of death are taxed and shows some steps which can be taken to help you develop an effective inheritance plan. In the last resort, it may even be possible for your heirs to rearrange gifts made to them under your will (or in

---

[2] Survey by NOP, 1998.

accordance with the law if you left no will) and Part 3 also takes a look at how these measures work.

Part 4 draws together some of the issues covered throughout the book which you should consider when contemplating special types of gift. First it looks at what is possibly your most valuable asset – your home. Although essentially your home is no different from any other asset, it is often the one which poses the most difficult questions over how best to balance your intention to give against the desire to avoid unnecessary tax. Secondly, Part 4 gathers together the planning points to consider when making gifts to children and grandchildren.

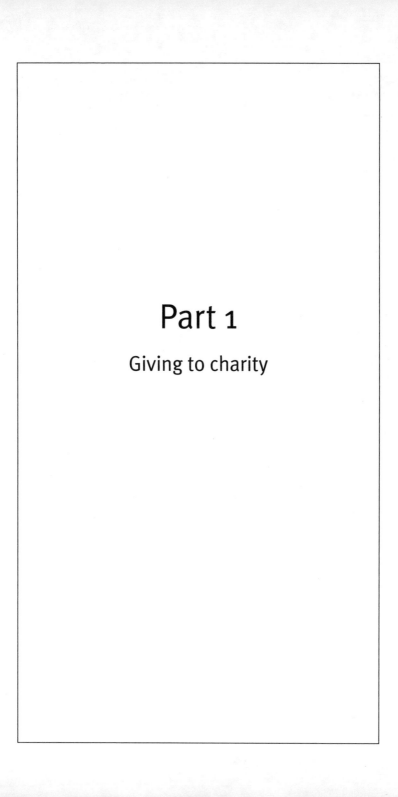

Part 1

Giving to charity

Chapter 2
Choosing the charities

IS IT A CHARITY?

'How odd,' said Mary, as she joined the rest of the family around the tea table. 'That phone call was from a man saying he was collecting money for a charity and would I make a donation over the phone with my credit card?'

Mary and Philip support several charities: they respond to regular postal appeals from Save the Children, buy Christmas gifts through an Oxfam catalogue, belong to the National Trust and often seek out bargains in the local charity shop. It is likely that their names are on various lists which are passed on to other charities, so Mary was not surprised to be contacted out of the blue. 'But I didn't like to give anything,' she said. 'I've never heard of the charity – though he did say it was registered, whatever that means. I had no way of knowing whether he was genuine . . .'

What is a charity?

Charities are part of the 'voluntary sector' of the economy. The voluntary sector is made up of a very diverse range of organisations – from youth clubs to poverty relief groups, from local fête committees to conservation groups – whose aim is to benefit some specified group or groups of people or society as a whole. Often voluntary groups are run by lowly paid or unpaid volunteers but others are large, highly organised concerns with paid workers and well-developed management systems. Voluntary groups often rely on fund-raising, gifts or grants for their finance.

Charities are distinct from the rest of the voluntary sector because they benefit from special tax status which makes them largely exempt from most taxes. There are over 186,000 registered charities in England and Wales[3] and maybe another 100,000 or more which are not registered. A high proportion of these are very small and many are thought to be inactive. Currently, in order to be a charity, an organisation must show that its purposes fall into at least one of the following areas:

- the relief of poverty
- the advancement of education
- the advancement of religion
- the pursuit of other aims which are judged beneficial to the community
- the promotion of urban and rural regeneration
- relief of unemployment
- the promotion of community participation in healthy recreation.

It is easy to think of examples of charities helping to relieve poverty that fit the first category: Oxfam, Save the Children, Shelter, Help the Aged. People are often surprised, however, at what counts as a charity in the other categories. For example, which of the following do *you* think are charities: Action on Smoking and Health (ASH), the National Anti-Vivisection Society, the Royal Opera House, the 'Moonies'? Table 2.1 gives you the answers; it shows the results of a survey carried out some time ago by *Which?* magazine to test its subscribers' perceptions of which organisations were charities.

More recently, a survey for the National Council for Voluntary Organisations (NCVO)★ found that 80 per cent of respondents did not know the Royal Opera House, Covent Garden, is a charity, and more than half of younger respondents thought incorrectly that the Child Support Agency is a charity.

The second category of charities – for the promotion of education – is not to be confused with education itself; its scope is much wider and it can cover virtually any field, including medical research, and making available musical and sporting activities, as well as actively passing on skills and knowledge. For example, this category covers charities as diverse as UK Cancer Research, the Royal Opera House

---

[3]Charity Commission 2003.

Table 2.1 *Which?* subscribers' perception of what counts as a charity

Subscribers were asked: which of the following do you think are registered charities?	Percentage of responses			Correct answer
	Yes	No	Don't know	
National Trust	68	16	14	Yes
The Unification Church ('Moonies')	28	47	23	Yes
Anti-apartheid Movement	6	54	37	No
Royal Opera House, Covent Garden	27	35	35	Yes
Child Poverty Action Group	73	7	19	Yes
National Anti-Vivisection Society	33	25	39	No
Shelter	82	4	12	Yes
Howard League for Penal Reform	26	20	52	Yes
Eton College	18	47	32	Yes
Action on Smoking and Health	21	38	38	Yes
Lord's Day Observance Society	21	30	46	Yes
National Canine Defence League	57	10	30	Yes

Source: *Which?* questionnaire, unpublished, 1990.

Covent Garden, British Red Cross Society and ASH, as well as more obviously educational bodies such as the Pre-school Learning Alliance and a number of schools.

The third category includes bodies such as the Salvation Army, Church Missionary Society and churches themselves. The fourth category enables charitable status to be given to bodies such as the National Trust, World Wide Fund for Nature and the Royal Society for the Prevention of Cruelty to Animals (RSPCA).

The next two categories are relatively new and could simply be covered by 'other aims which are judged beneficial to the community'. But recognising them as specific categories makes clear the increasing role in modern society of bodies that are trying to revive their communities and local economies and to ease unemployment – often the root cause of poverty in the UK.

In November 2001, 'the promotion of community participation in healthy recreation' was recognised as a separate charitable purpose. This is distinct from simply the promotion of sport which is not recognised as charitable. For sports bodies to qualify they must be capable of improving health and fitness and be open to anyone. However, sports clubs that do not fully meet these criteria or have chosen not to register as charities might still benefit from many of the tax advantages available to charities under arrangements for community amateur sports clubs introduced in the 2002 Budget – see Chapter 3.

Under present rules, organisations whose aims are partly or wholly political cannot be charities, even if part of their work falls into one or more of the categories above. But this does not mean that charities have to be totally apolitical. A charity is allowed to try to influence political decisions but only in the course of pursuing its charitable aims. It must not be too proactive in the means it chooses. This is a grey area and even well-established charities have fallen foul of the rules: for example, in 1991 Oxfam was warned that some of its campaigning to relieve distress and suffering in areas such as the Middle East and South Africa had unwittingly strayed too far over the line and amounted to advocating political change. In future it would have to curb such political activities.

To clarify the position, in 1995 the Charity Commission* published guidelines setting out what political activities charities can and cannot participate in. They are allowed to conduct political campaigns, provided the aims are charitable and the campaigns rely on reasoned, rather than emotive, arguments. To this end, charities can analyse and comment on party political electioneering, they can publish the voting records of MPs and they can give supporters ready-made letters to send to MPs or government ministers. Charities must not support any political party and may not participate in party political demonstrations.

Charities of the future

At the time of writing, the government was reviewing the way charitable status is defined and considering changes to the law to clarify what counts as a charity and increase the emphasis on such organisations providing public benefit.

The proposals include redefining charities as organisations that provide public benefit and have one or more of the following purposes:

- prevention and relief of poverty
- advancement of education

- advancement of religion
- advancement of health
- social and community advancement
- advancement of culture, arts and heritage
- advancement of amateur sport
- promotion of human rights, conflict resolution and reconciliation
- advancement of environmental protection and improvement
- other purposes beneficial to the community.

The inclusion of new categories, such as promotion of human rights, means that organisations such as Amnesty International would probably become eligible for charitable status. Charities would also be encouraged to campaign for social change.

With the increased emphasis on public benefit, charities which charge large fees for their services (with the effect that many people cannot afford them) – such as public schools – would be required to show how their activities have a public character in order to retain their charitable status.

It is not yet clear whether these proposals will be amended or when they might be implemented.

What does 'registered' mean?

In general, charities in England and Wales must be registered with the Charity Commission,★ which is the government body responsible for checking that an organisation's purposes really are charitable, investigating abuse (for example, fraud or negligent use of charitable funds) and helping charities to operate effectively. But, contrary to popular belief, not all charities must be, or indeed are, 'registered charities'.

Becoming registered is not the same as being granted charitable status. Many types of charities are excluded from the need to register but are still able to benefit from the special tax status. They include universities, voluntary schools, churches and many very small charities (for which the administrative burden of registration would be ridiculously great given the scale of their activities). Charity Commission figures show that, of the registered charities in England and Wales, nearly two-thirds have an income of less than £10,000 a year. Fewer than three charities out of every hundred take in more

Collector's certificate of authority and badge

<table>
<tr><td>

HOUSE-TO-HOUSE COLLECTIONS ACT
Collector's certificate of authority

NAME OF *Ivor Pound*
Penny Hill, Castle Canton

is hereby authorised to collect for

XYZ SOCIETY FOR THE RELIEF OF POVERTY
44 Almshouse Lane, London, NW10

IN DURING THE PERIOD *Penny Hill* 5–11 *May 2003*

Signed
I M Shakepot Director

Signature of Collector
Ivor Pound

</td><td>

HOUSE-TO-HOUSE
COLLECTIONS ACT

**XYZ SOCIETY FOR
THE RELIEF OF
POVERTY**

AUTHORISED
COLLECTOR'S BADGE

Signature of collector
Ivor Pound

**A registered charity
No. 123456**

</td></tr>
</table>

than £1 million a year. But these very large charities account for over three-quarters of all the income going to the registered charities.

In Scotland, the Scottish Charities Office★ is responsible for the regulation of charities. In Northern Ireland, this is the responsibility of the Charities Branch of the Department for Social Development.★

Checking out charity collections

Charities raise funds in a wide range of ways: street collections, door-to-door collections, donation boxes in shops and pubs, sponsorships, postal appeals, TV appeals, even telephone appeals.

Though the amounts given are generally small, surveys for the NCVO show that door-to-door and street collections and buying raffle tickets are probably the most commonly used methods of giving to charity. Whereas you might discard an appeal letter, say, it is hard to refuse a direct appeal for a small donation, even if you have never heard of the particular charity. So, how can you be sure that the collection is genuinely for charity?

If people arrive at your door collecting money, they must by law carry a collector's certificate of authority (see example above) showing the name, address and signature of the collector, the purpose of the collection and the time period during which the collection is to be made. Similarly, street collectors must carry a written authority from the organisation promoting the collection (which may be the charity or a specialist promoter). Door-to-door collectors and street collectors are also required to wear a prominent badge, which is provided by the charity, while they are collecting (see example opposite). Do not be afraid to ask to see a collector's authority and do not give money to anyone who cannot produce such a document.

You might be asked to help with a street or door-to-door collection. Before agreeing, satisfy yourself that the charity is genuine and that you are happy to collect for it. The charity will equip you with your certificate of authority and collector's badge, together with any equipment (for example, sealed collecting box or envelopes) and instructions to be followed during the collection such as always allow donors themselves to put money into the box or envelope. You may be required to deliver the money you collect to a branch member or direct to a bank – the instructions will cover this.

There is no simple way of checking the authenticity of an unsolicited telephone appeal, so you would be wise to be wary of giving by this means. If you want to donate, suggest that the caller sends you a letter identifying the charity and its aims and that you will post any donation you make.

Checking out the charities

You can check whether an organisation is a registered charity by consulting the Central Register of Charities kept by the Charity Commission.★ This can be done at the Commission's offices or over the Internet. If you want to check the more detailed file held about a particular charity, you will need to apply in writing.

The computer entry on the Register will tell you the charity's registration number, its address and briefly what the charity does. If an organisation is on the Register, you can treat this as confirmation that it is indeed a charity.

The Charity Commission cannot usually help if your enquiry concerns a charity that is not registered but there are a number of bodies which may be able to provide information about both registered and non-registered charities. To know whether or not an organisation has been granted charitable status, contact the Charity Division of the Inland Revenue.★

Your local authority will usually have details of charities operating in your area and may have its own register which you can inspect.

The Charities Aid Foundation (CAF)★ – which is itself a charity whose general aim is to promote growth in the flow of resources to the voluntary sector – operates a Charity Search service which can give you information about a specific charity or identify charities operating in a particular area or for a given cause.

Directories are produced by various organisations representing voluntary groups – not only charities. These organisations may be able to put you in touch with local sources of information about the charities in your area, and give you details of charities and other groups involved in particular activities or places.

The national bodies to contact for further information are the NCVO,★ the Northern Ireland Council for Voluntary Action,★ the Wales Council for Voluntary Action★ and the Scottish Council for Voluntary Organisations.★

But where does the money go?

Bear in mind that, although an organisation may be a charity, neither charitable status nor registration represents a 'seal of approval'. You may still want to satisfy yourself that any money you give will be used efficiently and as you had expected. Unfortunately, there is no easy way of checking this but a charity's financial accounts will give you some information.

All charities (whether registered or not) must prepare annual accounts describing the financial affairs of the charity over the year. They must provide you with a copy of these accounts within two months of your written request – the charity can charge you a reasonable fee for doing this. Many registered charities are required by law to provide the Charity Commission with copies of their accounts. Where accounts have been submitted to the Commission, they are available for the public to inspect. The Charity Commission keeps a publicly available list of charities that have persistently failed to send in their annual returns and reports. You should be wary of giving to any charity on this list – its failure to produce accounts might be due to financial problems or, at the very least, poor administration.

A charity's accounts will give you, *inter alia*, some idea about how the charity uses the funds it raises. One area of particular concern is how much of your money actually reaches the charitable cause. Inevitably, some funds must be spent on organising and running the charity itself. Research by CAF suggests people fear that nearly half of their donations might be going to pay for administration, whereas, on average, less than a fifth felt their donations should be used in this way. In fact, charities spend far less on management and administration than feared. CAF found that spending by the top 500 charities (by voluntary income) on these areas accounted for only 4.1 per cent of spending in 2000. A further 9 per cent was spent on fundraising. But, inevitably, there will be wide variation from one charity to another.

You need to take care when interpreting cost figures. A high level of costs may indeed suggest inefficiency but equally a low level of costs may be the result of the charity spending too little on administration and management. This may lead to inefficient use of resources. And a charity which has as its main activity giving advice, say, rather than passing on funds may justifiably have high running costs.

Charity Commission guidelines: giving safely to charity

The Charity Commission suggests you take the following precautions when giving to charity:

- ask the organisation if it is a registered charity and look for its registration number which should be printed on literature and collecting tins. Check the Central Register of Charities★
- check whether the person collecting is working directly for the charity or for a separate fundraising organisation. If the latter, ask to see a copy of the written agreement with the charity they are collecting for – they should have one and it should say what proportion of the money you give will be passed on to the charity
- check that the collector has an official badge or permit and do not be afraid to inspect it
- check that the collection tin is sealed and carries the charity's

name. It is illegal to collect in open tins, buckets and other containers

- only make out cheques to the charity itself, not to any other person or organisation
- if you think a collector is not genuine, tell the police or your local authority and do not give.

Chapter 3

Special schemes for giving to charity

GIVE MORE, PAY THE SAME

'Looks like a Save the Children appeal,' said Philip, bending to pick up a small envelope from the mat and passing it to his wife, Mary. 'We must give something,' she said. 'Oh, did you see this form printed on the back . . . "Add nearly 30 per cent to the value of your gift just by filling in your name and address". . . ? That sounds like a good deal if ever there was one. I wonder how it works?'

Tax benefits for charities

A great advantage to organisations of having charitable status is that they become eligible for a variety of tax benefits. As long as they meet certain conditions, charities currently enjoy complete freedom from income tax, capital gains tax (CGT) and corporation tax on their income and profits from most sources. In addition, when they receive donations, charities may be able to claim back income tax which has been paid by the giver (see below).

Whereas most businesses must pay business rates to their local authority, charities are given automatic relief against four-fifths of these rates and the local authority can exempt them from the remaining fifth if it chooses.

Charities are not completely free from tax; they are, in the main, treated like any other business when it comes to Value Added Tax (VAT). This can be a problem, especially for non-trading charities whose activities count as exempt from VAT. This means they cannot reclaim VAT paid on a wide range of items that they buy. Some things charities need – for example, equipment to be used for medical research, new building for charitable purposes and provision of toilet facilities in buildings run by charities for charitable purposes – can be purchased VAT-free. Spending on advertising is also normally VAT-free for charities.

Many charities receive dividends from funds which they invest in shares. Dividends are received after deduction of income tax together with a tax credit. Charities used to be able to reclaim the amount of the tax credit, so dividend income was tax-free. From 6 April 1999, the position changed. Charities are no longer able to reclaim the tax already deducted. However, to help them adjust, they receive compensation from the government for the lost tax credit. The compensation is given at a reducing rate over a five-year period, coming to an end in tax year 2003–4.

The other important benefit for charities is the ability to claim back tax relief on donations they receive through the gift aid system – see opposite.

Community amateur sports clubs

The definitions of charitable aims now specifically include the promotion of community participation in healthy recreation (see Chapter 2) which enables many sports clubs to acquire charitable status. However, clubs that are not eligible or do not want to go through the process of registering as a charity may still be able to enjoy many of the same tax benefits as charities if they qualify as 'community amateur sports clubs' (CASCs).

The concept of a CASC was introduced in the 2002 Budget. To qualify, a club must have as its main aim the promotion of or participation in an eligible sport, be organised on an amateur basis and be open to the whole community. An application must be made to the Inland Revenue,* which maintains a list of clubs that have CASC status.

The tax benefits for a CASC are not identical to those for charities but are very similar and include being able to claim back relief on gift aid donations (see opposite). But note that membership fees paid to a CASC do not count as donations and are not eligible for the gift aid scheme.

Advantages for donors

Major changes to the tax treatment of gifts to charity were made from 6 April 2000 onwards, and further changes were announced during 2002 which are being brought into effect on various dates.

Before April 2000, there was usually no tax benefit if you made ad hoc donations to charity – to give efficiently, you had to plan ahead and either give regularly or give a fairly substantial sum. The three main ways to give tax-efficiently were: by covenant, gift aid or payroll giving.

From 6 April 2000 onwards, covenants have been taken into the gift aid scheme. In addition, gift aid has become much more flexible, enabling you to get tax advantages even on small, irregular gifts. But, if you pay little or no tax, watch out – you could end up with an unexpected tax bill from the Inland Revenue. Further changes to gift aid were announced in 2002, allowing donations to be carried back to the previous tax year and enabling tax refunds to be donated to charity through your tax return.

The limit on gifts via payroll giving has been removed and, for four years until 5 April 2004, the government adds a bonus to any gifts you make this way.

Also from 6 April 2000, you are able to claim income tax relief on gifts you make to charity of shares, unit trusts and similar investments. From 6 April 2002, this has been extended to gifts of land and buildings as well.

The details of these various schemes are explained below.

Gift aid

You can get tax relief at your highest rate on money you give to charity or a community amateur sports club (see opposite) through the gift aid scheme. From 6 April 2000 onwards, you can make gifts of any amount this way. (Before that date, gifts had to be at least a given size: £250 from 16 March 1993 to 5 April 2000; £400 from 7 May 1992 to 15 March 1993; £600 before 7 May 1992.)

The amount you give is treated as having had tax relief at the basic rate (22 per cent in 2003–4) already deducted. The charity then claims the tax relief from the Inland Revenue and adds it to your gift. In this way, every £10 you give in 2003–4 is worth £10 / (100% –

22%) = £12.82 to the charity. Put another way: for every £10 you want the charity to receive, you pay only £7.80 – the government pays the rest.

If you are a higher-rate taxpayer, you can claim extra tax relief equal to the difference between relief at the higher rate (40 per cent in 2003–4) and the basic-rate relief you have already deducted from the gift. Higher-rate relief is either given through an adjustment to your pay-as-you-earn (PAYE) code or through the self-assessment system.

Before 6 April 2000, you had to complete a special form to use the gift aid scheme. But, from that date onwards, the administration has been much more straightforward. You simply need to make a declaration (see example opposite) that includes:

• the name of the charity
• a description of the gift
• your name
• your address including your postcode.

The declaration should normally be in writing and can be made in any way, including fax or Internet. Alternatively, if you are making a donation by phone, you can give the details orally and the charity must send you a written record of your declaration – you then have 30 days in which to change your mind about making the gift.

The declaration can cover a single gift or series of gifts if you are making regular donations.

In 2001–2, individuals gave £1,463 million to charity using the gift aid scheme and charities were able to reclaim a further £413 million.

The amount given in this way has more than trebled since the changes made in April 2000.

Example of a gift aid declaration

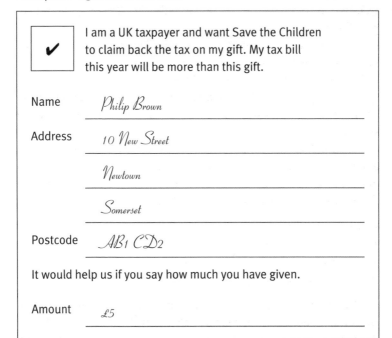

I am a UK taxpayer and want Save the Children to claim back the tax on my gift. My tax bill this year will be more than this gift.

Name *Philip Brown*

Address *10 New Street*

Newtown

Somerset

Postcode *AB1 CD2*

It would help us if you say how much you have given.

Amount *£5*

EXAMPLE 3.1

In August 2003, Philip and Mary decide to respond to a Save the Children appeal. They put £5 in the collecting envelope and fill in the form on the back. Save the Children will be able to claim tax relief from the Inland Revenue of £5 x 22% / (100% − 22%) = £1.41, bringing the total gift to £6.41. Mary is a basic rate taxpayer but Philip is a higher-rate taxpayer, so it is more tax efficient if the gift is in his name, since he can claim extra relief. Tax relief at 40 per cent on the gross gift of £6.41 would be £2.56 but Philip has already had basic-rate relief by deducting it from his donation. Therefore, Philip claims extra relief of £2.56 − £1.41 = £1.15. In this way, Save the Children receives £6.41 at a cost to Philip of just £5 − £1.15 = £3.85.

EXAMPLE 3.2

Following the death of a close friend from cancer, Philip gives £78 to the UK Cancer Research in 2003–04. He makes the donation by phone. The charity asks him for his name and address and to confirm that he is a taxpayer. A few days later, Philip gets a copy of these details. The charity is able to claim back basic-rate tax relief of £78 x 22% / (100% – 22%) = £22, bringing the total it receives to £100. Through his self-assessment tax return, Philip claims higher-rate relief which comes to 40% x £100 – £22 = £18. The charity has received £100 at a cost to Philip of just £78 – £18 = £60.

EXAMPLE 3.3

Mary is not a regular churchgoer but likes to go to a service from time to time. Last Sunday, she noticed a pile of envelopes as she entered the church with 'Gift Aid' printed across the top. The steward explained that, provided she was a taxpayer, instead of just putting cash direct on the collection plate, she could first put her offering in one of these envelopes, filling in the form on the front. That way the church could claim back tax relief on whatever she gave. Mary put £3 in the envelope. The church can claim back £3 x 22% / (100% – 22%) = 85p, bringing the total offering to £3.85 at a cost to Mary of just £3.

Gift aid and age allowance

If you're aged 65 or over, you qualify for a higher age-related personal allowance – see Table 3.1. And, if you are a married man and you or your wife were born before 6 April 1935, you can qualify for married couple's allowance which includes an age-related addition. However, if your 'total income' exceeds a given limit (£18,300 in 2003–4), your age-related allowances are reduced until they reach a basic amount. The rate of reduction is £1 for every £2 by which total income exceeds the limit.

'Total income' is basically your income from most sources (excluding tax-free income, for example from a cash ISA or National

Table 3.1 Age allowances and income limits[1] at which they are lost in 2003–4

Age you reach during the tax year	If you are married, age your wife reaches during the tax year	Maximum personal allowance	Maximum married couple's allowance	Income limit at which extra age-related allowance(s) lost
Single person or married woman[2]				
Under 65	Not applicable	£4,615	Not applicable	Not applicable
65–74	Not applicable	£6,610[3]	Not applicable	£22,290
75 or over	Not applicable	£6,720[3]	Not applicable	£22,510
Married man[2]				
Under 65	Under 68	£4,615	Not applicable	Not applicable
	68–74	£4,615	£5,565[4]	£25,130
	75 or over	£4,615	£5,635[4]	£25,270
65–67	Under 68	£6,610[3]	Not applicable	£22,290
	68–74	£6,610[3]	£5,565[4]	£29,120
	75 or over	£6,610[3]	£5,635[4]	£29,260
68–74	Under 75	£6,610[3]	£5,565[4]	£29,120
	75 or over	£6,610[3]	£5,635[4]	£29,260
75 or over	Any age	£6,720[3]	£5,635[4]	£29,480

Notes: [1]You start to lose £1 of age-related allowance for every £2 by which your 'total income' exceeds £18,300 in 2003–4.
[2]In 2003–4, you can elect for either £2,150 or £1,075 of the married couple's allowance to be transferred to the wife (not shown in this table) but the age-related addition always stays with the husband and any reduction is based on his income.
[3]The personal allowance is never reduced below a basic amount – £4,615 in 2003–4.
[4]The married couple's allowance is never reduced below a basic amount – £2,150 in 2003–4.

Savings & Investments Certificates) less certain expenses that qualify for tax relief. Gift aid donations are one such expense.

If you are in the income bracket where you are losing (or have just lost) age allowance, making donations by gift aid is especially tax-efficient. In addition to the charity claiming back relief on your gift, you will get an increase in your allowance that will reduce your tax bill.

EXAMPLE 3.4

Mary's dad, Stan, is 73 and a widower. In 2003–4, Stan has an income of £22,300 from his state and private pensions. This is too high for him to qualify for any age-related personal allowance, so he gets just the basic personal allowance of £4,615. His tax bill for the year is £3,655.50.

But then Stan decides to give £156 to the Royal Naval Benevolent Trust. The charity is able to claim back £156 x 22% / (100% – 22%) = £44, so the 'grossed-up' donation is £156 + £44 = £200. This reduces

Stan's 'total income' to £22,300 – £200 = £22,100. This is £22,100 – £18,300 = £3,800 more than the age allowance income limit and means the maximum age allowance for someone of his age of £6,610 is reduced by £3,800 / 2 = £1,900 to £4,710 – slightly more than the basic allowance. As a result his tax bill falls to £3,634.60. Stan saves £20.90 in tax. In other words, the charity gets £200 at a total cost to Stan of £135.10.

Gift aid and tax credits

From 6 April 2003, two new state benefits – working tax credit and child tax credit – have been introduced. They are integrated with the tax system in the sense that the amount of credit you can get depends broadly on your income for tax purposes. If you are a couple, credits are based on your joint income. Gift aid donations are deducted from income in assessing how much you can get in tax credits.

Working tax credit is designed to help people who work but have only a low income. Households with no children would be unlikely to qualify if their income exceeds around £11,000 (single person) or £15,000 (couple) in 2003–4. However, households with children can qualify for either both credits, or just child tax credit, up to much higher levels of income. In 2003–4 you can get at least some child tax credit if your income is up to £58,175 (or £66,350 if you have a child under one year old).

In particular, a basic family element of child tax credit equal to £525 in 2003–4 (or £1,050 if you have a child under one year old) is paid until your household income reaches £50,000. The family element is reduced by £1 for every £15 above that limit. Therefore, if your income is above £50,000, a gift aid donation can be very tax-efficient if it also increases the child tax credit you get.

Note that, due to an oversight, the 2003–4 tax credit application form does not mention gift aid donations. However, these charity donations are deductible and you should subtract them from the figure you provide in the income section of the form.

EXAMPLE 3.5

Andrea and Bob have one child and an income of £53,000 in 2003–4. The full tax credit is £525 but this is reduced by (£53,000 – £50,000) /

£15 = £200 to £325. If Bob gives £500 to charity through gift aid, the charity receives £500 / (100% – 22%) = £641.03. Bob is a higher-rate taxpayer and so also gets higher-rate tax relief of (40% – 22%) x £641.03 = £115.39. But the couple's income for child tax credit is also reduced by the gross gift aid donation (rounded up to the nearest £1) to £53,000 – £642 = £52,358. Their child tax credit is now reduced by only (£52,358 – £50,000) / £15 = £157.20 to £367.80. In total, tax relief and extra credit come to £299.21 which is 46.7 per cent of the gross gift aid donation. Looked at another way, the charity gets £641.03 at a cost to Bob and Andrea of just £341.82.

Carrying back gift aid donations

For gift aid donations made on or after 6 April 2003, you can elect to have the gift treated for tax purposes as if it had been paid in the previous tax year.

Your election must be made to the Inland Revenue in writing on or before the date on which you deliver your tax return for the year to which the donation is being carried back. There is space on the tax return to make this election.

For example, suppose you make a donation during 2003–4 which you want to carry back to the 2002–3 tax year. Your tax return for 2002–3 must be filed no later than 31 January 2004. This means you have until 31 January 2004 to both pay the donation and file your return. You cannot carry back the donation if you make it after 31 January 2004. Moreover, if you file your return early – say, by 30 September 2003 – you cannot carry back a donation made after that date.

To use the carry back election, you must have either income or capital gains in the earlier year on which you have paid tax.

Using the election affects only the tax relief you get and not the amount that can be reclaimed by the charity or sports club. It still claims back relief based on the basic tax rate for the year in which the donation was actually paid.

Carrying back a donation might save you tax in the following situations:

- you are a non-taxpayer or starting-rate taxpayer this tax year (see overleaf) but paid tax at the basic or higher rate last year

- you are a basic-rate taxpayer this year but paid tax at the higher rate last year
- your income last tax year was in the range where you were losing age allowance.

Note that carrying back a gift aid donation does not affect a claim for tax credits because for this purpose the donation continues to be deductible for the year the donation was paid, not the year to which it was carried back.

For donations in 2003–4 only, carrying back a donation could also save you tax if in 2002–3 you were eligible for children's tax credit but only at a reduced rate because some of your income was taxed at the higher rate. (The children's tax credit was replaced from April 2003, so carrying back donations in later years will not have the same effect.) You could qualify for the children's tax credit in 2002–3 if you were caring for one or more children. The amount of the credit was reduced by £2 for every £3 by which your income fell into the higher-rate tax band. Higher-rate tax relief on gift aid donations is given by extending your basic-rate band. This has the effect of reducing the amount of your income taxed at the higher rate and, therefore, incidentally could also increase your children's tax credit.

Gift aid if you pay little or no tax

Do not use gift aid if you are a non-taxpayer or will have only a very low income tax and/or capital gains tax bill for the year in which you pay the donation (or the year to which you elect to carry it back).

If you are a non-taxpayer, the charity will still claim the relief from the Inland Revenue. But the Revenue will then ask you for tax equal to the relief given.

Similarly, if your tax bill for the year is less than the amount of tax relief that you are treated as having deducted from your donation, the charity will still claim full tax relief on the donation, but the Revenue will ask you for tax equal to the excess relief given.

In working out how much tax you have paid, some reliefs are ignored – for example, tax credits on dividends, and allowances like married couple's allowance given as a reduction in your tax bill.

EXAMPLE 3.6

Philip's mum, Lucy, is 78. She has an income of £7,660 a year from her state pension, a small widow's pension and a small amount of savings. Tax on her income is expected to be £94 in 2003–4. In September 2003, Lucy decides to give £400 to The Friends of Verrington Hospital, a local charity supporting the hospital where her late sister was nursed through her final illness. If Lucy makes the donation through gift aid, she will be treated as having deducted tax relief from the gift of £400 x 22% / (100% − 22%) = £112.82. This is £112.82 − £94 = £18.82 more than her expected tax bill for the year, so she can expect her tax office to adjust her bill to collect the extra £18.82. To avoid this, Lucy makes the gift without using the gift aid scheme.

Other points to note about gift aid

You can't combine gift aid with any other tax-efficient advantageous way of giving to charity. For example, you can't claim gift aid relief for donations made through a payroll giving scheme (see page 43).

Your gift will not qualify for gift aid if you (or someone connected with you, such as a family member or close business associate) in return gets some benefit as a result of the gift and the benefit exceeds the limits shown in Table 3.2. However, there is a special exception that means you don't count the following benefits:

• the right to free or reduced-price entry to properties preserved for the public benefit, where maintaining such properties is the main or sole purpose of the charity and the opportunity to benefit is publicly available
• the right to free or reduced-price entry to observe wildlife, where the conservation of such wildlife is the sole or main purpose of the charity and the opportunity to benefit is publicly available.

From your April 2004 tax return onwards, if you are due a tax refund you will be able to donate some or all of it to a charity of your choice by making a nomination in your tax return. You will also be able to specify whether gift aid should apply to the donation. The Inland Revenue will then pay the refund direct to the charity. You don't have to be a higher-rate taxpayer to use this facility. And any charity is eligible *provided* it is based in the UK — it does not have to be a registered charity.

Table 3.2 Maximum benefit allowed as a result of a gift if it is to qualify for gift aid

Size of your gift	Maximum benefit allowed	Example
up to £100	25% of the value of the gift	You give £50; any benefit must be worth no more than £50 x 25% = £12.50
over £100 up to £1,000	£25	You give £500; the maximum benefit is £25
over £1,000	2.5% of the value of the gift	You give £1,500; any benefit must be worth no more than £1,500 x 2.5% = £37.50
AND		
All gifts to the same charity during the same tax year	£250	You make 20 gifts of £100 to the same charity. In line with the rule above, 25% of each gift would give a total potential benefit of 20 x £25 = £500, but this rule caps that benefit at £250.

Covenants

A covenant is a legally binding promise to give something to someone (or to do or refrain from doing something). In the past, it has been a common way of agreeing to make regular donations to a charity and, providing certain conditions were met, the donations qualified for tax relief under rules that applied specifically to covenants.

From 6 April 2000 onwards, the special rules no longer apply. Instead, covenanted donations come under the normal rules for gift aid (see pages 33–42). You can still make gifts by deed of covenant if you want to, but there is no tax reason for doing so.

If you are making donations (or paying subscriptions to a charity such as the National Trust) via a covenant drawn up before 6 April 2000, donations from that date will automatically come under the gift aid rules — you do not need to do anything. Under both the old covenant tax rules and the current gift aid rules, the payments you make are treated as if tax at the basic rate has been deducted from the amount you pay. However, the covenant may have been drawn up in one of two ways:

- **net covenant** You agree to give a set amount to the charity regularly. If the basic rate of tax changes, there is no change to the amount you give but the charity claims a different amount of tax relief
- **gross covenant** You agree that the charity will receive a set amount regularly. If the basic rate of tax changes, the charity receives the same sum overall but you must adjust the amount you give. This continues to be the case, even after 6 April 2000 when payments are covered by the gift aid rules.

If your covenant started on or after 6 April 2000, you must complete a gift aid declaration (see page 34) in order for the gifts to qualify for tax relief.

It is likely that the use of covenants as a way of making gifts to charity will become increasingly rare.

Payroll giving schemes

Payroll giving (also called 'Payroll deduction') is a method of making regular gifts to charity out of your pay-packet. It is open only to employees and only to those whose employer operates a payroll giving scheme. From 6 April 2000 onwards, you can give any amount using this scheme. Before that, there was an upper limit on your donations (£1,200 each tax year from 6 April 1996 to 5 April 2000; £900 a year between 6 April 1993 and 5 April 1996; £600 a year before 6 April 1993). Moreover, for donations you make between 6 April 2000 and 5 April 2004 (originally 2003 but extended for an extra year) inclusive, the government will add a bonus equal to 10 per cent of the amount of your donation. For example, if you agree to give £100 a month, the charity will receive £110 a month including the government bonus.

The scheme works like this. Your employer sets up an arrangement with an agency approved by the Inland Revenue (in fact, a few employers have set up their own agencies). You then tell your employer how much you want to give each payday and to which charity or charities. The employer deducts the specified amount from your pay and hands it over to the agency, which arranges for the money to be transferred to the charities you picked. (The agency may make a charge – for example, 5 per cent of the donations it handles – to cover its own running costs, but sometimes there is no charge or your employer might separately cover any administration costs.) Your donation is deducted from your pay before tax (but not National Insurance), so you automatically get full income tax relief. Payroll giving is popular with charities because they receive the whole (gross) donation direct from you, avoiding any paperwork and delay involved in claiming tax relief from the Inland Revenue.

However, payroll giving has been slow to catch on with employees. In 2001–2, only 504,000 employees were giving this way (out of a total of nearly 28 million employees in the UK). The amount they gave was £73 million on which they received £25 million tax relief. The government's hopes that the changes to payroll giving from April 2000 would kick-start the scheme and encourage its adoption as a mainstream way of giving to charity have not really materialised. The number of people giving in this way fell by around a third between 1999–2000 and 2001–2. Though the amount donated nearly doubled, it remains very low compared with gift aid.

One of the largest agencies running payroll giving schemes is the Charities Aid Foundation (CAF),★ which operates a scheme called Give As You Earn (GAYE). It offers three different options:

- **Direct donation** Each employee chooses the charities to receive his or her donation each month
- **CAF Charity Account** Donations are paid into a special account from which you can make donations of any size to any charities. See page 50 for more details
- **Staff charity fund** Employees pool their individual donations to form a single account from which donations of any size can be made to any charities.

EXAMPLE 3.7

Mary earns £700 a month, before tax, working in the local branch of a national building society. The society operates a payroll giving scheme through which Mary gives £10 a month each to Help the Aged and

Barnardo's. Normally, Mary would pay £49.79 a month in income tax (during the 2003–4 tax year) but after deducting the payroll giving from her pay, the tax bill is reduced to £45.39 a month. In other words, she gets tax relief of £4.40 a month, which reduces the cost to her of the £20 she gives to charity to just £15.60.

If your employer operates a payroll giving scheme, he or she can provide you with details and an application form.

You do not have to keep up your donations for any minimum period of time. You stop making them whenever you like simply by informing your employer of your wishes.

Payroll giving cannot be used in combination with any of the other tax-advantageous ways of giving to charity. So, for example, you cannot claim gift aid relief on donations made through a payroll giving scheme. Inland Revenue rules do not allow payroll giving to be used to pay subscriptions entitling you, for example, to membership benefits from a charity.

Giving things rather than cash

You do not have to give just cash as a charitable donation. You could instead give something you own: for example, land, premises, a car, furniture or investments such as shares. As described in Part 2, normally you might have to pay capital gains tax (CGT) and even inheritance tax (IHT) when you give something away. But gifts to charities and, from 6 April 2002, community amateur sports clubs, are generally completely free of these taxes.

For the exemption from IHT to apply, you must relinquish all your rights to whatever it is that you are giving. For example, there might well be a tax bill if you gave the freehold of your home to a charity but continued to live there. For more details about the way CGT and IHT work, see Chapters 5–7.

In addition to the CGT and IHT reliefs described above, gifts of some types of assets to charities – but not community amateur sports clubs – can also qualify for income tax relief. Since 6 April 2000, this applies to gifts of shares and similar investments and, from 6 April 2002 onwards, it also applies to gifts of land or buildings.

Gifts of shares or similar investments

You can claim income tax relief when you give any of these investments to a charity:

- shares or securities listed on a recognised stock exchange
- unlisted shares or securities dealt in on a recognised stock exchange (including the Alternative Investment Market)
- units in an authorised unit trust
- shares in an open-ended investment company (OEIC)
- an interest in an offshore investment fund.

You can claim the market value of the shares or units you give (plus any costs of disposal you incur) as a deduction from your income. This means you get income tax relief up to your top rate. If you receive anything for the shares or units – either cash or a benefit in kind – this is deducted from the amount you can claim.

This relief is available not only for gifts to charities but also to the National Heritage Memorial Fund, the Historic Buildings and Monuments Commission for England, the British Museum and the Natural History Museum.

Giving shares or units direct to charity, rather than selling them first and giving cash, can be very tax-efficient where you would stand to make a gain on the shares or units if they were sold. If the shares or units are standing at a loss, it can be more efficient to sell them first and give cash.

Note that you can only claim this income tax relief against your income and not against any capital gains you make on other sales or gifts. This means giving shares or units will not be tax-efficient if you do not have enough income against which to set the relief. (Companies are treated differently – see page 56.)

EXAMPLE 3.8

Harry, who is a higher-rate taxpayer, wants to make a substantial donation to the Arthritis Research Campaign (ARC). He is considering funding his donation by selling some HBOS plc shares.

Harry could sell the shares for £2,500, of which £1,000 would be taxable. He has already used up his CGT allowance for the year (see page 95), so he would have to pay tax of 40% x £1,000 = £400. This would leave £2,500 – £400 = £2,100 to give to ARC. The gift would qualify for gift aid (see page 33), so ARC would claim back basic-rate tax relief on the £2,100 and Harry would get higher-rate relief on the gift. This would mean ARC received £2,692 in total at an overall cost to Harry of £2,100 + £400 – £485 = £2,015.

Instead, Harry could give the shares direct to ARC. There is no CGT to pay on gifts to charity. And Harry can claim income tax relief on the market value of the gift which is £2,500. This means Harry gets income tax relief of 40% x £2,500 = £1,000. The charity sells the shares to realise the full £2,500. In this way the charity gets £2,500 at a cost to Harry of £2,500 – £1,000 = £1,500. Therefore, giving the shares direct is the better option.

EXAMPLE 3.9

Melanie, a higher-rate taxpayer, is considering giving some shares to the Woodland Trust. The market value of the shares is £1,000 but if Melanie sold them she would make a loss of £200. She could set this loss against gains on other assets, which would save her up to 40% x £200 = £80 in capital gains tax (less if she could claim taper relief – see page 81). If she gives the £1,000 proceeds from the sale to the Woodland Trust, the gift would qualify for gift aid (see page 33). The Trust could claim back basic-rate relief, bringing the total value of the gift to £1,282. Melanie could claim higher-rate relief of £231, reducing the total cost to her to £1,000 – £80 – £231 = £689. Put another way, the charity receives £1.86 for every £1 it costs Melanie.

Instead, Melanie could just give the shares direct to the Woodland Trust. There is no capital gain or loss on gifts to charities. However, Melanie could claim income tax relief on the market value of the shares, which comes to 40% x £1,000 = £400. The Trust sells the shares to realise £1,000. In this way, the charity gets £1,000 at a cost to Melanie of £1,000 – £400 = £600. Put another way, the charity receives £1.67 for every £1 it costs Melanie, so selling the shares and donating the cash raised would be more tax-efficient.

Gifts of land or buildings

Income tax relief is available on a gift of land or buildings to charity – but not community amateur sports clubs – made on or after 6 April 2002. Giving land or buildings works in much the same way as giving shares (see page 46). So you can claim the market value of the property plus any disposal costs less anything you receive in exchange.

The property must be in the UK but can be either freehold or leasehold. You must completely give up your ownership rights and, if you own the property jointly with other people, you must surrender your rights to the charity.

In general, relief is withdrawn if, within five years of 31 January following the tax year in which you give the property away, you acquire any interest or right in the property. There are two exceptions: first, if you acquire the interest through the death of someone; and second, if you pay the full going rate for the interest or right – for example, if you live in the property but pay the full market rent.

To claim the relief, you must have a certificate from the charity concerned describing the property, the date it was given and stating that the charity has accepted the gift.

As with a gift of shares, giving land or buildings direct to a charity will generally be tax-efficient if you would otherwise make a taxable gain on selling the property. But, if selling it would realise a loss, it will be more tax-efficient to sell the land or buildings first and then donate the proceeds to charity using gift aid.

Chapter 4
Other ways of giving to charity

PAY NOW, GIVE LATER

Mary stood chatting to her neighbour, Jack, about charity appeals. 'I set aside a certain amount for charities,' he said, 'but I bide my time about which charities I give to. You see, I have a special charity account – I pay money in, the account claims a bit extra from the taxman, and I have a sort of debit card and cheque book. When I want to donate to a cause, I simply give my card number or write out a cheque drawn on my account. And, if I want to check the account, that's easy – I can do it online.'

'What a great idea,' Mary commented. 'Who runs this charity account?'

Apart from the special schemes outlined in Chapter 3, there are a number of other ways of giving to charity that can give either you or the charity some tax advantage. Some are sophisticated schemes, really only suitable if you have a large sum to give. Others can be used to give even small sums. This chapter also looks briefly at a couple of common ways of giving to charity that do not benefit from tax advantages: the National Lottery and affinity credit cards.

Charitable bequests

If you leave money or assets to charity in your will, your estate pays no IHT on the gift. (Your estate is all your possessions less any debts at the time of death.)

A bequest to charity can also save IHT in a second way, because the value of your estate is reduced by the amount of your gift to charity. This can mean less IHT on the estate as a whole. Bear in mind, though, that making a bequest to charity cuts down the amount of the estate left for your survivors to inherit, so you should not use this as a tax-saving method unless you intend to make philanthropic gifts anyway.

All gifts from your estate when you die – whether to charity or to other organisations or to people – are free of CGT.

A solicitor can help you to insert an appropriate clause in your will to leave a bequest to charity. Some charities offer you help in making your will – for example, paying the cost – in the hope that you will leave something to the charity. For the will to be legally watertight, it is essential that there can be no question of the charity having brought undue influence to bear on you. If it was thought that a charity had pressurised you into leaving it a bequest, your will could be challenged by other beneficiaries and, in the end, your gift to the charity might not be made after all. To avoid any problems of this sort, you should ensure that:

- you have written details of the arrangement by which the charity is helping you to make your will and the procedures to be followed
- you do not proceed if the charity's help is conditional on your making it a bequest
- the solicitor takes instructions from you alone and not the charity
- no details of your will are disclosed to the charity without your consent
- you do not proceed if you feel in any way pressurised to include the charity in your will.

See Part 3 for more information about gifts made at the time of death.

CAF Charity Account

The Charities Aid Foundation (CAF)* is a charity whose aim is to promote charities generally and give them support and assistance. One of the services it runs is the CAF Charity Account.* This is like a bank account with the sole purpose of making gifts to charity. The advantages of the Charity Account are that the money you give is increased by tax relief and you have a convenient, flexible way of giving to a wide range of charities. CAF makes a charge for running the account. It works as follows.

You pay money into your Charity Account using the tax-efficient means already discussed: gift aid (see page 33), payroll giving (see page 43) or gifts of shares and similar investments (see page 46). Because CAF is itself a charity, it is able to claim tax relief on the money you pay in using gift aid and it adds this to your account. With payroll giving you qualify for tax relief directly as normal and, until 5 April 2004, the government adds a 10 per cent bonus of whatever you pay. With gifts of shares, your gift is free of CGT and you can claim income tax relief. CAF sells the shares and then credits the proceeds to your account.

CAF sets minimum limits on the amount you can pay into the account of either £100 as a lump sum or £10 a month if you pay in regularly. In 2003, CAF's charges for running the account were 4 per cent of sums up to £13,500 and 1 per cent of any excess up to £74,000, and a part of the amount you pay in is donated to the National Council for Voluntary Organisations (NCVO).* The money in the account does not earn interest.

When you want to make a donation to charity from your account, you can do this in several ways:

- online transfer, where you access your account over the Internet and carry out a variety of transactions including making donations
- phone transfer
- by post using a Charity Account chequebook
- by standing order, if you want to make regular donations to a particular charity.

You can make donations to any charity, whether registered or not.

Note that you do not get any further tax relief when you make the donation, because it has already had the benefit of tax relief when you first paid the money into the Charity Account.

The normal rules which apply to gift aid and payroll giving apply when you are paying into the CAF Charity Account. For example, the CAF Charity Account is not suitable if you pay little or no tax and would receive a bill from the Inland Revenue for the tax relief paid over to CAF by gift aid (see page 40).

EXAMPLE 4.1

Jack puts money into his CAF Charity Account using gift aid (see page 33). Under the scheme, he pays an after-tax amount of £150 a year into the account. When each payment is made, CAF reclaims basic-rate tax relief of £42.31 (at 2003–4 tax rates), bringing the total which is paid into the account each year to £192.31. (Jack is a basic-rate taxpayer, so he cannot directly reclaim any tax himself.)

CAF deducts a charge of £7.69 a year, leaving £184.62. Out of this, Jack has a standing order to pay £50 a year to the Royal National Institute for Deaf People. He makes other donations online: for example, last year he gave to Oxfam and the Royal Society for the Prevention of Cruelty to Animals (RSPCA) and used a cheque to make a donation to his local scout group.

Discretionary trusts

A trust is a special legal arrangement where money, shares or other property are held for the benefit of others. Trustees have the duty of seeing that the property in the trust and any income and gains from it (which together make up the 'trust fund') are used as set out in the trust deed and rules. With a 'discretionary trust', the trustees are given the power to decide how the trust fund is used (within any constraints imposed by the trust rules).

Special tax rules apply to trusts (see Chapter 10) but it is worth noting here that gifts to charity from a discretionary trust can be very tax-efficient. The charity will be able to reclaim all the income tax – usually at 34 per cent (in 2003–4) rather than just the basic rate – that the trust has paid on the income it gives. If the trust makes a gift to charity of capital, there will be no CGT or IHT to pay.

Charitable trusts

Many charities are organised as 'charitable trusts': that is, trustees hold money for the benefit of others and use or distribute it according to the rules set out in the trust deed. The trust also qualifies for special tax treatment because it meets the requirements for charitable status (see Chapter 2). It is not just organisations that can use charitable trusts; you can, in effect, set up your own charity to give funds to other charities. This would be worth doing if:

- you wanted to give a large sum to charity or to give regular sizeable amounts
- you wanted to split the donation between different charities and/or
- you had not yet decided to which charities you wished to give some or all of the money.

Using your own charitable trust is worthwhile only if you want to give a large sum to charity – at least £10,000, say. It can be used to make gifts both during your lifetime and to continue your donations after your death, possibly with the addition of further funds under the terms of your will.

Setting up a charitable trust yourself is a complicated and costly business and you will need the help of a solicitor. Typically, you would set up a trust – usually a discretionary trust (see Chapter 9 for more about these) – often with yourself as one of the trustees. Once the trust deed has been drawn up (but before it is completed), you need to send it to the Charity Commission,★ which, in consultation with the Inland Revenue,★ will decide whether the trust will qualify as a charity. As long as it does, you can go ahead and set up the trust and it will be exempt from most taxes in the same way as a normal charity (see Chapter 3). This means that you will be able to make tax-efficient donations into the trust to be passed on to the charities you choose. For example, you could donate a lump sum under the gift aid scheme. The trust would be able to claim back tax on the payments in the same way as a normal charity. But, when the trust itself makes payments to a charity, it cannot use a special scheme, such as gift aid – you cannot get tax relief twice!

Fortunately, there is a simpler way to set up a charitable trust. CAF★ can set up your own trust for you without initial fees or legal costs, just an annual administration fee. Your money (usually a minimum of £10,000) is paid into a CAF investment fund. You can choose between funds focusing on income, growth or deposits. CAF provides the trustees and, since CAF is itself a registered charity, there are no formalities to complete with the Charity Commissioners. You can add to your trust at any time. Income earned by your trust fund is paid into an account where it can be paid out to charities as you direct. CAF provides you with regular income statements and an annual capital statement showing your fund's investments.

EXAMPLE 4.2

Daisy married a wealthy landowner but was widowed many years ago. Daisy's 'good causes' are famous in her family. One of her projects is a charitable trust to which she pays £10,000 a year by gift aid. The £10,000 she pays into the trust is treated as a gift from which tax relief at the basic rate has already been deducted. The charitable trust can claim back that relief which, at the 2003–4 rate of 22 per cent, comes to £10,000 x 22% (100% – 22%) = £2,821. So the trust receives £12,821 in total.

Daisy has received basic-rate relief on her donation but she can claim extra relief because she is a higher-rate taxpayer. The gross donation was £12,821. Higher-rate tax relief at 40 per cent less the basic-rate relief already given comes to £12,821 x 40% – £2,821 = £2,307. So the charitable trust has received £12,821 at a cost to Daisy of just £10,000 – £2,307 = £7,693.

The trust is a discretionary trust. Daisy is a trustee and largely decides how the trust money will be used. The trust aims to help people who are in sudden and urgent need: for example, in 2003 it paid £5,000 to charities helping people in Afghanistan and Iraq and £3,000 to give aid to famine victims in Africa. If the trust does not pay out the full amount donated in any year, the remainder is invested to be used for charitable causes in future years.

You can set up a charitable trust in your will to receive a bequest. The bequest would reduce the size of your estate for tax purposes and could mean there is less IHT to be paid (see Part 3). The deed and rules of the charitable trust would specify how the bequest is to be used: for example, you might want the capital to remain invested, while the income from it is donated to charity, or you might want the trustees to decide to which charities the capital and/or income are to be given. You can even set up a 'temporary charitable trust' where the trust funds are used for charitable purposes for a specified period but then revert to a non–charitable use: for example, you might direct that income be donated to charity until your grandchildren come of age when the trust money is to be split between them. When a temporary charitable trust stops being used for charitable purposes, there will be an income tax bill and possibly a CGT bill. The rules are complex, so seek professional advice before setting up this type of trust.

There is always a risk that a trust set up under a will might not be recognised by the authorities as charitable even though it was your intention that it should be. To avoid this risk, you could set up the trust during your lifetime, paying just a small amount into it now; this gives you the chance to alter the trust if the Inland Revenue is not satisfied that it meets the requirements for a charity. Once charitable status has been secured, you can safely make a bequest to the trust in your will.

Gifts from businesses

If you run your own company or you are self-employed, there are a number of tax-efficient ways in which you can give to charity. Similarly, a club which is set up as a limited company can use the methods outlined in this section.

Ideally, you would be able to treat a gift to charity as an allowable business expense since this would reduce your profits and thus tax on them. But normal business rules apply and your gift would have to be made 'wholly and exclusively for the purposes of trade' in order to be allowable. Most charitable gifts just do not fit the bill. However, a number of quirks and concessions in the tax rules mean that you should be able to treat the following sorts of gifts to charities as an allowable expense:

- small gifts of money, or gifts in kind, to support a local charity provided the gift has a business purpose – for example, donations to a local charity that benefits your employees in some way
- sponsorship of a charity event as long as it provides you with advertising
- all the costs of employing someone, even though seconded temporarily to work for a charity rather than working for you.

Most business gifts to charity are *not* allowable expenses but businesses can use gift aid (see page 33) to make gifts in much the same way as an individual. If you operate as a sole trader, you simply use the gift aid scheme in the normal way, so your donation is treated as net of tax at the basic rate. The charity claims back the tax and you claim any higher-rate relief through your tax return. If you are in partnership, a gift from the partnership will normally be treated as divided in equal shares between the partners and gift aid will then apply individually to each partner. This means each partner needs to fill in a gift aid declaration (see page 34).

Since 1 April 2000, gifts from companies through gift aid are treated differently. The gift is made 'gross' – in other words without any tax relief deducted. The charity does not claim back any relief and the company gets tax relief by deducting the gift from its profits used to work out the corporation tax due.

Like individuals, businesses can also claim tax relief on gifts of shares, unit trusts and similar investments and gifts of land or buildings given to charity (see pages 46 and 48). (However, companies cannot claim income tax relief on a donation of their own shares.) Sole traders and partners claim relief through their self-assessment tax returns in the normal way. Companies deduct the value of the gift from their profits used to work out corporation tax.

To find out more about the tax treatment of business donations to charity, contact any Inland Revenue★ tax office or enquiry centre.

Although covenants now come under the tax rules for gift aid, they can still be a useful legal device for making gifts to charity, particularly if, say, you want to give a certain proportion of your profits each year to charity rather than a set amount.

EXAMPLE 4.3

Jack is the treasurer of a car racing club which meets regularly during the summer months. At the meetings, both members and spectators are charged an entrance fee and there are other takings for refreshments. The club always gives the income from these meetings, after deducting costs, to a charity.

The club is set up as a limited company. In order to take advantage of the tax relief available on charitable giving, it decides to use the gift aid scheme. But, because it wants to have a formal agreement that its income is used in a specified way, it makes a covenant to pay the profits from each season's race meetings to the Cancer and Leukaemia in Childhood charity (CLIC). Despite the fact that the profits vary and cannot be known at the time the covenant is drawn up, this is a valid form of covenant.

Businesses (whether sole traders, partnerships or companies) can also claim tax relief on items they give to charity that are either:

- goods they make or sell in the course of their trade, or
- machinery or plant used in the trade.

Relief is given by excluding the value of the donated items from trading receipts or as a disposal at nil value for capital allowances.

Community investment tax relief

Although not a way of giving to charity as such, this new scheme, which started in January 2003, is another way of helping disadvantaged communities. The scheme lets you claim tax relief on loans you make to, or shares you buy in, a community development finance institution (CDFI).

CDFIs are bodies accredited by the Inland Revenue and set up to provide finance for small businesses and social enterprise projects.

You do not invest directly in the businesses and projects yourself. Instead you lend to, or invest in, the CDFI and claim income tax relief at your highest rate on up to 5 per cent a year of the amount involved for a maximum of five years. (Relief is restricted to the amount needed to reduce your tax bill for the year to zero, so could come to less than 5 per cent relief.) To claim the tax relief, you must have a certificate from the institution. An Inland Revenue booklet, *Community investment tax relief (CITR) scheme: A brief guide for investors* (no reference number), is available from tax offices★ and the Inland Revenue★ website.

The National Lottery

The National Lottery was launched in 1994. Although part of the money it raised was earmarked for 'good causes', charities did not welcome the Lottery. They were concerned on three counts:

- would the Lottery be seen as a substitute for giving to charity?

- would people play the National Lottery instead of charity-run lotteries that could not offer such large prizes?
- would loose change that once found its way into collecting boxes instead be spent on Lottery tickets?

The National Council for Voluntary Organisations (NCVO)★ ran a series of surveys to track the impact of the Lottery. It found that between 1993 and 1997, individuals' average monthly donations to charity fell by nearly a quarter. Although it was not possible to prove a direct link to the Lottery, it was generally thought to be the most likely cause of the slump. However, since the low point in 1997, average donations have increased. Part of the increase since 2000 is probably due to the tax changes (see Chapter 3) designed to encourage charitable giving.

The overall impact of the Lottery varied from charity to charity depending on the extent to which their donations were hit by competition from the Lottery and to which they benefited from the distribution of Lottery money to good causes. In recent years, public participation in Lottery games has tailed off and so the total money going to the good causes has also fallen. Figures from the National Lottery Commission show that in 2000–1 the Lottery raised £1.55 billion for good causes compared with £1.75 billion at its peak in 1997–8.

Since the start, 28p of each £1 you spend on Lottery games has gone to good causes. This is not the same as saying 28p in the £1 goes to charity, because not all the recipients of Lottery money are charitable. But charities can benefit, and some of the other recipients, although not charities, have similar purposes. At the time of writing, there were six good causes:

- **The Arts Councils** support the arts. Some of the recipients are charities
- **The Sports Councils** aim to foster sporting excellence and attract major sporting events to the UK. Some of the recipient bodies are charities
- **The Community Fund** (formerly the National Lottery Charities Board) makes grants to charities and to benevolent and philanthropic organisations which fall outside the legal definition of 'charity', provided they have the essential attributes of a charity and meet various other requirements

- **The Heritage Lottery Fund** aims to safeguard and enhance the national heritage which is widely defined and includes historic buildings, museums, galleries, parks, gardens, the countryside, local history and so on
- **the New Opportunities Fund** covers health, education and environmental causes
- **the Millennium Commission** was set up to fund community projects to mark the millennium. Although it no longer receives any new money, the Commission is still distributing its remaining funds to projects which benefit individuals and their communities.

Chart 4.1 How 'good causes' money was split between the distributing bodies in 2002–3

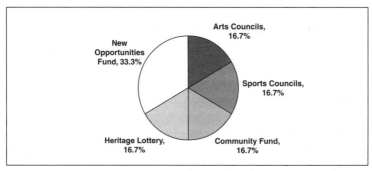

Some of the bodies listed above jointly contribute towards a funding programme called Awards for All, which makes small grants to a very wide range of projects that involve bringing communities together to enjoy art, sport, heritage or other activities. In addition, a £200-million lump sum of Lottery money was used to set up the National Endowment for Science, Technology and the Arts (NESTA), which aims to foster talent by investing in outstanding ideas and people.

In February 2003, the government announced that The Community Fund and the New Opportunities Fund would be merged to form a new body whose priorities would be improving the quality of life in communities and promoting social inclusion. The newly merged body will receive over 50 per cent of the Lottery money raised for good causes.

Table 4.1 lists the total volume and value of Lottery awards made up to February 2003.

Table 4.1 Lottery awards made up to February 2003

Distributing body	Number of projects	Amount
Arts Councils	25,949	£2,080.3 million
Sports Councils	21,387	£1,801.5 million
Community Fund	51,394	£2,470.2 million
Heritage Lottery Fund	9,241	£2,140.9 million
New Opportunities Fund	8,741	£896.5 million
Millennium Commission	2,268	£1,986.6 million
Awards for All	9,999	£36.8 million
TOTAL	128,979	£11,412.8 million

By playing the Lottery you are helping to create a huge fund of money to benefit a variety of good causes, including many smaller projects that might not be eligible for traditional charity funds. On the other hand, an increasing proportion of the money has been directed to areas such as health and education which some would view as more appropriately funded out of mainstream taxation. In addition, pound for pound, more of your money reaches charity if you give direct rather than by buying Lottery tickets – especially if you use one of the tax-efficient schemes for charitable giving. Moreover, if you give direct, you can choose the charities you want to benefit rather than handing that decision to the various bodies responsible for distributing Lottery money.

Donation cards

A number of charities and credit card companies have combined forces to issue donation cards (also called 'affinity cards'). These are normal credit cards but the card company promises to make donations to charity (or sometimes non-charitable bodies, such as football clubs and political parties) linked to your use of the credit card. For example, if you take out an HSBC National Trust Visa card, the bank donates £10 to the Trust at the time you open the card account and donates a further 5p each time you make a transaction through the card. Co-operative Bank offers a range of donation cards linked to Help the Aged, Oxfam, Save the Children and the Royal Society for the Protection of Birds among other bodies (some charitable, some not). With all these, the Co-operative

Bank gives £10 or £15 to the organisation when you first take out the card and donates further sums equal to 0.25 per cent of the value of the transactions made using the card. Bank of Scotland and MBNA are two of the largest donation card issuers, with cards linked to over 600 and 800 organisations, respectively.

The credit card company can use a donation card scheme to make tax-efficient donations to charity, but it is, of course, a marketing exercise for the company, attracting customers and helping to project a caring image. If you use a credit card anyway, a donation card is a way in which you can play an indirect role in giving to charity but compare interest rates and other terms with standard credit cards before you commit yourself. It may be better to choose a low-cost ordinary card and arrange to make your donations direct to charity. If you do not normally use a credit card, you should be wary of taking out a donation card: do not run up debts that you cannot afford.

Part 2

Lifetime gifts to
family and friends

Chapter 5

Tax-free gifts

THE CHOICE OF GIFT MATTERS

'Sylvia,' Jeffrey turned solemnly to his wife, 'I think we should give Tom a helping hand to buy a home now that he's settling down.'

'I couldn't agree more. But to be fair to the girls, we ought to set aside some money to help them later on too,' replied Sylvia.

'It doesn't have to be money, of course – they might like to have one or two of those paintings my mother left me. I wonder if it makes a tax difference? I do believe that we could give Tom a bit of money as a wedding present without running into tax problems . . .'

You need to be aware of two main taxes when making a gift to someone: capital gains tax (CGT) and inheritance tax (IHT). Some gifts can also affect your income tax position – an aspect which can be to your advantage as long as you arrange the gift in a suitable way (see Chapter 8). This chapter looks at gifts you can make during your lifetime that are either free of CGT, free of IHT or completely free of both taxes. Subsequent chapters look at gifts which may be taxable.

Capital gains tax

When you give someone something that you own, you are treated for tax purposes as making a 'disposal' of an 'asset'. An asset is simply something you own. Disposal means ceasing to own the asset, however this comes about – the tax position when you give away an asset is essentially the same as if you had sold it.

If an asset's value at the time you give it away is greater than its value at the time you first started to own it, there *could* be a CGT bill. But do not panic! Often, you will not have to pay any CGT, because:

- some assets are outside the scope of CGT
- gains from some transactions are always tax-free.

The scope of capital gains tax

CGT is a tax on the disposal of *assets*. Assets cover virtually all types of possessions: land, buildings (including your home), stocks and shares, paintings, furniture, patents and copyrights, debts owed to you. Assets, for CGT purposes, do not include sterling currency – so a gift of money cannot result in a CGT bill. By an interesting quirk of the law, sovereigns minted after 1837 still count as sterling currency and are therefore outside the CGT net. (Sovereigns minted before then count as 'chattels' – see below.)

Certain other assets are specifically exempt from CGT. These are looked at in the following sections.

Chattels

These are tangible, movable property – basically your personal belongings, such as clothes, books, compact discs and your household goods, as well as things like jewellery, antiques, paintings and many other collectibles. An item in this category is exempt from CGT provided it has a predicted useful life of 50 years or less and you have not used it in a business.

For chattels with an expected life of more than 50 years, any gain is exempt if the value of the item at the time you dispose of it is no more than £6,000. If a chattel's value is more than £6,000, any gain can be worked out in a special way which may reduce the CGT bill (see Example 6.3 on page 85). There are rules to prevent you reducing the CGT payable by splitting up a set – for example, a set of chairs – and then giving all the parts of the set to the same person.

If you give away or sell a decoration awarded (e.g. to you or a relative) for valour or gallantry, there is no CGT on any gain, unless you had originally bought the decoration or exchanged something of value for it.

Your home

There is no CGT to pay when you dispose of part or all of your only, or main, home. This exemption includes your garden up to a reasonable size (usually half a hectare – about 1.25 acres – but it can be more if the style and size of house warrants a larger garden).

If you have more than one home, you will have to nominate one as your main home for CGT purposes. A husband and wife who live together can have only one main home between them. This is so even if they each spend a lot of time in separate homes (for example, because they live apart during the week for work purposes).

You may lose part of the exemption if part of your home was set aside exclusively for business. There may also be a CGT bill when you dispose of your home, if you have lived away for long periods.

EXAMPLE 5.1

Daisy has decided that Hadley Hall where she has lived since her marriage is now too large for her needs. She plans to give the Hall to her only son, Albert, and buy a cottage nearby. When Daisy inherited the Hall on her husband's death, it was worth £150,000. It is now worth three times that but there will be no CGT bill because:

- the Hall is Daisy's only home, and
- although the garden runs to over two acres, the Inland Revenue has agreed that this is in keeping with the house.

However, Daisy does need to consider her position with regard to inheritance tax (see Chapter 7).

Motor vehicles

There is no CGT on gains from selling or giving away a private car (including vintage or classic cars), a motorbike or other private motor vehicle. This exemption can also apply to a vehicle used for business provided it was 'commonly used as a private vehicle'. However, the exemption does not stretch to vehicles that are not commonly used as private vehicles and are unsuitable for use in that way – so watch out if you are tempted by surplus Ministry of Defence tanks or similar exotica!

A vehicle you sell or give away might have a personalised or cherished number plate. The right to use the combination of letters and numbers shown on the plate is an 'intangible' asset that is not covered by the CGT exemption for motor vehicles. If the value of the vehicle you sell or give away includes an amount in respect of the personalised plate, you need to apportion the proceeds between the value of the vehicle and the value of the right to use the registration shown on the plate, and there could be CGT to pay on the latter.

Foreign currency
There is no CGT on gains from buying and selling foreign money which you have obtained for your own use – for a holiday abroad, say, for buying or running a holiday home abroad or for use during a business trip.

Some investments
Gains on some investments are completely free from CGT: for example, National Savings & Investments products including Premium Bonds, gilts, many corporate bonds, and shares held through an Individual Savings Account (ISA) or a Personal Equity Plan (PEP). Provided certain conditions are met, gains on shares bought through an Enterprise Investment Scheme (EIS) or its forerunner the Business Expansion Scheme (BES) are also CGT-free. Similarly, gains on shares in Venture Capital Trusts (VCTs) are also free of CGT provided you invest for at least three years (five years for shares bought before 6 April 2000).

Insurance policies
Payment from a life insurance policy, whether on maturity, early surrender or even through selling the policy to someone else, is usually exempt from CGT. The exemption does not apply, however, if you bought the policy from someone else, for example through an auction.

Your rights to certain payments
If you dispose of your right to receive an income under an annuity or a covenant, say, there is usually no CGT on any gain you make as a result. Similarly, if you give away your right to benefit under the terms of a trust or your right to repayment of money you have lent

someone, there is usually no CGT – but there could be, if in the first place you had bought these rights.

Tax-free transactions

Some *transactions* are also exempt from CGT. This means that the following types of gift are free of CGT.

Gifts between husband and wife

Gifts between husband and wife are free of CGT provided the couple are living together.

Gifts to charities and certain other bodies

Donations and gifts to charity, and to various other institutions, including many museums and art galleries, local authorities, government departments and universities, and, from 6 April 2002, community amateur sports clubs (see page 32) are CGT-free.

Gifts of national heritage property

The sale or gift of certain property, such as works of art, to a museum, art gallery, the National Trust or similar body, university, local authority or government department, may be exempt from CGT. So, too, is the acceptance by the Inland Revenue of such property in lieu of inheritance tax (see page 213). The sale price or valuation must take into account the tax you have saved.

Eligible property can include pictures, prints, books, manuscripts, works of art, scientific objects, provided they are 'pre-eminent' for their national, scientific, historic or artistic interest. Buildings and land of outstanding scenic, historic or scientific interest and items associated with them are also eligible.

A gift of eligible property to anyone else can be free of CGT if it also qualifies as conditionally exempt from inheritance tax (see page 71) or would do so if it did not count as a potentially exempt transfer (see page 76). To qualify, the person receiving the gift must agree certain conditions with the Inland Revenue including that the gifted property will stay in the UK, it will be properly maintained and preserved, and the public will have reasonable access to it. The exemption from CGT is lost if the property is subsequently sold, unless this is to a museum, art gallery, the National Trust or similar body, university, local authority or government department.

If the gift is not exempt, you might instead be able to claim hold-over relief (see page 100).

Gifts if you move abroad

Since 17 March 1998, if you leave the UK to take up residence abroad, you can give away assets you acquired while still in the UK without paying any CGT but only if you are resident abroad for at least five tax years (see page 169).

Gifts on death

When you die, you are deemed to make a gift of all you then own to your heirs but, whatever, and however much, you leave, it is always free of CGT.

Your heirs are treated as acquiring the assets at their market value at the time of your death, so any previous capital gains that had built up while the assets were in your hands are wiped out.

Inheritance tax

IHT is a tax on the 'transfer of value' from one person to another. This means a gift (or other transaction) which reduces the value of the possessions (the 'estate') owned by the person making the transfer. In theory, IHT could apply to any gift but, as with CGT, there are exemptions and adjustments. This means that on most lifetime gifts there is no IHT to pay, because:

* various types of gift are always free of IHT
* some gifts, called 'potentially exempt transfers' (PETs), are free of tax, provided the giver lives on for seven years after making the gift (see page 76).

Gifts which are always free of IHT

The scope of IHT is, on the face of it, wider than that of CGT because IHT covers all assets – including money, as well as houses, land, pictures and furniture. Gifts made in certain circumstances or between certain people or bodies are free of IHT. This applies to the following gifts, whether you make them during your lifetime or as bequests in your will (see Chapter 12):

Gifts between husband and wife

Gifts between husband and wife up to any amount are tax-free as long as the couple are not divorced. Even a husband and wife who are separated benefit from this exemption. If the husband or wife receiving the gift is not 'domiciled' (see box below) in the UK, the exemption is limited to a total of £55,000.

DOMICILE

Your place of domicile is broadly where you make your permanent home and intend to end your days. However, for the purposes of inheritance tax you are treated as still UK-domiciled during the first three years after you have acquired a domicile in another country, or if you have been a UK resident for 17 of the last 20 tax years.

Gifts to charities and certain other bodies

This exemption from IHT is similar to the equivalent one for CGT (see page 69). It covers outright donations and gifts of any amount to UK charities, national museums and art galleries, universities, local authorities, government departments and a number of other bodies, including, from 6 April 2002, community amateur sports clubs (see page 32).

Gifts of national heritage property

The gift of certain property, such as works of art, to a museum, art gallery, the National Trust or similar body, university, local authority or government department may be exempt from IHT. The transfer of such property to the Inland Revenue in lieu of paying IHT (see page 213) is also exempt.

Eligible property can include pictures, prints, books, manuscripts, works of art, scientific objects, provided they are 'pre-eminent' for their national, scientific, historic or artistic interest. Buildings and land of outstanding scenic, historic or scientific interest and items associated with them are also eligible.

A gift of eligible property to anyone else can be conditionally exempt from inheritance tax. To qualify, the person receiving the gift must agree certain conditions with the Inland Revenue, including that the gifted property will stay in the UK, it will be properly maintained and preserved, and the public will have reasonable access to it.

You can't claim conditional exemption for a gift that is a potentially exempt transfer (see page 76) but you can apply if the gift subsequently becomes chargeable because the giver died within seven years.

A claim for conditional exemption must be made within two years of the gift (or death in the case of a potentially exempt transfer). You (and/or your husband or wife) must have either owned the property for at least six years or inherited it on the death of the previous owner with a conditional exemption also applying to that transfer.

Gifts to political parties

A gift to a political party is exempt from IHT, provided the party has at least two MPs or polled at least 150,000 votes at the most recent general election.

Housing Associations

Gifts of land to a Registered Housing Association are exempt.

Lifetime gifts which are free of IHT

The following gifts are free of IHT only when they are made during your lifetime (i.e. not in your will).

Normal expenditure out of income

If you can show that a gift you are making is one of a regular pattern of similar gifts and that you are making it out of your income (rather than from your savings or other capital), the gift will be exempt from IHT.

Gifts made under a legally binding agreement, such as a deed of covenant, will usually be treated as regular gifts. So too will premiums you pay for an insurance policy or contributions to a pension scheme that is for the benefit of someone else: for example, a policy on your life which would pay out to your children in the event of your death. If the gifts are not made under any formal agreement but you intend that they will be regular gifts, they can still qualify for the exemption. The first gift or two might not be treated as exempt at the time you make them but, once a regular pattern has been established, they can be reassessed as tax-exempt.

The gifts must be made out of your income, so you need to be able to show that you have enough income left to meet your day-to-day living expenses. The income can be from any source – a job, interest from investments, dividends from shares. But bear in mind that the capital element of a 'purchased life annuity' (see Glossary) is not income nor are withdrawals from 'single-premium life insurance bonds' (see Glossary).

Normally, the gifts would be cash. If you make gifts which are not cash, you will have to be able to prove that the things you are giving were bought out of your income.

EXAMPLE 5.2

Stan, who is 73, would like to give some money to his grandson, Ed (aged 14), to help him later in life. Stan arranges a stakeholder pension scheme for Ed to which Stan pays £50 a month. Stan's payments count as normal expenditure out of income, so his gift to Ed is free of inheritance tax. The gift is also tax-efficient in other ways: the contributions are treated as being made after deduction of tax relief at the basic rate and the pension company claims back the relief to add to the scheme, so each £50 is boosted to £64.10 at 2003–4 tax rates; the investment grows largely tax-free; part of the eventual proceeds can be taken as a tax-free lump sum.

The main drawback from Ed's point of view is that he will not be able to touch the money until he reaches at least age 50 (or 55 if government proposals to increase the minimum pension age go ahead) and, at that time, most of the proceeds must be taken in the form of a pension. That does not seem attractive to Ed at age 14. Later in life he will probably appreciate Stan's gift because pension contributions made so early in life have a long time to grow and can be expected to accumulate to a sizeable sum.

Gifts for the maintenance of your family

Money or things which you give to provide housing, food, education, or some other form of maintenance, for your husband or wife, ex-husband or ex-wife, children or a dependent relative are outside the IHT net.

As far as husband and wife are concerned, the normal exemption for gifts between married couples (see page 71) would usually apply rather than this exemption. But if either husband or wife are domiciled (see page 71) abroad, this exemption could be useful. This exemption will usually cover maintenance agreements made as a result of a marriage breakdown.

The definition of children is very wide, covering stepchildren, illegitimate and adopted children but it does not extend to grandchildren. Usually a child is considered to be adult when he or she reaches the age of 18 but, if he or she goes on to full-time education or training after that age, the IHT exemption carries on.

A 'dependent relative' can be any relative of you or your husband or wife who is unable to maintain him or herself because of old age or infirmity. It also includes your mother or mother-in-law, even if not elderly or infirm, if they are widowed, separated or divorced. As a concession, this exemption is also extended to gifts to your mother if she is unmarried, provided she is financially dependent on you.

Lottery syndicates and similar arrangements

There is no inheritance tax to pay on the transfer of winnings to members of a syndicate set up to share wins from schemes such as the National Lottery and football pools, provided the money is shared out according to an agreement that was drawn up in advance of the win. The agreement could be just oral but it is better to have a written agreement. So, if you and your family or friends often daydream about how you would give each other part of a really big win, it might be a good idea to draw up a formal arrangement now.

Yearly tax-free exemption

Every tax year, you can give away £3,000-worth of gifts without their counting in any way for IHT purposes. This exemption is in addition to the other exemptions, so a gift which qualifies for some other exemption does not count towards the £3,000 annual limit.

If you do not use up the full exemption one year, you can carry it forward to the next year – but not to any subsequent year. This means that, if you used none of last year's exemption, you could make up to £6,000-worth of gifts this year that qualify for the exemption. Gifts always use up the exemption for the tax year in which they are made first *before* using up any carried-forward exemption.

EXAMPLE 5.3

Albert is not altogether pleased at being given Hadley Hall by Daisy (see page 67). She has paid little attention to the house in the last 20 years and now the roof needs re-slating and all the exterior woodwork is in dire need of a new coat of paint. After several heated discussions, Daisy finally agrees to give Albert £5,000 towards the cost of the work. Albert persuades Daisy to pay the money to a company which he runs rather than direct to him.

A gift from a person to a company would usually be taxable under the IHT rules. But, in this case, there is no IHT to pay because Daisy has not used her annual exemption for either this year or last year. The gift to Albert uses up the full £3,000 exemption available for this year and £2,000 of the exemption carried forward from last year. There remains £1,000 of last year's exemption which can be set against any other chargeable gifts made this year but it cannot be carried forward any further.

Small gifts

You can make as many gifts as you like of up to £250 to each person, and these will be exempt. You cannot combine the small gift exemption with another exemption to give more than £250 to *one* person but you can, say, give £3,000 to one recipient and gifts of £250 to any number of *other* people.

This exemption will generally cover birthday and Christmas presents, and any other small gifts you make during the year.

Wedding gifts

As a parent, you can give up to £5,000 to the happy couple free of IHT. A grandparent (or other ancestor) can give up to £2,500. Anyone else can give up to £1,000. The bride and groom can give up to £2,500 to each other but this limit will not be relevant if both are domiciled (see page 71) in the UK, since the exemption for married couples will apply.

The exemptions apply to each giver: for example, assuming both sets of parents of the bride and groom were still living, the couple could receive a maximum of £20,000 from their parents without incurring IHT.

The exemptions under this section can also apply to a marriage settlement which aims to benefit the bride or groom, their children or the husbands or wives of their children.

Potentially exempt transfers

A potentially exempt transfer (PET) is a gift from a person either to another person or to certain types of trust (see Chapter 9) that is not covered by some other IHT exemption. As long as the person making the gift survives for seven years after the date of the gift, there is no IHT to pay. If the giver dies within seven years, there may be an IHT bill. PETs are looked at in detail in Chapter 7.

EXAMPLE 5.4

Daisy's gift of Hadley Hall to Albert is valued at £450,000. Despite the substantial value of the gift, there is no IHT to pay at the time of the gift, because it counts as a PET. As long as Daisy survives for seven years, there will be no IHT at all. But if she does die within that time, the gift will be reassessed and tax may then be due, calculated using the value of the Hall at the time of the original gift (i.e. £450,000), Daisy's overall IHT position at that time and IHT rates at the time of death (see page 114).

Combining CGT and IHT exemptions

Some types of gift are specifically exempt from both CGT and IHT: for example, gifts to charities and museums and gifts of national heritage property. Other gifts will be completely tax-free as long as they fall within an IHT exemption *and* you give cash or other assets which are not liable for CGT. Chapters 6 and 7 describe other situations in which either CGT or IHT may not be payable. You can make use of the exemptions in these situations, too, to ensure that your gifts are free of both taxes.

EXAMPLE 5.5

Jeffrey gives his son, Tom, £4,000 in cash as a wedding gift to help him and his new wife buy a home of their own. There is no CGT on a gift of cash and no IHT on a wedding gift of this size.

Jeffrey also wants to give his youngest daughter, Ruth, a gift of similar value. She decides she would like to have a watercolour – a family heirloom – which is valued at £4,500. This counts as a chattel (see page 66) and, since its value is less than £6,000, there is no CGT liability. The gift is a PET under the IHT rules and so, since Jeffrey is expected to live a good many years longer, the gift is likely to be completely free of IHT.

Chapter 6

Capital gains tax on lifetime gifts

AND STILL NO TAX TO PAY

'Congratulations!' Frederick raised his glass and drank his son's health. 'And now you are come of age, it's time you had some financial responsibility . . . Happy birthday.'

Frederick handed an envelope to his son. Inside was a statement for £12,300-worth of unit trusts. 'I don't know what to say, Dad,' gasped Colin in surprise.

'Well, thank-you might be a start. It's not a trivial gift, you know – though at least I didn't have to pay any capital gains tax on it,' Frederick chuckled, with a satisfied smile on his face.

The way capital gains are taxed changed from April 1998 onwards. Indexation allowance (see page 83) was replaced by taper relief (see page 81). This reduces a taxable gain according to the length of time you have held an asset but there is no longer any distinction between 'gains' purely due to increases in the general price level and 'real' gains in value.

A knock-on effect of taper relief was an end to share-pooling – see 'Shares and unit trusts', page 90 – which means extra paperwork for you. And the government took the opportunity also to abolish 'bed-and-breakfasting' – see page 168 – though there are some ways around the problem.

The initial impact of the changes was to make capital gains tax (CGT) more onerous than it was under the pre-1998 regime. However, this has been offset by further changes. The government has aligned the treatment of capital gains with the treatment of savings income, so that, from 6 April 1999 onwards, for many people gains are taxed at the savings rate instead of basic rate of tax and, since 6 April 2000, the starting rate has applied to gains (see page 98). But the most significant relaxation has been the treatment of business assets. Since April 2002, these qualify for maximum taper relief once they have been held for just two years (compared with ten for non-business assets) and the definition has been changed bringing most employee shares and most shareholdings in unlisted trading companies within its scope.

No tax to pay?

Chapter 5 looked at gifts that are specifically exempt from CGT. But even if your gift is not covered by one of the exemptions – for example, if you are giving away shares, a second home or a valuable heirloom – there could still be no tax to pay, because:

- from 6 April 1998 onwards, your gain could have been reduced by taper relief, with the greatest relief given to the assets you have held the longest
- increases in the value of an asset in line with inflation up to April 1998 are not taxed
- you reduce gains by deducting losses made on various other assets
- everyone has an 'annual exempt amount' – a tax-free slice of several thousands of pounds of gains which are automatically tax-free each year.

Your first step in working out what tax might be due is to calculate the basic gain on the asset you are giving away. What happens next will depend on when you first acquired the asset and the period over which you have held it.

The basic gain

- Take the 'final value' of the gift. This will usually be the price you would have received if you had sold the asset on the open market.
- Deduct the 'initial value'. This is the price you originally paid for it or its market value at the time you first became the owner.
- Deduct any allowable expenses. These are costs you incurred in acquiring and disposing of the asset (e.g. commission paid to a

broker, the cost of an expert valuation or solicitor's fees) and any expenses associated with enhancing the value of the asset (e.g. adding an extension to a property) but not spending on maintenance and repairs.

Assets acquired on or after 1 April 1998

For an asset acquired on or after 1 April 1998, the result of the calculation above is your 'chargeable gain' (if the answer is greater than zero) or your 'allowable loss' (if the answer is less than zero).

Where you have made a chargeable gain, you must deduct any losses you have made during the same tax year in which the gift is made. You also deduct any losses brought forward from earlier tax years but no more than are needed to reduce your gains to the amount of the tax-free slice (see page 96 for more about losses). The resulting figure is your 'net chargeable gain'.

You do not necessarily pay tax on the whole of your net chargeable gain. The government wants to encourage people to hold investments for the longer term in the belief that this provides a healthier environment for British business. Therefore taper relief reduces the amount of your net chargeable gain with the largest reduction given to the assets you have held for the longest – see Table 6.1. For non-business assets, there is no reduction at all until you have held the asset for three years. The reduction then depends on the number of complete years since 5 April 1998 for which you have held the asset. The maximum reduction is given after ten complete years. Taper relief is more generous if the asset you are giving away counts as a business asset (see page 102).

If you make a gift to your husband or wife and he or she subsequently disposes of the asset, taper relief at the time of disposal is counted from the period when you first started to own the asset not from the later date when the gift was made.

Table 6.1 CGT taper relief for non-business assets

If you have held the asset for this many complete years after 5 April 1998:	Your net chargeable gain is reduced by this percentage:	Only this percentage of your gain counts as chargeable:	For example, a net chargeable gain of £5,000 is reduced to:
0	No reduction	100%	£5,000
1	No reduction	100%	£5,000
2	No reduction	100%	£5,000
3	5%	95%	£4,750
4	10%	90%	£4,500
5	15%	85%	£4,250
6	20%	80%	£4,000
7	25%	75%	£3,750
8	30%	70%	£3,500
9	35%	65%	£3,250
10 or more	40%	60%	£3,000

EXAMPLE 6.1

Carole bought a holiday cottage in May 1998 for £65,000. The buying costs amounted to £1,200. In August 1998, Carole added a conservatory to the cottage at a cost of £1,700. In June 2003, Carole gives the cottage to her niece, Becky. It is then valued at £92,000 and the costs incurred in making the transfer to Becky amount to £1,020. Carole is deemed to have made a chargeable gain on the gift as follows:

Final value of the cottage	£92,000
less initial value	£65,000
less allowable expenses (£1,200 + £1,700 + £1,020)	£ 3,920
Chargeable gain	£23,080
less allowable losses	£ 0
Net chargeable gain before CGT taper relief	£23,080

Number of complete years for which cottage held (May 1998 to May 2003)	5 years
Percentage taper	85%
Net chargeable gain after taper relief (85% x £23,080)	£19,618

CGT on gifts of assets acquired before 1 April 1998 but after March 1982

If you give away an asset which you started to own on or after 31 March 1982 but before 1 April 1998, work out the basic gain as on page 80. Divide your period of ownership into two:

* holding period 1: date of acquisition up to April 1998
* holding period 2: 6 April 1998 up to date when gift is made.

Holding period 1: indexation allowance

In respect of holding period 1 (date of acquisition up to April 1998), you can deduct indexation allowance. Take the initial value of the asset (see page 80) and each allowable expense and multiply each of these values by the appropriate indexation factor. Add the result together and the total is the indexation allowance.

The indexation factor for the initial value and each expense is derived from the change in the Retail Prices Index (RPI) since the expense was incurred up to 5 April 1998 (or, if earlier, the date on which the gift was made). This is described on page 88.

The effect of the indexation allowance is to strip out any gains which are simply the result of inflation – i.e. do not represent any real increase in your wealth. However, since 6 April 1995, the indexation allowance can at most wipe out the whole gain – it cannot be used to create or increase a loss for CGT purposes.

Deducting the indexation allowance from your basic gain gives you your 'indexed gain'.

Holding period 2: taper relief

Having found your indexed gain, you next work out how much taper relief you qualify for in respect of holding period 2 (6 April 1998 to date of gift) using the rules described on page 81 with one exception: you are allowed to add one extra year to the holding period for any non-business asset which you already owned on 17 March 1998 (the Budget day on which taper relief was announced).

EXAMPLE 6.2

On his 18th birthday on 1 September 2003, Colin is given a portfolio of unit trusts by his father, Frederick. Frederick originally bought the units in July 1991 for £4,700. They are now worth £12,300. As Frederick is disposing of the units, there could be a CGT bill. To work out whether he has made a chargeable gain, Frederick makes the following calculations:

Basic gain

Final value of units	£12,300
less initial value	£4,700
less fee paid to investment adviser at time units were bought	£150
	£7,450

Indexation allowance

Initial value and allowable expenses incurred at time of acquisition	£4,850
Indexation factor (see page 89)	0.215
Indexation allowance for period to April 1998 (0.215 x £4,850)	£1,043
Indexed gain (£7,450 − £1,043)	£6,407
less allowable losses	£0
Net chargeable gain before taper relief	£6,407

Taper relief

Number of complete years since 5 April 1998 for which asset held	5
Plus one year because asset acquired before 17 March 1998	6
Percentage taper (see page 82)	80%
Net chargeable gain after taper relief (80% x £6,407)	£5,125

Gifts made before 1 April 1998

If you gave away an asset before 1 April 1998, taper relief does not apply at all. Indexation allowance will apply for the whole period you owned the asset from 31 March onwards. The allowance is given as described on page 88 but calculated only up to the date of the gift (rather than to April 1998). For details about calculating the indexation allowance, see page 90.

EXAMPLE 6.3

In February 2004 Sylvia and Jeffrey decide to give their elder daughter, Hazel, an oil painting she had always liked. It has been in Jeffrey's family for several generations and in February was valued at £7,000.

The gift counts as a disposal of a chattel with a predicted life of more than 50 years. Its value is greater than £6,000, so there may be a CGT bill (see page 66) but special rules apply in calculating the chargeable gain: the gain will be the *lower* of either five-thirds of the excess of the disposal value over £6,000 or the gain (before deducting any losses or taper relief but after deducting any indexation allowance) worked out in the normal way.

When Jeffrey inherited the painting in February 1987, it was valued at £3,500. Jeffrey can claim an indexation allowance (see page 88) of 0.620 x £3,500 = £2,170. For simplicity, assume there are no allowable expenses. The two calculations are as follows:

Method 1

Final value	£7,000
less £6,000	£6,000
	£1,000
5/3 x £1,000	£1,667

Method 2

Final value	£7,000
less initial value	£3,500
less indexation allowance	£2,170
	£1,330

Method 2 gives the lower answer, so Jeffrey's chargeable gain is £1,330.

CGT on gifts of assets acquired before April 1982

Gains due to inflation were not always tax-free. The legislation taking them out of the CGT net is effective only from the end of March 1982 onwards. For an asset which you started to own *before* 1 April 1982 (or 6 April 1982 in the case of shares), the sums are slightly different from those outlined in the previous section. There are two methods of calculating your chargeable gain, as follows:

- **Method 1**   The initial value is usually taken to be the value of the asset on 31 March 1982, and the indexation allowance for the initial cost is based on inflation since that date. Any allowable expenses incurred before 31 March 1982 are ignored; allowable expenses after that date are indexed in the normal way
- **Method 2**   If working out your chargeable gain using Method 1 would result in a higher CGT bill than taking into account the full period during which you have owned the asset including the pre-March 1982 period, you can instead work out the chargeable gain based on the whole period. In this case, the initial value is the actual value at the time you first acquired the asset. The indexation allowance is worked out based on either the initial value *or* the asset's value on 31 March 1982 but adjusting for inflation only since March 1982.

If Method 1 and Method 2 both result in a gain, your chargeable gain will be the lower of the two amounts. If both methods give a loss, your allowable loss is the smaller amount. If one gives a gain and the other a loss, you are deemed to have made neither a gain nor a loss – there will be no CGT to pay but no loss to offset against gains on other assets. If Method 2 would, in any case, have produced neither a gain nor a loss, that method is used whatever the result of using Method 1 would have been. The comparison of the outcomes of Methods 1 and 2 is called the 'Kink test'.

You can choose to use just Method 1. If you do, *all* your assets will be covered by the election. The effect is as if you had sold all your assets on 31 March 1982 and immediately rebought them. It will usually be worth making this choice if the values of all or most of your assets were higher on 31 March 1982 than they were at the time you first acquired them.

EXAMPLE 6.4

Tom's grandmother, Emily, gives Tom some shares as a wedding present in June 2003. She originally bought them in 1979 for £1,500 and they are now worth £11,000. On 31 March 1982, they were valued at just £1,000. Emily's chargeable gain is worked out using Methods 1 and 2 as follows:

Method 1

Final value of shares	£11,000
less value of shares on 31 March 1982	£1,000
less indexation allowance for period March 1982 to April 1998 (see below)	£1,047
Chargeable gain (before losses and taper relief)	£8,953

Method 2

Final value of shares	£11,000
less initial value of shares	£1,500
less indexation allowance	£1,571
Chargeable gain (before losses and taper relief)	£7,929

Indexation allowance

Indexation factor for inflation from 31 March 1982 to April 1998	1.047
Indexation allowance using value at 31 March 1982 (1.047 x £1,000)	£1,047
Indexation allowance using initial value (1.047 x £1,500)	£1,571

The result is smaller using Method 2, so Emily's net chargeable gain is £7,929.

Working out your indexation allowance

Your indexation allowance is the appropriate indexation factor multiplied by the relevant initial value or allowable expense. The indexation factor depends on the month when you first acquired the asset or incurred the expense. Until April 1998, the factor also varied according to the month in which you disposed of the asset. But, since indexation allowance now runs only up to April 1998, there is just one set of indexation factors which applies to all disposals you make from April 1998 onwards. These are shown in Table 6.2. Look along the left-hand side to find the year in which you acquired the asset or incurred the expense; run your eye across to the column for the relevant month. This is the indexation factor you should use. See Example 6.5.

EXAMPLE 6.5

In September 2003, Christina gives her daughter Michelle some jewellery which Christina inherited from her own mother in February 1990. She needs to work out what indexation allowance she can claim for the period February 1990 to April 1998. Using Table 6.2, she finds the year 1990 along the left-hand side and runs across to the column for February. The entry tells her that the indexation factor to use is 0.353.

Table 6.2 Indexation factors for gifts or disposals you make from April 1998 onwards

	Jan	Feb	Mar	April	May	June	July	Aug	Sept	Oct	Nov	Dec
1982	–	–	1.047	1.006	0.992	0.987	0.986	0.985	0.987	0.977	0.967	0.971
1983	0.968	0.960	0.956	0.929	0.921	0.917	0.906	0.898	0.889	0.883	0.876	0.871
1984	0.872	0.865	0.859	0.834	0.828	0.823	0.825	0.808	0.804	0.793	0.788	0.789
1985	0.783	0.769	0.752	0.716	0.708	0.704	0.707	0.703	0.704	0.701	0.695	0.693
1986	0.689	0.683	0.681	0.665	0.662	0.663	0.667	0.662	0.654	0.652	0.638	0.632
1987	0.626	0.620	0.616	0.597	0.596	0.596	0.597	0.593	0.588	0.580	0.573	0.574
1988	0.574	0.568	0.562	0.537	0.531	0.525	0.524	0.507	0.500	0.485	0.478	0.474
1989	0.465	0.454	0.448	0.423	0.414	0.409	0.408	0.404	0.395	0.384	0.372	0.369
1990	0.361	0.353	0.339	0.300	0.288	0.283	0.282	0.269	0.258	0.248	0.251	0.252
1991	0.249	0.242	0.237	0.222	0.218	0.213	0.215	0.213	0.208	0.204	0.199	0.198
1992	0.199	0.193	0.189	0.171	0.167	0.167	0.171	0.171	0.166	0.162	0.164	0.168
1993	0.179	0.171	0.167	0.156	0.152	0.153	0.156	0.151	0.146	0.147	0.148	0.146
1994	0.151	0.144	0.141	0.128	0.124	0.124	0.129	0.124	0.121	0.120	0.119	0.114
1995	0.114	0.107	0.102	0.091	0.087	0.085	0.091	0.085	0.080	0.085	0.085	0.079
1996	0.083	0.078	0.073	0.066	0.063	0.063	0.067	0.062	0.057	0.057	0.057	0.053
1997	0.053	0.049	0.046	0.040	0.036	0.032	0.032	0.026	0.021	0.019	0.019	0.016
1998	0.019	0.014	0.011	–	–	–	–	–	–	–	–	–

If you need the indexation factor for a disposal made before April 1998, you can work it out from the Retail Prices Index (RPI). This index is the most commonly used measure of the level of prices in the UK. Table 6.3 lists the RPI from March 1982 up to April 1998. The latest RPI figure you will need for CGT calculations is that for April 1998.

To work out the appropriate indexation factor, take the RPI figure for the month in which you disposed of the asset – call this R_D. Then take the RPI figure for the month in which you acquired the asset (or incurred the expense) or for March 1982, whichever is appropriate, and call this R_I. Now make the following calculation:

$$\text{Indexation factor} = \frac{R_D - R_I}{R_I}$$

Indexation factors are rounded to the nearest third decimal place.

EXAMPLE 6.6

Jack gave his mother, Rachel, some shares in February 1998. He originally bought them in August 1981 but he can claim indexation allowance only since March 1982. To work out the allowance, he takes the RPI for February 1998 which is 160.3 (see Table 6.3) and the RPI for March 1982 which is 79.44. He does the following sum:

$$\text{Indexation factor} = \frac{R_D - R_I}{R_I} = \frac{160.3 - 79.44}{79.44}$$
$$= 1.018$$

The indexation factor Jack needs to use is 1.018. The indexation allowance he can claim is the factor multiplied by the relevant initial value or allowable expense.

Shares and unit trusts

If you give away identical shares, unit trusts or other securities that you acquired all at the same time, the CGT rules apply in the same way as for any other asset. However, suppose you own shares in one

Table 6.3 Retail Prices Index (Base: January 1987 = 100)

	Jan	Feb	Mar	April	May	June	July	Aug	Sept	Oct	Nov	Dec
1982	–	–	79.44	81.04	81.62	81.85	81.88	81.90	81.85	82.26	82.66	82.51
1983	82.61	82.97	83.12	84.28	84.64	84.84	85.30	85.68	86.06	86.36	86.67	86.89
1984	86.84	87.20	87.48	88.64	88.97	89.20	89.10	89.94	90.11	90.67	90.95	90.87
1985	91.20	91.94	92.80	94.78	95.21	95.41	95.23	95.49	95.44	95.59	95.92	96.05
1986	96.25	96.60	96.73	97.67	97.85	97.79	97.52	97.82	98.30	98.45	99.29	99.62
1987	100.0	100.4	100.6	101.8	101.9	101.9	101.8	102.1	102.4	102.9	103.4	103.3
1988	103.3	103.7	104.1	105.8	106.2	106.6	106.7	107.9	108.4	109.5	110.0	110.3
1989	111.0	111.8	112.3	114.3	115.0	115.4	115.5	115.8	116.6	117.5	118.5	118.8
1990	119.5	120.2	121.4	125.1	126.2	126.7	126.8	128.1	129.3	130.3	130.0	129.9
1991	130.2	130.9	131.4	133.1	133.5	134.1	133.8	134.1	134.6	135.1	135.6	135.7
1992	135.6	136.3	136.7	138.8	139.3	139.3	138.8	138.9	139.4	139.9	139.7	139.2
1993	137.9	138.8	139.3	140.6	141.1	141.0	140.7	141.3	141.9	141.8	141.6	141.9
1994	141.3	142.1	142.5	144.2	144.7	144.7	144.0	144.7	145.0	145.2	145.3	146.0
1995	146.0	146.9	147.5	149.0	149.6	149.8	149.1	149.9	150.6	149.8	149.8	150.7
1996	150.2	150.9	151.5	152.6	152.9	153.0	152.4	153.1	153.8	153.8	153.9	154.4
1997	154.4	155.0	155.4	156.3	156.9	157.5	157.5	158.5	159.3	159.5	159.6	160.0
1998	159.5	160.3	160.8	162.6	–	–	–	–	–	–	–	–

company, all of the same type but bought at different times. Special rules are needed to identify which particular shares you are disposing of, so that you can use the correct initial value and indexation allowance (if applicable) in your calculations.

Gifts made on or after 6 April 1998

With the introduction of the CGT taper, it is important to know exactly when each asset was acquired. So, for gifts and other disposals made on or after 6 April 1998, the shares, unit trusts or other securities which you give away are matched to the ones you own in the following order:

- shares you bought on the same day
- shares purchased within the following 30 days. This rule was introduced to curb a practice called 'bed-and-breakfasting'. You used to be able to realise a capital gain or loss by selling shares one day and buying them back the next – such a move could be very tax-efficient (see page 168). Now, you will need to leave at least 30 days between selling the shares and buying them back – a risky strategy when the stock market might move against you. However, there are alternative ways to bed-and-breakfast (see page 168)
- shares bought on or after 6 April 1998, identifying which are the most recent acquisitions first – this is called a last-in-first-out (LIFO) basis
- shares in your '1982 pool' (see Batch 3, opposite)
- shares in your '1965 pool' (see Batch 4, page 94)
- shares you acquired before 6 April 1965, starting with the shares you bought most recently – i.e. LIFO basis. You can opt to have quoted shares treated as part of your 1965 pool instead.

There are two important points to note about the rules for identifying shares (and unit trusts and other securities):

- you must keep accurate records of your share purchases and sales, recording the dates of transactions, quantity and price of the shares involved
- the LIFO rules tend to minimise the amount of taper relief which you can claim.

EXAMPLE 6.7

Connie received 300 Alliance & Leicester shares when the building society was demutualised in April 1997 and she bought further shares in the company as follows:

9 April 1998	1,700 shares
2 November 1999	500 shares
16 July 2000	700 shares

In October 2003, she decides to give half her Alliance & Leicester shares to her niece, Harriet. The 1,600 shares she gives away are matched in the following order:

16 July 2000	700 shares
2 November 1999	500 shares
9 April 1998	400 shares
Total	1,600 shares

Any subsequent gifts or other disposals would be matched against the remaining 1,300 shares bought on 9 April 1998 and then her original 300 shares.

Gifts made before 6 April 1998

For gifts and other disposals you made before 6 April 1998, the problem of identifying which shares were being given away or sold was solved mainly by pooling all the identical shares and working out an average price and indexation allowance. Your shareholding was divided into a maximum of five 'batches':

- **Batch 1**   Your disposal was matched first to shares which you bought on the same day as the disposal. You could not claim any indexation allowance
- **Batch 2**   Next, your disposal was matched to shares which you bought within ten days before the disposal. You could not claim any indexation allowance
- **Batch 3**   Next, the disposal was matched to a 'pool' made up of all shares you acquired on or after 6 April 1982. To find the initial value of the shares and your indexation allowance, you need to

work out the value of the shares after indexation *for the pool as a whole* (see Example 6.8 below)

- **Batch 4**   Next, the disposal was matched to a 'pool' made up of all the shares you bought in the period 6 April 1965 up to 5 April 1982. Again, to value the shares, you need to look at the pool as a whole. The indexation allowance is calculated only from March 1982, but based either on the actual purchases you made or on the value at 31 March 1982, unless you have elected to have all your assets rebased to this date (see page 86)
- **Batch 5**   Finally, the disposal was matched to any shares which you acquired before 6 April 1965, starting with the shares you bought most recently and working backwards. You can opt to have quoted shares treated as part of batch 4 instead.

EXAMPLE 6.8

In January 1997, Gerald gave his sister Dot 1,000 shares in a company, valued at £3,000. These were part of a holding which Gerald originally acquired in two lots: 1,000 shares for £1,500 in June 1982 and 2,000 shares for £4,000 in March 1988. The shares formed a 'batch 3 pool'. The initial value of the pool after indexation was worked out as follows:

Cost of 1,000 shares bought in June 1982	£1,500
plus indexation allowance for period June 1982 to	
January 1997 (0.886 x £1,500)	£1,329
plus cost of 2,000 shares bought in March 1988	£4,000
plus indexation allowance for period March 1988 to	
January 1997 (0.483 x £4,000)	£1,932
Indexed value of pool	£8,761

Gerald gave away 1,000 of the 3,000 shares in the pool. The indexed value of the shares he gave away was deemed to be 1000/3000 x £8,761 = £2,920. Gerald's chargeable gain on the gift to Dot was worked out as follows:

Value of shares at the time of the gift	£3,000
less indexed value of the shares	£2,920
Chargeable gain	£80

The indexed value of the shares remaining in the pool was 2000/3000 x £8,761 = £5,841 as at January 1997. Further indexation allowance accrued up to the time Gerald disposed of these shares or April 1998 if that was sooner. After that the pool was 'closed'.

From 6 April 2000 onwards, the definition of 'business asset' for taper relief was expanded (see page 80) and now includes certain types of shareholdings even if you are not closely involved in running the business concerned. In particular, most shares acquired through employee share schemes and most shares in unlisted trading companies (including those quoted on the Alternative Investment Market) count as business assets. As such, they are treated very favourably for taper relief purposes – see page 102 for details.

How much tax?

If you are deemed to have made a chargeable gain on an asset you give away, there could be some tax to pay, but not necessarily. Everyone has a tax-free slice – more formally called the 'annual exempt amount'. This means that the first slice of chargeable gains which you make each year is tax-free. In 2003–4, you can have net chargeable gains of £7,900 before any CGT becomes payable. The tax-free slice for earlier years is shown in Table 6.4.

Table 6.4 Tax-free slice for capital gains

Tax year	Tax-free slice
1997–8	£6,500
1998–9	£6,800
1999–2000	£7,100
2000–1	£7,200
2001–2	£7,500
2002–3	£7,700
2003–4	£7,900

Claiming allowable losses

If you make a loss on something you give away or otherwise dispose of, you set the loss against gains you have made on other assets in the same tax year. You have no choice about this. Any capital losses made in the same year must be set against any gains to the extent that your gains are reduced to zero. This means that any taper relief and tax-free slice may then be wasted.

If your losses come to more than your gains for the tax year, you carry forward the unrelieved losses to future years. In general, you can never carry them back to earlier years – although, when you die, your executors can.

If your losses come to less than your gains for the tax year, you next deduct any losses you have brought forward from earlier years. Once again, you have no choice – you must set off any losses brought forward but, this time, only to the extent that your net chargeable gains are reduced to the amount of the tax-free slice. This means that, although taper relief may be wasted (see Example 6.9), your annual tax-free slice is not. Any losses not used up continue to be carried forward to be relieved in future years.

Since 6 April 1998, where you make a gift you deduct any losses you are claiming before applying the CGT taper and before deducting the tax-free slice. This means that losses, as well as gains, are reduced by the taper relief. But you do set off the losses in the way which benefits you most. This means, if you have made gains on several assets in the same year, setting losses against the gain(s) which qualify for the lowest taper relief – see Example 6.10.

Where you made the disposal before 6 April 1998, losses made in the same tax year were claimed after deducting indexation allowance but before the tax-free slice; losses carried forward from an earlier year were deducted after subtracting the tax-free slice for the year. But there was no need to claim any more in losses than was needed to reduce the gains to the amount of the tax-free slice. This ensured that no allowances or reliefs were wasted.

EXAMPLE 6.9

In 2003–4, Sally has gains before taper relief of £8,500 and carried-forward losses of £1,300. The tax-free slice for the year is £7,900.

Sally must set enough of her carried-forward losses against the gains to reduce them to the level of the tax-free slice. In other words: £8,500 – £600 = £7,900. She qualifies for 10 per cent taper relief on her gains, reducing them to 90% x £7,900 = £7,110. But this is now £790 less than her tax-free slice for the year, so £790 of her reliefs have been wasted. She pays no tax on her gains and continues to carry forward the remaining £700 of losses.

If instead Sally had made gains of only £7,900 for the tax year, there would have been no tax to pay on them because they would be covered by the tax-free slice and she would have continued to carry forward the full £1,300 of losses.

EXAMPLE 6.10

In November 2003, Liam gives two plots of land to his son. The first was inherited in 1989. The gain on this plot after indexation allowance but before taper relief is £20,300. He qualifies for six years' taper relief on this gain. This means the gain can be reduced by 20 per cent.

Liam bought the second plot in September 2000. The gain on this is £4,500 before taper relief. He has held the land for three complete tax years, which qualifies him for 5 per cent taper relief.

Liam is carrying forward losses of £3,000 which he made on share sales several years ago. Consider the impact of setting these losses against each gain:

Losses set against gain on plot 1

Gain on plot 1	£20,300
Less loss relief	£3,000
Gain on plot 1 before taper relief	£17,300
Less taper relief for plot 1 @ 20%	£3,460
Plus gain on plot 2	£4,500
Less taper relief for plot 2 @ 5%	£225
Chargeable gains after loss relief and taper relief	£18,115

Losses set against gain on plot 2

Gain on plot 2	£4,500
Less loss relief	£3,000
Gain on plot 2 before taper relief	£1,500
Less taper relief for plot 2 @ 5%	£75
Plus gain on plot 1	£20,300
Less taper relief for plot 1 @ 20%	£4,060
Chargeable gains after loss relief and taper relief	£17,665

Liam has lower chargeable gains and so pays less tax if he sets his carried-forward losses against the gain on plot 2 – in other words, the gain which qualifies for the lower rate of taper relief. This is because taper relief reduces the losses by less.

Working out the tax bill

If, after following these steps, you are left with a gain, there will be tax to pay. CGT is charged at three rates in 2003–4: the 10 per cent starting rate, the lower rate of 20 per cent and the higher rate of 40 per cent. To see which rate applies to you, add your taxable gains (after all the adjustments described above) to your taxable *income* for the year. The result of this sum tells you what rate of CGT is payable:

Table 6.5 Tax rate on chargeable gains 2003–4

This tax rate applies	If your gains plus taxable income equal:
10 per cent	Up to £1,960
20 per cent	From £1,961 to £30,500
40 per cent	More than £30,500

If your taxable income is below a threshold given in Table 6.5 and adding the gain to the income takes the total above the threshold, you will pay the lesser tax rate on part of your gain and the greater rate on the rest. For example, if you have taxable income of £29,600 in the 2003–4 tax year and taxable gains of £2,000 (a total of

£31,600), you would pay 20 per cent CGT on £900 of the gain and 40 per cent CGT on the £1,100 of gain above the higher-rate threshold.

EXAMPLE 6.11

Frederick made a chargeable gain of £5,125 on the unit trusts he gives to Colin (see page 84). But after taking account of chargeable gains on other assets he has disposed of during the tax year, Frederick still has £6,000 of his tax-free slice unused. He can set this against the gift to Colin, which means there will be no CGT to pay.

EXAMPLE 6.12

In the 2003–4 tax year, Emily has net chargeable gains of £8,329. She deducts the tax-free slice of £7,900, leaving taxable gains of £429. Emily's taxable income for the year is £30,100. The tax on her gains is worked out as follows:

Slice of gains in excess of £30,500 threshold	£29
Slice of gain within basic-rate band	£400
CGT at 40 per cent on £29	£11.60
CGT at 20 per cent on £400	£80.00
Total CGT bill	£91.60

Gifts between husband and wife

As described in Chapter 5, a gift to your husband or wife is normally free of capital gains tax. The recipient takes over the initial value, allowable expenses, indexation allowance and taper relief period of the original owner. Therefore, the gift of an asset to your husband or wife can save capital gains tax if he or she has unused losses, unused tax-free slice, or would pay tax on a gain at lower rate(s) than you.

Hold-over relief

With a few gifts you make, you could face bills for both CGT and IHT at the time the gift is made. Alternatively, you might face a CGT bill and have to use some or all of an IHT exemption which could trigger an IHT bill on a later gift. 'Hold-over relief' lets you avoid this potential for a double tax bill. The way it works is that, instead of being treated as having realised a gain on the asset you give away, you – in effect – give away your CGT liability along with the asset. Gifts which qualify for this relief must be made between individuals or trusts. They include:

- gifts which count as chargeable gifts for inheritance tax purposes (see Chapter 7) or would do so if they were not covered by the yearly tax-free exemption (see page 74) or the tax-free slice (see page 108). Gifts which are potentially exempt transfers (PETs) (see page 114) do not qualify for relief, unless they become chargeable because the person making the gift dies within seven years
- gifts of national heritage property – land, buildings, a work of art and so on – though you will not need to claim hold-over relief if the property qualifies as exempt from CGT (see page 69)
- gifts to political parties (see page 72)
- gifts made from accumulation-and-maintenance trusts at the time a beneficiary becomes entitled to the trust property or a life interest in it (see Chapter 9).

Hold-over relief is not given automatically. If you are making a gift to a person, both you and that person jointly claim the relief using the form in Inland Revenue Helpsheet IR295. If you are putting the gift into trust, only you need claim.

Relief is given in the following way. The chargeable gain you have made on the asset up to the time of the gift is worked out. That amount is deducted from your total chargeable gains for the year – so you pay no CGT on the gain. The chargeable gain on the asset is also deducted from the recipient's initial value of the gift. This increases the likelihood of a chargeable gain when the recipient comes to dispose of the gift (though whether or not any tax would be payable then would depend on the availability of reliefs and exemptions, such as unused tax-free slice or further hold-over relief). For the purposes of calculating CGT taper relief when the recipient eventually disposes of the asset, the clock starts ticking from the date on which the recipient became the new owner of the asset.

Before 14 March 1989, hold-over relief applied to a much wider range of gifts, including those which counted as PETs under the IHT legislation. The restrictions now applying to the relief mean that it is mainly useful when you are making gifts to a discretionary trust (see page 145) or where you become entitled to receive property from such a trust.

Hold-over relief may be clawed back if the person receiving the gift ceases to be a UK resident within six years of the end of the tax year in which the gift was made. The recipient will then be liable for CGT on the held-over gain but, if he or she doesn't pay, the Inland Revenue can seek to recover tax from the person who made the gift, which could land you with an unexpected CGT bill. If there is a possibility that the person to whom you are making the gift might move abroad, you could take out insurance to cover the possible CGT bill.

Giving away a business or business assets

Hold-over relief is also available when you give away assets used in your business or shares in an unlisted trading company. However, to counter tax avoidance, hold-over relief ceased to be available from 9 November 1999 onwards where shares or securities are transferred to any company.

Relief must be claimed, in most cases, jointly by both the giver and the recipient – use the form in Inland Revenue Helpsheet IR295. It works by enabling the giver to deduct the gain which would otherwise be payable from their chargeable gains, and the recipient deducts the same amount from the initial value at which he or she receives the assets or shares.

If the assets concerned have not been used in the business for the whole time that they were owned by the giver, then the amount of hold-over relief available may be scaled down proportionately (and the relevant period of ownership includes any time before 31 March 1982).

If hold-over relief is available on the assets anyway because they are subject to an IHT charge (see above) then the IHT-related hold-over relief applies rather than the business-related relief. Similarly, if the assets or shares qualified for 'retirement relief' (which until April 2003 reduced or eliminated a CGT bill that would otherwise be payable when you dispose of your business in order to retire), this was given in preference to hold-over relief.

Hold-over relief can also be claimed on gifts of agricultural property. If the land or property is not currently in use as part of your business, then relief may still be granted if the property also qualifies for relief from IHT (see page 121).

If you give away or otherwise dispose of business assets, a higher than normal rate of taper relief applies in respect of periods since April 1998 during which you held the asset. Taper relief for business assets was made more generous for disposals from 6 April 2000 and again from 6 April 2002 – Table 6.6 shows the rates that apply from 6 April 2002 onwards.

Table 6.6 CGT taper relief for business assets

If you have held the asset for this many complete years after 5 April 1998:	Your net chargeable gain is reduced by:	Only this percentage of your gain counts as chargeable:	For example, a net chargeable gain of £5,000 is reduced to:
0	No reduction	100%	£5,000
1	50%	50%	£2,500
2 or more	75%	25%	£1,250

Business assets can be:

- something used in your business if you are a sole trader or partner
- from 6 April 2004 onwards, something used in a business carried on by some other individual or partnership
- something used by a 'qualifying company' (see below)
- something you are required to have as a result of your employment
- shares in a qualifying company (see below).

The definition of a qualifying company changed from 6 April 2000 onwards. Before that date, it meant:

- a trading company where you controlled at least 25 per cent of the voting rights, or

- provided you were a full-time officer or employee of the company, a trading company where you controlled at least 5 per cent of the voting rights.

From 6 April 2000 onwards, the definition has been widened so that now it means:

- any unlisted trading company
- a quoted trading company where you control at least 5 per cent of the voting rights, or
- provided you are an officer or an employee (full- or part-time), any quoted company whether a trading or non-trading company.

'Unlisted' means that none of the company's shares are quoted on a recognised stock exchange. For this purpose, shares traded on the Alternative Investment Market (AIM) count as unlisted. 'Trading company' is a company carrying on one or more trades, professions or vocations in order to make a profit. It excludes simply holding investments (except where they do not make up a substantial extent of the company's activities) but specifically does include letting out furnished holiday accommodation on a commercial basis.

If you give away an asset which counted as a non-business asset before 6 April 2000, but a business asset from then on, you have to apportion any capital gain between the two periods and claim the relevant taper relief for each part – see Example 6.13. This can have the perverse effect of allowing more taper relief on an asset held for a shorter period of time than available on an asset held for a longer period – see Example 6.14.

As the two examples show, where an asset qualified as a business asset only from 6 April 2000 onwards, you may get higher taper relief if the period of ownership started on or after 6 April 2000. This begs the question: if you held such an asset before 6 April 2000, is there any way to reset the clock so that your taper relief period starts only from that date? The answer is: yes, there may be a way – for example, by transferring the asset to a trust (claiming hold-over relief – see page 100 – to transfer your gain to the trustees). This would start a new taper relief holding period in the hands of the trustees. Since 6 April 2002, this will generally be worth doing in the case of expensive assets because the trust needs to hold them for only two years in order to qualify for maximum business taper relief. But for smaller assets, bear in mind that there are usually costs involved in setting up a trust and, as time goes by, the two-year period from April 1998 to April 2000 will make up a smaller and smaller proportion of the total time you have held the asset, and so have a decreasing impact on the tax bill.

EXAMPLE 6.13

Since 6 April 1998, Bella has held 3 per cent of the ordinary shares of Hammerson Ltd, an unquoted electronics company. Until 6 April 2000, this holding did not count as a business asset but from that date it does.

On 10 May 2003, Bella decides to give the shares to her granddaughter, Phoebe. She realises a taxable profit of £12,000. For taper relief purposes, she has held the shares for five complete years. This entitles her to 15 per cent taper relief at the non-business rate and 75 per cent at the business taper rate.

During three of these years (6 April 2000 to 5 April 2003), the shares counted as a business asset. Therefore, 75 per cent taper relief is applied to 3/5th of £12,000, reducing that part of the taxable gain to 3/5th x £12,000 x 25% = £1,800.

During the period 6 April 1998 to 5 April 2000 the shares counted as non-business assets. Therefore 15 per cent taper relief is applied to 2/5th of £12,000, reducing that part of the gain to 2/5th x £12,000 x 85% = £4,080.

Bella's taxable gain after taper relief is £1,800 + £4,080 = £5,880.

EXAMPLE 6.14

Bella's husband, Richard, also has a 3 per cent holding in Hammerson Ltd (see Example 6.13). Neither Bella nor Richard work for the company. They look at whether it would be more tax-efficient if Richard instead of Bella gave shares to Phoebe.

Richard first acquired his shares on 6 April 2000. Coincidentally, on 10 May 2003, Richard would also have a gain of £12,000 if he gave away the shares. The shares count as a business asset throughout the three complete years that Richard has held them and so qualify for 75 per cent taper relief. This reduces Richard's taxable gain to £12,000 x 25% = £3,000.

Even though Richard has not held Hammerson shares for as long as Bella, his taxable gain is significantly lower (£3,000 compared with Bella's £5,880). It would, therefore, be more tax-efficient for Richard to make the gift to Phoebe.

Where something is used partly for business and partly privately, the gain will be divided pro rata and the appropriate taper relief applied to each part.

If you are planning to give away your business or farm, you should seek advice from your accountant and solicitor.

Telling the taxman

If you receive a tax return asking about income and gains you have made in 2002–3, give the information asked for and send the return to your tax office by 30 September 2003 if you want your tax office to work out the tax for you or by 31 January 2004 if you are happy to work out your own tax bill. For gains made in 2003–4, you have until 31 January 2005 to submit details to your tax office.

If you owe less than £2,000 tax for, say, the 2002–3 tax year, instead of paying a lump sum by 31 January 2004 the tax can be collected through pay-as-you-earn (PAYE), which means your payment is spread throughout the tax year beginning on 6 April 2004. To do this you must normally submit your tax return by 30 September 2003, but if you file your return online you have until the end of December.

If you do not receive a tax return, you have six months from the end of the tax year in which you made any chargeable gains to tell your tax office. For example, if you owe tax on gains made in 2002–3, you must notify your tax office by 5 October 2003. It will then send you a tax return to complete. Under self-assessment, where tax returns are sent out after 31 October, you have a full three months to send them back, rather than being tied to the normal 31 January deadline. If you have not made any chargeable gains, there is no requirement for you to report any disposals to your tax office.

If you do not let the Revenue know about chargeable gains you have made, you can be fined up to the amount of the tax due and unpaid by 31 January following the end of the tax year in which the gains were made. (If you pay the tax on time, you cannot be fined, even if you still haven't given the tax office details of the gains.)

You are required to keep a record of any information needed to calculate your tax bill. The information may be original documents or copies and, by law, must be kept for one year following the date on which you filed your tax return with your tax office. Your tax office can ask to see these documents. However, it is prudent to hold on to your records for longer than this, because, if you discover an error, you can go back up to five years from 31 January following the year of assessment to claim back tax overpaid.

The rules about keeping documents are different for businesses. If you are self-employed or a partner, you must keep any records relating to business gifts for five years from 31 January following the end of the tax year to which they relate. For information about the tax treatment of gains on gifts made by companies and the record-keeping requirements, talk to your accountant.

EXAMPLE 6.15

Unexpectedly, Emily did not receive a tax return for the 2002–3 tax year. However, she knows that she has some capital gains tax to pay. She must tell her tax office by 5 October 2003, so that it can send her a tax return to complete. Emily or her accountant should calculate the amount of CGT due and ensure that it is paid by 31 January 2004. Alternatively, Emily can ask her tax office to work out the tax bill but if the return reaches the office after 30 September 2003 it cannot guarantee to let Emily know the amount of CGT due in time for the 31 January 2004 payment date. To avoid any fine, Emily should pay an estimated amount by 31 January 2004 even if she does not know the exact bill by then.

Chapter 7

Inheritance tax on lifetime gifts

A TAX NO-ONE PAYS?

'Do you have to pay any inheritance tax when you give me Hadley Hall?' asked Albert.

'It's none of your business,' snapped Daisy, 'though if you'd bothered to learn anything useful you'd know that there's no inheritance tax on a gift from one person to another – it's a PET! I suppose you think that's a furry animal.'

'As it happens I *do* know about PETs,' retorted Albert, 'and there could be a tax bill – what's more I could end up having to pay it. So it really is my business too.'

Throughout the lifetime of the Labour government which came to power in 1997, rumours have abounded that it would make radical changes to the inheritance tax (IHT) system, closing off exemptions and killing the much-loved PET (potentially exempt transfer). Each budget has been an anti-climax and the inheritance tax regime, bar a little tinkering, has – so far – been left intact.

Chapter 5 listed the many exemptions from IHT for gifts made during your lifetime – so many in fact that IHT is sometimes referred to as a voluntary tax. That is not quite true. Two types of gift could result in an IHT bill during the giver's lifetime:

- gifts to or from a company
- gifts to a 'discretionary trust' (see Chapter 10).

Gifts from one person to another, which counted as PETs when they were made (see page 114) can also cause an IHT bill if the person making the gift dies within seven years. You must also be careful if you make 'gifts with reservation': that is, giving away something from which you continue to benefit.

Gifts which are taxable when they are made

The scope of inheritance tax

The forerunner of IHT was called capital transfer tax (CTT). The two taxes were virtually the same, with one very important difference: CTT applied to virtually *all* gifts, whereas under the IHT system, gifts between *individuals* (and certain types of trust) count as PETs. These are tax-free as long as the giver survives for seven years after making the gift. However, even under the present system, some gifts – that is, those which are *not* between individuals (and certain trusts) – can prompt an immediate tax bill. In tax language, such gifts are called 'chargeable transfers' and they comprise mainly gifts involving companies and gifts to discretionary trusts. In this book, chargeable transfers are also referred to as 'chargeable gifts'.

How a chargeable transfer is taxed

IHT does not apply to each gift you make in isolation. It is based on all the chargeable transfers you have made over the last seven years. Adding all these gifts together gives you a 'cumulative total' – called your 'running total' in this book. The first slice of the running total – up to £255,000 for the 2003–4 tax year – is tax-free. You pay tax only on gifts which take you above that limit. The tax-free slice is normally increased each tax year in line with inflation up to the previous September but the changes have sometimes been more erratic. Table 7.1 shows the amounts for recent years.

The IHT rate on lifetime gifts is set with reference to the rate of tax which may apply to your estate when you die (see Chapter 13). The death rate for the 2003–4 tax year is 40 per cent; the lifetime rate is half this, in other words 20 per cent.

Table 7.1 Rates of inheritance tax

Tax year	Tax-free slice	Rate of tax on running total in excess of the tax-free slice	
		Death rate	Lifetime rate
1996–7	£200,000	40%	20%
1997–8	£215,000	40%	20%
1998–9	£223,000	40%	20%
1999–2000	£231,000	40%	20%
2000–1	£234,000	40%	20%
2001–2	£242,000	40%	20%
2002–3	£250,000	40%	20%
2003–4	£255,000	40%	20%

Tax due on a lifetime gift can be paid either by the person (or trust or company) making the gift or by the person (or trust or company) receiving the gift. If the person making the gift pays, the tax itself counts as part of the gift, which increases the value of the transfer to be taxed. A gift where the giver pays the tax is called a 'net gift'; if the recipient pays the tax, it is called a 'gross gift'. You can work out how much tax is due on a net or gross gift using the calculators below and overleaf.

CALCULATOR FOR INHERITANCE TAX ON A NET GIFT 2003–4

A What is your running total before making the gift (including any tax paid by you)?

B Work out the tax due on your running total:
If **A** is £255,000 or less, the tax due is 0.
If **A** is more than £255,000, the tax due is 20% x [**A** – £255,000].

C Subtract **B** from **A**. This gives you your net running total.

D Enter value of gift – use the amount the recipient will receive.

E Add **C** and **D**. This gives you your new net running total.

F Work out the tax due on your new running total:
If **E** is £255,000 or less, the tax is 0.
If **E** is more than £255,000, the tax due is 25% x [**E** – £255,000].

G Subtract **B** from **F**. This is the amount of tax (to be paid by the giver) on the current gift.

CALCULATOR FOR INHERITANCE TAX ON A GROSS GIFT 2003–4

A What is your running total before making the gift (including any tax paid by you)?

B Work out the tax due on your running total:
If **A** is £255,000 or less, the tax due is 0.
If **A** is more than £255,000, the tax due is 20% x [**A** – £255,000].

C Enter the current gift – use the amount you are giving.

D Find your new running total by adding **C** and **A**.

E Work out the tax due on your new running total:
If **D** is £255,000 or less, the tax due is 0.
If **D** is more than £255,000, the tax due is 20% x [**D** – £255,000].

F Subtract **B** from **E**. This is the amount of tax (to be paid by the recipient) on the current gift.

EXAMPLE 7.1

Frederick has a grown-up daughter, Louise, who has a learning disability. She lives largely independently and has a modest income from a job in a supermarket but she would not be able to cope with large sums of money or complicated planning for the future.

Frederick wants to make sure that Louise will always be financially secure and to provide a 'last resort' emergency fund which would also be available to his son Colin if the need arose. Frederick decides to set up a discretionary trust for the benefit of his children, making himself and his sister the trustees who will decide when Louise or Colin need help and how much help they should receive. (For more about discretionary trusts, see Chapter 9.)

Frederick sets up the trust in October 2003 with a gift of £70,000. He will pay any tax due on this, so it is a net gift. As Frederick has not used any of his annual exemption of £3,000 for 2003–4 (see page 74), only £67,000 counts as a chargeable transfer. Over the seven years from November 1996 to October 2003, he has made other chargeable transfers of £200,000. He uses the calculator for net gifts (see page 109) to work out his inheritance tax position as follows:

A	Frederick's running total before making the gift (including any tax paid by him)	£200,000
B	Tax due on his running total: If **A** is £255,000 or less, the tax due is 0 If **A** is more than £255,000, the tax due is 20% x [**A** – £255,000]	£0
C	Subtract **B** from **A**. This gives you Frederick's net running total	£200,000
D	Enter value of gift – the amount the trust will receive	£67,000
E	Add **C** and **D**. This gives Frederick's new net running total	£267,000
F	Tax due on his new running total: If **E** is £255,000 or less, the tax is 0 If **E** is more than £255,000, the tax due is 25% x [**E** – £255,000] (i.e. $\frac{1}{4}$ x £12,000)	£3,000
G	Subtract **B** from **F**. This is the amount of tax (to be paid by Frederick) on the gift to the trust.	£3,000

Frederick's gift to the trust is made up of the £70,000 plus £3,000 he pays in tax – £73,000 in total.

EXAMPLE 7.2

Suppose, in Example 7.1 above, that Frederick decided to pay £70,000 into the trust, but to leave the trust to pay any tax. In this case, the chargeable transfer of £67,000 would be a *gross* gift. Using the calculator for gross gifts (see page 110), the inheritance tax position would be:

A	Frederick's running total before making the gift (including any tax paid by him)	£200,000
B	Tax due on his running total: If **A** is £255,000 or less, the tax due is 0. If **A** is more than £255,000, the tax due is 20% x [**A** – £255,000]	£0
C	Enter the current gift – the amount Frederick is giving	£67,000
D	Frederick's new running total is found by adding **C** and **A**	£267,000
E	Tax due on his new running total: If **D** is £255,000 or less, the tax due is 0. If **D** is more than £255,000, the tax due is 20% x [**D** – £255,000]. (i.e. 20% x £12,000)	£2,400
F	Subtract **B** from **E**. This is the amount of tax (to be paid by the trust) on the gift to the trust.	£2,400

The trust would receive £70,000 but £2,400 would have to be used to pay the IHT bill due on the transfer leaving £67,600 in the trust fund.

Death within seven years

Tax on a lifetime gift which is a chargeable transfer is usually charged at a rate of 20 per cent (in 2003–4). But, if the person making the gift dies within three years, the gift is reassessed and tax is charged at the full death rate current at the time of death (i.e. 40 per cent for 2003–4). If the giver dies more than three years but less than seven years after making the gift, the gift is still reassessed for tax but at less than the full death rate due to the effect of IHT taper relief. Table 7.2 shows the rates which would apply.

The extra tax due will be charged to the person who received the gift but, if they cannot or will not pay, the giver's estate must pay the bill.

Table 7.2 New tax rate if giver dies within seven years of making a gift

Years between gift and death	% of full death rate which applies	% rate of tax on the gift (at 2003–4 rates)
Up to 3	100	40
More than 3 and up to 4	80	32
More than 4 and up to 5	60	24
More than 5 and up to 6	40	16
More than 6 and up to 7	20	8
More than 7	0	no extra tax

At first sight, you might assume that there will never be any extra tax to pay if the giver dies more than five years after making the chargeable transfer, since the rate of tax which would then apply (16 per cent assuming 2003–4 rates) is lower than the 20 per cent rate at which tax is paid on lifetime gifts. However, the position is not so simple: in reassessing the gift, it is looked at in relation to the running total at the time the gift was made; since PETs may also be reassessed (see page 114) when the giver dies, a PET made within the seven-year period but before the chargeable transfer being considered would increase the running total. Also, bear in mind that the original tax on the gift was charged at the tax-free slice and rates applicable at the time of the gift, whereas tax due on reassessment is charged at the tax-free slice and rates applicable at the time of death – and a change in rates may result in extra tax becoming due. Equally, a relaxation in IHT rates may seem to imply a reduction in the tax bill, but none of the tax paid at the time the gift was made is refundable – see Example 7.3 on page 116. For a summary of tax-free slices and tax rates applicable in earlier years, see Table 7.1 on page 109.

Potentially exempt transfers (PETs)

Most of the gifts that you make during your lifetime are free of IHT. Even if they are not covered by one of the specific exemptions outlined in Chapter 5, they will count as potentially exempt transfers (PETs). As the name suggests, these gifts are exempt but with a proviso: the giver must survive for seven years after making the gift. The purpose of this rule is to prevent people escaping tax on their estates by giving away their possessions shortly before death.

If the giver does die within seven years of making a gift, the gift loses its exempt status and is reassessed as a chargeable gift. This has two effects, which are quite separate though unfortunately often confused:

- first, because the PET is now treated as chargeable, the taxman steps back in time and asks: at the time this gift was made, given that we now know it is chargeable, should any tax have been paid? What happens if the answer is 'yes' is described under 'How the PET is taxed' below
- second, because the PET has become a chargeable gift, it enters into your running total, which may mean that extra tax becomes due on subsequent chargeable gifts, other PETs being reassessed and the estate left at the time of death – see Example 7.3 on page 116.

How the PET is taxed

If the giver dies within seven years, the PET is treated as if it had originally been a chargeable transfer. Of course, this does not necessarily mean tax is due, because:

- in the tax year you made the gift, you might not have used your yearly £3,000 tax-free exemption (see page 74). And, if you had not used the exemption in the previous year either, you might have the scope to give up to £6,000 in that tax year in chargeable gifts without having any tax to pay

- as with any other gift which might be taxable, it is not looked at in isolation. It is included in your running total over the seven years up to the date of the gift in question. Only if the running total exceeds the relevant tax-free slice will any tax become due. In the case of a reassessed PET, the relevant tax-free slice is the amount in force at the time of death (not at the time the gift was made) – i.e. £255,000 if the giver died in the 2003–4 tax year.

It is important to note that PETs up to seven years before death are reassessed and gifts in the seven years up to the making of the PET are looked at in deciding whether tax is due. This means that gifts made during the *14* years before death could be relevant.

If the running total up to the making of the reassessed PET does come to more than the tax-free slice at the time of death, then IHT is due at the rates current at the time of death – i.e. 40 per cent in 2003-4. However, if the giver died more than three years after making the gift, the amount of tax payable is reduced by the effect of IHT taper relief. Table 7.3 shows the effect of this relief.

Table 7.3 How IHT taper relief reduces tax on a reassessed PET

Years between making the PET and death	% of full death rate which applies	Effective % rate of tax on the gift (at 2003–4 rates)
Up to 3	100	40
More than 3 and up to 4	80	32
More than 4 and up to 5	60	24
More than 5 and up to 6	40	16
More than 6 and up to 7	20	8
More than 7	0	no tax

Bear in mind that taper relief only reduces any tax due on the reassessed PET. If there is no tax payable on the PET (for example, because the running total including the PET is less than the tax-free slice), then taper relief has no relevance. And taper relief cannot be used to reduce tax on the estate of the deceased giver, even if that tax bill was created or increased because of the inclusion of the reassessed PET in the running total up to the time of death.

Who pays the tax?

Any tax which becomes due on a reassessed PET is first charged to the person who received the gift. If he or she cannot or will not pay, the late giver's estate must pay the bill. It is possible to take out insurance to cover the potential tax bill on a PET.

EXAMPLE 7.3

Godfrey dies on 1 January 2004 leaving an estate of £250,000. He made the following gifts during his lifetime (assuming the annual tax-free exemptions have already been used in each case):

1 January 1994	Chargeable transfer	£100,000 paid into a discretionary trust
1 January 1996	Chargeable transfer	£50,000 paid into a discretionary trust
1 February 1997	Chargeable transfer	£68,000 paid into a discretionary trust
1 June 1999	PET	£80,000 given to nephew, John

On his death, chargeable transfers and PETs made within the seven years before death – i.e. in the period 2 January 1997 to 1 January 2004 – are reassessed as follows:

- chargeable transfer made on 1 February 1997. Tax was originally paid in 1996–7 on a running total of £100,000 + £50,000 + £68,000 = £218,000. The tax-free slice then was £200,000 and the trust paid tax at 20 per cent on the £18,000 of the February 1997 gift which exceeded that slice – i.e. tax of 20 per cent x £18,000 = £3,600. When the gift is reassessed on Godfrey's death, there is no tax to be paid because the running total of £218,000 is less than the tax-free slice in force at the time of death – i.e. £255,000. However, no refund is allowed of the tax already paid in Godfrey's lifetime
- PET made on 1 June 1999. No tax was charged on the PET at the time it was made. When it is reviewed on Godfrey's death, the PET becomes the top slice of £80,000 on a running total of £100,000 + £50,000 + £68,000 + £80,000 = £298,000. Earlier gifts have used up £218,000 of the tax-free slice of £255,000. £37,000 of the PET exhausts the remaining tax-free slice. This leaves £43,000 to be taxed

at the death rate of 40 per cent. So tax is initially calculated as 40% x £43,000 = £17,200. However, taper relief applies because the PET was more than three years before Godfrey's death. Only 60 per cent of the tax is payable – i.e. 60% x £17,200 = £10,2320.

Although more properly the subject of Chapter 13, it is worth noting here what impact the reassessed chargeable transfers and PETs have on tax on the estate. The estate counts as the top slice of £250,000 on a running total of £68,000 + £80,000 + £250,000 = £398,000. The earlier gifts use up £148,000 of the £255,000 tax-free slice. And £107,000 of the estate uses up the remaining part of the tax-free slice. This leaves £143,000 of the estate to be taxed at 40 per cent – i.e. 40% x £143,000 = £57,200. Note that taper relief is not relevant to this tax bill which is payable in full – by the estate, unless the will specifies otherwise.

Fall in value

There is some tax relief if the value of a PET or chargeable transfer has fallen since the time it was first made. Whoever is paying the tax is allowed to deduct the fall in value from the original value of the gift. Bear in mind, however, that the original value of a gift was the loss to the giver *not* the value to the recipient, so even a large percentage fall in the value of the item in the recipient's hands might have only a small impact on the value of the item for IHT purposes (see Example 7.4). The fall-in-value relief is not given automatically; the person paying the tax must make a claim to the Capital Taxes Office.*

EXAMPLE 7.4

In September 2001, Dorothy gave her niece, Charlotte, one of a pair of rare antique vases. As a pair, the vases had a market price of £110,000 but individually they were each worth only £40,000. The value of the gift was the loss to Dorothy. In other words, the difference between the market price of the pair and the price of the remaining vase: £110,000 – £40,000 = £70,000. The gift counted as a PET and so there was no tax to pay.

In February 2004, Dorothy dies and Charlotte receives a demand for tax on the gift of the vase. She has the vase valued by a local dealer who puts a market price of only £35,000 on the vase now. Charlotte agrees to the reduced value of the gift which is worked out as the original loss to the giver less the fall in value: £70,000 – £5,000 = £65,000.

Tax now due on the gift is calculated as follows. Just before she made the gift to Charlotte, in September 2001, Dorothy's cumulative total of gifts, including other PETs that have become chargeable since her death, came to £193,000. Adding the value of the vase brings the total to £193,000 + £65,000 = £258,000. This is £3,000 more than the 2003–4 tax-free slice of £255,000, so IHT is payable at 40% x £3,000 = £1,200. As fewer than three years have passed since Dorothy made the gift, taper relief does not apply.

Protection from IHT on a PET

Life insurance can be used to protect the person receiving a PET from a possible IHT bill (see page 223 for how this would work). The insurance could be taken out by the person making a PET, in which case the insurance would itself count as a gift but might qualify for one of the IHT exemptions (see Chapter 5). Another option would be for the person receiving the PET to pay premiums him or herself for a term insurance policy based on the life of the giver.

Life insurance can also be used in just the same way to protect the recipient of a gift that counts as a chargeable transfer from the possibility of an extra tax bill, should the giver die within seven years.

For more information, seek advice from an insurance broker* or an independent financial adviser.*

Gifts with reservation

Problems can arise if you give something away but continue to benefit from it in some way. A 'gift with reservation' occurs in the following circumstances:

- if the person to whom you give the gift does not really take possession of it: for example, you might give a valuable painting to someone but insist that it carries on hanging in your home

- if you carry on deriving some benefit from the thing you give away unless you pay a full market rate – or the equivalent in kind – for your use of the asset. This might occur, for example, if you give your home to your children but you retain the right to live in part of the property rent-free. (See Chapter 15 for more about this.)

Special rules apply to gifts with reservation. However, if the gift is covered by one of the IHT exemptions outlined in Chapter 5 at the time the gift is made, the special rules do not normally apply and there is no IHT to pay. But you cannot claim the 'expenditure out of normal income' exemption against a gift with reservation and you cannot use your £3,000 yearly exemption against the gift at the time it is made.

Unless the gift counts as a chargeable transfer, there is no IHT to pay when the gift is made but there may be later on. The special rules come into operation at the time the person who made the gift dies. If, at the time of death, the giver still benefited from the gift with reservation, the possessions they gave are treated as if they are still part of the giver's estate and were given away only at the time of death (see Chapter 13). If the giver stopped benefiting from the possessions some time before his or her death, the gift with reservation is treated as a PET made at the time the giver's benefit stopped. Provided that this was more than seven years before death, IHT will not apply. On the other hand, if that time was within the seven years before the giver's death, the normal PET rules apply and there may be an IHT bill on the gift. But, in the event that the giver had unused yearly exemption for the year in which the gift stopped being a gift with reservation, it is the Inland Revenue's (controversial) view that the exemption cannot be set against this PET.

If the gift with reservation counted as a chargeable transfer, IHT may have been paid when the gift was made – this would apply, say, to a gift you made to a discretionary trust. The special rules still apply when the giver dies but other rules prevent IHT being payable twice over on the same gift. For example, suppose you give £10,000 to a discretionary trust designed to benefit your whole family, including yourself. Because you are a beneficiary of the trust, you are still able to benefit from the £10,000, so it counts as a gift with reservation.

As a gift to a discretionary trust, it is a chargeable transfer on which IHT may be payable. But, if you continue to be a beneficiary of the trust right up to the time you die, the £10,000 will continue to be deemed as part of your estate and treated as if it was given outright to the trust only on the date of your death. At that time, the gift may again give rise to an IHT bill but special rules give relief against the double charge (though not against other tax charges relating to the trust, see Chapter 10).

A gift is not a gift with reservation if you continue to benefit but you pay for the right to do so.

If you can carve up a possession which you intend to give so that you can keep a distinct part of it, you can give away the remainder without that part counting as a gift with reservation. However, your scope to adopt this approach to gifts of land has been severely limited by the Inland Revenue's reaction to the success of a tax case, Ingram and Another *v* Inland Revenue Commissioners. Lady Ingram owned the freehold to her house and land. She divided this into a rent-free lease which she kept and a separate freehold, subject to the lease, which she gave away (an arrangement known as a 'lease carve-out'). The Inland Revenue claimed that the gift of the freehold was a gift with reservation since Lady Ingram retained the right to live in the house without paying any rent. The case took nine years and finally reached the House of Lords. The Lords decided that the rent-free lease was *not* a reservation of benefit in relation to the gift of the freehold. This was a triumph for the taxpayer and looked set to open the way for many similar schemes. The Inland Revenue was not amused. In the 1999 Budget, new rules were introduced to ensure that such schemes are after all caught by the reservation of benefit rules. The rules apply to gifts of an interest in land made on or after 9 March 1999.

As mentioned above, the gift with reservation rules do not apply if a gift is already covered by certain of the exemptions described in Chapter 5. A recent court case (Commissioners of the Inland Revenue *vs* Eversden and Another) highlighted how the exemption for gifts between husband and wife could be used to circumvent the reservation rules. A wife transferred her home to a trust which gave her husband a right for life to receive the income of the trust fund, after which the trust property passed to various discretionary trusts. A class of beneficiaries that included the wife could benefit from the discretionary trusts. Until her death, the wife continued to live in the trust property. It was agreed that the initial gift to the trust in favour of the husband was not a gift with reservation because it was covered by the exemption for a gift from one spouse to the other. The Inland Revenue argued that the subsequent transfers were separate events that did fall foul of the gift with reservation rules because the wife could benefit from the transfers. However, the court disagreed and held that the initial gift of the life interest to the husband took the whole arrangements outside the scope of the reservation rules.

The Revenue is going to appeal to ask the courts to reconsider this judgment. In the meantime, it was thought that the government might introduce measures in the 2003 Budget to close this route for saving tax, but no change was made and so for now this type of arrangement can still be effective. If you are attracted to anything along these lines, it is essential that you get advice from a solicitor★ or tax adviser★ to ensure that the trust wording achieves your objectives and that any tax pitfalls are avoided.

Giving away the family business

If you pass on your business or farm during your lifetime, you may qualify for relief against IHT on the value of the transfer. Basic details of the schemes are given in Chapter 13, which looks at passing on your business or farm in your will. The application of the scheme is broadly the same in the case of lifetime gifts, with one important exception, outlined below.

Whether your gift of business or agricultural property counts as a PET or as a chargeable transfer, the relief will be clawed back, if:

- you die within seven years of making the gift, and
- the recipient no longer owns the business or farm, and
- the recipient does not fully reinvest the proceeds in – in the case of business property relief – a new business, or – in the case of agricultural property relief – a new farm.

Relief will also be clawed back if the recipient dies before you and no longer owns the business or farm.

In view of this clawback, it is extremely important that you plan carefully and that you take expert advice from your accountant★

and a solicitor,* before making a gift of part or all of your business or farm.

Telling the taxman

You do not have to tell the tax authorities about any lifetime gifts you make which count as PETs but you should keep a record of them. Put a copy of the record where it would be found by whoever would handle your estate if you were to die – for example, in the same place as your will. It would be the responsibility of that person to pass these details on to the Capital Taxes Office so that PETs could be reassessed.

If you make gifts which count as chargeable transfers – i.e. gifts to discretionary trusts or involving companies – you do not need to tell the tax office, provided:

- your total chargeable transfers during the year come to no more than £10,000, and
- your running total of gifts during the last ten years – probably the government intended to reduce this to seven years but so far the change has been overlooked – comes to no more than £40,000.

If you have made a chargeable transfer that should be reported, you need to complete **form IHT100**, which is available from the Capital Taxes Office.* Normally, you must send in the completed form within 12 months of the end of the month in which you made the gift but tax will usually have to be paid before this.

In the case of lifetime chargeable gifts, IHT is normally due to be paid six months after the end of the month in which the gift was made. But, if the gift was made in the period 6 April to 30 September inclusive, tax is due on 30 April of the following year.

Should extra tax become payable on a chargeable gift, or should the PET become chargeable because of the death of the giver within seven years of making the gift, the tax is due six months after the end of the month in which the death occurs. In some limited cases, it may be possible to pay the tax in ten equal yearly instalments.

Chapter 8

Income tax and gifts

WHOSE TAX IS IT ANYWAY?

'I don't believe this,' Michael exploded, waving the tax assessment he had just opened. 'The Revenue have charged me income tax on Rebecca's savings account.'

Rebecca looked on quizzically. 'But you opened the account for me, Daddy. Isn't it mine any more?'

There is no income tax as such on a gift but just as a gift to charity can affect the income tax position of the giver and the recipient, so too can gifts between individuals. If you are aware of the types of gift that affect income tax and the pitfalls to watch out for, you are then well placed to arrange your giving in the most tax-efficient way.

Gifts between husband and wife

Independent taxation

An important date in the tax calendar was 6 April 1990, because, from the 1990–1 tax year onwards, 'independent taxation' was introduced. A married couple had up to then been treated as a single unit for tax purposes but now husband and wife are each treated as individuals responsible for their own tax. This means that:

• you are taxed on your own income, regardless of your spouse's income

• you claim your own tax allowances to set against your income

- you have your own tax-free slice for capital gains tax (CGT) purposes. (You also have your own inheritance tax – IHT – running total and exemptions, but this was the case even before independent taxation was introduced.)

Before independent taxation, it mattered little from an income tax point of view whether it was you or your husband or wife who owned the family assets – house, savings, chattels. It seems amazing in this age of equality that any income from such assets used always to be treated as that of the husband even if legally it belonged to the wife. Nowadays, the system is much fairer: your individual tax bills will take account of income from the assets that each of you in fact owns. This means that who owns what is important and rearranging the family assets – for example, through gifts between husband and wife – could reduce the income tax bill of the family as a whole. Bear in mind that there is no CGT or IHT to pay on gifts between husband and wife but the pattern in which you hold the family assets could affect IHT later on (see Chapter 14).

EXAMPLE 8.1

In August 2003, Ray inherits a substantial portfolio of corporate bonds and government stocks from his late aunt. The portfolio produces a healthy income which Ray welcomes but he is dismayed at having to pay tax on it at his top rate of 40 per cent. His wife, Joyce, has no income or savings of her own, so it makes sense for Ray to give some of his investments to her. He transfers enough so that Joyce receives an investment income of around £4,615 – the amount of her unused personal allowance in 2003–4. No IHT or CGT is payable on the gift from Ray to Joyce.

Although some of the investments pay out income with some tax already deducted, Joyce is able to claim the tax back, so the income is tax-free in her hands.

Jointly owned assets

Like many married couples, you may well have bank accounts, savings accounts and investments that are jointly held by you and your husband or wife. In England and Wales there are two ways of holding assets jointly: under a 'joint tenancy' or as 'tenants in common'. These are legal terms which can apply to any type of asset and not only to the way you share a home. (Different arrangements apply in Scotland – see page 128.)

Under a joint tenancy, you and your spouse both own the whole asset, you have identical interests in it, and you cannot sell or give away the asset without the agreement of the other person. In the event of one of you dying, the other automatically becomes the sole owner of the asset (though the deceased person's share still counts as part of his or her estate).

Under a tenancy in common, you and your spouse both have the right to enjoy or use the whole asset, but you each have your own distinct share in the asset and the shares need not be equal. On your death, your share of the asset does not automatically pass to your husband or wife and you can leave it to anyone you choose.

Some solicitors advise that you need a formal, signed and witnessed deed in order to switch from a joint tenancy to a tenancy in common. In fact, that is not the case. The law simply requires that one joint owner gives the other notice *in writing*. The notice does not have to be in any particular form – a letter would do – nor do you have to use any particular words. But your intention must be clear. To make matters doubly clear, you might consider drawing up a joint statement which you both sign.

EXAMPLE 8.2

Richard and Bella are married and own their home as joint tenants but they realise that they could plan their tax affairs more efficiently if they each had a distinct half-share in the home as tenants in common. To achieve this, Richard sends Bella a letter as follows:

3 Tosca Drive
Hampton
Lancs
DT56 6PP
29 August 2003

Mrs Bella Ringer
3 Tosca Drive
Hampton
Lancs
DT56 6PP

Dear Bella,

Please accept this letter as notice of my desire to sever as from today the joint tenancy in our property known as 3 Tosca Drive, Hampton, Lancs DT56 6PP now held by us as joint tenants both at law and in equity, so that from now on this property shall belong to us as tenants in common in equal shares.

Yours sincerely,

Richard

Richard Ringer

Switching from a tenancy in common to a joint tenancy does require a formal deed, which a solicitor can draw up for you.

For income tax purposes, the Inland Revenue will at first assume that any assets you hold jointly are held under a joint tenancy. This means that you will each be treated as receiving half of any income from the asset. If you want the income to be treated differently, you need to send your tax office a completed **form 17** setting out how the income is to be shared between you. You can get form 17 from your usual tax office* or a local tax enquiry centre.*

However, be warned that the way the income is split for tax purposes *must* reflect the actual shares that you and your spouse have in the income-producing asset. You cannot just choose the most convenient income split if it does not match the real shares and you cannot choose one split for income purposes and another for capital. Joint bank and building society accounts are almost always held as joint tenants, so can only ever be held on a 50-50 basis, but of course there's nothing to stop you transferring cash to your husband or wife so they can pay into an account in their own name. If, exceptionally, you do hold an account as tenants in common, you must send the Inland Revenue proof of this arrangement at the time you submit **form 17**.

In the case of other assets, you do not need to send in proof with form 17 but, if requested to do so, you should be prepared to provide the Inland Revenue with proof of the shares you each have in an asset and thus your share of the income. The proof might be copies of application forms or documents you signed when you first had the asset or copies of deeds or letters stating the relative shares.

Consider giving some of your assets to your husband or wife or giving away part of your share of an asset, if to do so would mean that together you pay less tax, as in the following circumstances:

- if one of you pays income tax and the other does not, give income-producing assets to the non-taxpayer (as in Example 8.1 on page 124). But note that since April 1999 non-taxpayers can no longer reclaim the tax already deducted from income from shares, share-based unit trusts and similar investments. In 2003–4, this type of income is paid with tax at 10 per cent already deducted. Higher-rate taxpayers have extra to pay but for all other taxpayers there is neither more tax to pay nor any tax to reclaim

- if one of you pays tax at the higher rate and the other pays tax at the basic or starting rate, give income-producing assets (including shares, unit trusts and cash that can be invested in a bank or building society account) to the taxpayer paying at the lesser rate. Income from most investments is paid with tax (at the savings rate of 20 per cent or at the shares rate of 10 per cent in 2003–4) already deducted. Starting- and basic-rate taxpayers have no further tax to pay, but higher-rate taxpayers must pay extra tax

- if one of you has income tax allowances that are being reduced because your income exceeds a given threshold, give enough income-producing assets to the other, so that the allowances are restored to the full amount. This may affect you if you are receiving married couple's allowance (available to couples where husband and/or wife was born before 6 April 1935) or age-related personal allowance (available to anyone aged 65 or over)

- if one of you regularly uses up your capital gains tax-free slice but the other does not, give assets whose value is expected to rise to the person with the unused slice.

Joint assets in Scotland

In Scotland, jointly owned assets are nearly always held as tenants in common – i.e. with each person owning a distinct share of the asset. However, if the owners have agreed on it, there can be a 'survivorship destination clause' written into the ownership documents. Like joint tenancy in England and Wales, the survivorship destination clause ensures that the share of a co-owner who dies automatically passes to the remaining owner(s) – even if the will stipulates that something different should happen. Note that the clause can only be cancelled with the consent of all the owners and it requires a formal deed which can be drawn up by a solicitor.

Anti-avoidance rules

There are tax rules that aim to catch the artificial transfer of income from one person to another. They operate where a 'settlement' comes into being. A settlement is any transfer where there is an element of 'bounty' – in other words, you do not get your full money's worth in return for the transfer. Trusts – see Chapter 9 – are examples of settlements, but so too can be many other types of arrangement, including informal gifts.

If a gift you make is treated as a settlement, any income from this will continue to be treated as yours if either of the following applies:

- you or your husband or wife can benefit from the gift or income from it
- the gift was to your own child who is unmarried and under the age of 18 (except that income which does not exceed £100 a year can be treated as that of the child).

The rules do not apply to an outright gift between husband and wife provided there are no strings attached.

The anti-avoidance rules mean that you can't reduce the family income tax bill by, say, shifting assets to your children. Unfortunately, they also catch genuine gifts you might want to make to your child – for more information, see Chapter 16. However, bear in mind that the rules apply only to income, not capital gains – and not to some types of tax-free income. So, for example, gifts to children can still be effective provided that, instead of producing income, they generate capital gains.

The rules also catch gifts you put into trust if you or your husband or wife are actual or potential beneficiaries – see Chapter 10.

The Inland Revenue argues that the anti-avoidance rules may apply where, say, a husband gives his non-working wife shares in his company and the company then pays dividends to the wife. Business planning is outside the scope of this book, and you should seek professional advice if you are considering gifts of shares in a family company.

EXAMPLE 8.3

Michael had not realised, when he opened a building society account for his daughter Rebecca, that income from the £20,000 he had placed in the account would count as his own for tax purposes.

He decides to close the account and put £1,000 into a National Savings Children's Bonus Bond for Rebecca and the rest into a growth unit trust for her (see Chapter 16 for more information).

Chapter 9

Using trusts

PLANNING FOR THE FUTURE

Ruth and David have become grandparents for the first time. 'I want to give the baby a nest egg for her future,' David explains to his solicitor. 'Of course, she's too young to handle money now, but I can put it in trust, can't I?'

'Yes, indeed,' replied the solicitor. 'You probably require what is known as an accumulation-and-maintenance trust. That would enable her to receive the money when she is adult, but gives the option to use it for her benefit in the meantime. Let us have a look at your precise circumstances and wishes.'

Trusts are legal arrangements that let you give away assets but retain some control over how they are used. They are also frequently used as a way of reducing inheritance tax (IHT) that might otherwise be payable on death. Trusts can be set up during your lifetime or under a will. (Trusts are also sometimes referred to as 'settlements' though for tax purposes 'settlement' includes many other types of arrangement.)

What is a trust?

A trust is an arrangement where the legal owners of assets (which can be things, money, land, buildings and so on) hold, and must use, them for the benefit of someone else. There are three conditions that must be met for the creation of a trust: the intention to create it must be clear from the words used, the trust property must be identified, and it must be clear who is to benefit from the trust. (In Scotland, there is a further requirement that trust assets or evidence of their ownership is physically delivered to the trustees or alternatively that the trust is registered in the Books of Council and Session.) It is common to set out this information and other conditions in a written deed, but trusts can, and do, come into being without anything being put into writing.

There are three main participants in a trust:

- **the settlor (called the truster or granter in Scotland)** This is the person who gives away the assets to be placed in the trust. A trust may have more than one settlor and this does not have to be an individual. For example, the settlor could be a company or another trust

- **the trustees** There is usually more than one trustee (see below) and these are the legal owners of the trust property. So the property is registered in their names, and they are responsible for holding it safely and accounting for it. The settlor can be a trustee, so too can a beneficiary

- **the beneficiaries** There might be one beneficiary or more. These are the people who will – or might – share the trust property and any income from it. Beneficiaries can be individuals, companies, charities or other bodies. Different beneficiaries may have different rights – see below for more information. The settlor can be a beneficiary of the trust, but this has tax implications – see Chapter 10.

Why use a trust? *(for giving)*

A trust can be useful in many situations, for example:

- **giving to children** You might want to make a gift now to a child to be available to him or her later, for example, when they reach an age you specify

- **maintaining control** The person you want to benefit might not be good at handling money, for example, they have learning difficulties or a tendency to be spendthrift

- **giving to a group** Maybe you want to give to a group of people that is not yet complete – for example, your grandchildren including those yet to be born

- **retaining flexibility** Perhaps you're not sure at this stage who should benefit from your gift or you want to be able to change who benefits or the amount they get if circumstances change. Provided you specify the range of *potential* beneficiaries now, you can leave these decisions until later
- **separating income from capital** This lets you specify that someone will have your assets in the end but, in the meantime, someone else has the income from them or the use of them. This can be particularly useful in family situations – for example, if you want a widow or widower to be financially secure but ultimately want your children (maybe from a former marriage) to benefit
- **giving on special occasions or in set circumstances** You might want to make a gift only on the occasion of some possible but indeterminate event, such as a marriage or birth. Similarly, you might want someone to benefit now but for your gift to pass to someone else if, say, the first beneficiary goes bankrupt
- **maintaining confidentiality** A beneficiary does not have to know that you have arranged a gift to be made at some future time. Similarly, a beneficiary in receipt of income or capital from a trust does not have to know who the settlor was
- **tax-efficiency** Sometimes a gift into trust can save you tax, or avoid tax problems that would arise with an outright gift. See Chapter 10 for a detailed discussion of the tax treatment of trusts.

How do you create a trust?

It is best to use a formal, written trust deed that makes your intentions crystal clear. This is not a job for the DIY enthusiast – get professional help either from a solicitor★ or an accountant,★ tax adviser★ or independent financial adviser (IFA)★ (who can advise on the appropriate trust and explain the pros and cons but will normally use a solicitor to draw up the deed itself). Creating a trust in this way can be costly, so check that the benefits warrant the financial outlay.

Life insurance products are very often used in conjunction with trusts. They can be particularly suitable because they pay out on death and special tax rules enable capital to be drawn from a policy during your lifetime without immediate tax implications (see page 226). As a result, many life insurance companies can provide you with off-the-shelf trust documents that let you very simply, and usually at no extra cost, opt to have a life policy written in trust (see Chapter 14). You can either arrange this direct with the insurance company or through an IFA.*

More about the participants

The settlor

The settlor makes the gift to the trust and specifies what he or she wants the trust to do, who the beneficiaries are, and what powers the trustees will have.

However, there are some constraints on what, as settlor, you can do. For example, the law generally sets the maximum lifetime of a trust – usually 80 years – and the maximum period over which income can be accumulated within a trust before it has to be paid out to one or more beneficiaries. Many statutory rules come into play only if your trust deed fails to specify what should happen. Provided a solicitor draws up the deed for you, there should be no nasty surprises.

It is usual – but not required – that the settlor appoints the first trustees. It is common for a settlor to want to retain some control over the trust property and the decisions concerning it. There are various ways of approaching this:

- even though you are the settlor, you can also be a trustee. But be aware that you are bound by the terms of the trust just like any other trustee
- obviously, at the outset, you should choose trustees who you think are sympathetic to your aims. And, if the deed is worded appropriately, you can retain the right to appoint new trustees in future. This will help you to ensure that the trustees remain sympathetic
- you can give the trustees an expression of your wishes. This needs to be carefully written so that it does not legally bind the trustees (since this could alter the nature of the trust with consequent tax implications).

The settlor can be a beneficiary of the trust, in which case it becomes a 'settlor-interested trust'. This may seem tempting as it could give you an opening to get your money or assets back if circumstances change, but there are serious tax drawbacks, as described in Chapter 10.

The beneficiaries

As described below, there are two main types of trusts: those with an interest in possession and those without. In an interest-in-possession trust, there are two types of beneficiary:

- **life interest (called life rent in Scotland)** A beneficiary with a life interest is called a life tenant (life renter in Scotland) and is entitled to the income produced by the trust assets or to the use of the assets (for example, the right to live in a home owned by the trust). But a life tenant has no right to the trust assets him or herself so, for example, the trustees cannot give this beneficiary the trust assets or the proceeds of selling them
- **reversionary interest** A beneficiary with a reversionary interest (sometimes called a 'remainderman') will eventually become entitled to the trust assets but only when the life interest comes to an end.

Where there is no interest in possession, the trustees may have discretion to distribute income, capital or both to the beneficiaries who might be named individuals or people within a specified 'class' such as your grandchildren.

If you are the settlor and a beneficiary of the trust is your own child who is unmarried and under the age of 18, any income paid out to the child or used for his or her benefit (for example, to pay school fees) will count as your own income for tax purposes. Except in the case of bare trusts, this does not apply if the income is accumulated within the trust. See Chapter 10 for details.

Beneficiaries might have a contingent interest so that they benefit only when a particular, specified event takes place, such as reaching a particular age, outliving someone else, or perhaps if the current beneficiary becomes bankrupt.

A trust might have a single beneficiary or many. Unless the trust deed specifies otherwise, multiple beneficiaries share an interest in equal shares. For example, if a life interest is given to two beneficiaries, and the trust deed does not say otherwise, they will each receive half the income from the trust.

Modern trusts are often flexible, giving the trustees the power to change the beneficiaries after the trust has been set up. For example, a trust might initially give a life interest to one person but give the trustees the power to revoke this and assign the interest to someone else. Trusts that give the trustees these very wide powers are often called 'flexible trusts' or 'flexible power of appointment trusts'.

As a beneficiary, you have the right to inspect the trust deed and rules, the general records of meetings and the trust accounts. But you do not have any right to see records of the reasons behind the decisions of trustees in exercising their discretionary powers.

Beneficiaries do not have the right to alter the actions or decisions of trustees, provided that the trustees have acted within their powers. But, if as a beneficiary you believe the trustees are in breach of their duties – for example, by failing to look after the trust assets properly, investing them unsuitably, or making decisions that conflict with the powers in the trust deed – you can take court action to challenge the actions of the trustees.

If certain conditions are met, the beneficiaries can direct the trustees to hand over the trust property and the trust then comes to an end. The conditions are that: all the beneficiaries can be identified, there is no possibility of further beneficiaries (for example, children who have not yet been born), they have all reached age 18 and are all of sound mind.

The trustees

If a trust holds land, the maximum number of trustees is four. There is no minimum, but as two trustees are required to give a valid receipt for the proceeds from selling land, two is the practical minimum. (The exception is where there is a sole corporate trustee.) For trusts not holding land, there is no minimum or maximum number but more than four trustees of a family trust would be unusual.

Anyone can be a trustee, provided they are at least 18 years old and of sound mind – even someone who is bankrupt or has been convicted of a serious offence. However, a court can remove trustees it deems to be unfit. Beneficiaries can be trustees, though usually this is not a good idea as trustees should not normally profit from a trust and should be wary of acting if they have a conflict of interest.

(However, in some types of trust – for example, pension schemes – it is normal for some of the trustees to be beneficiaries.)

Usually, the settlor appoints the first trustees. If you set up a trust in your will, it is normal to appoint the same people to be executors of the will and trustees of the trust, but you can choose different people if you want to.

Someone cannot be forced to act as a trustee. Having taken on the job they can usually resign, but this may be subject to either a replacement being found or at least two trustees remaining (or a single corporate trustee).

The trust deed may specify how trustees are to be appointed – for example, the deed may name one or more people as 'appointers' who have the job of choosing trustees as and when the need arises. If not, the remaining trustees have the power to appoint new trustees when required. If the last trustee dies, his or her personal representative inherits this power.

Usually there is no automatic right of the beneficiaries to remove a trustee – the beneficiaries would have to ask a court to do this.

Being a trustee is an onerous task, not to be taken on lightly. As a trustee, various Acts of Parliament (in particular the Trustee Act 1925 and, in England and Wales, the Trustee Act 2000) give you certain powers and also impose duties. In several areas, these are often varied by the rules of the particular trust, so an important first job as a trustee is to read the trust rules and make sure you understand them. Some of the main statutory powers and duties are briefly outlined below.

The trustees' powers

Advancement
The power to give ('advance') capital to a beneficiary, subject to the rules of the trust and rights of other beneficiaries.

Maintenance
The power to use the income of the trust for the maintenance, education or benefit of a beneficiary. This clearly applies where a beneficiary has the right to receive the trust income. It can also apply to a beneficiary who has the right to receive trust assets, say, at a given age – in the meantime, they may have the right to income earned by those assets.

Charging

Trustees are not allowed to profit from their role but they can set reasonable expenses against the trust income or capital. In addition, professional trustees – such as solicitors or a bank – can be paid a reasonable sum for their services.

Delegation

Trustees generally can delegate any of their administrative functions (managing investments, paperwork, keeping assets safe etc.), but they may not delegate their distributive functions, such as:

- deciding how the trust assets should be distributed among the beneficiaries
- deciding whether expenses etc. should be paid out of income or capital (since this affects the distribution of the trust assets between beneficiaries with an interest in the income and those with an interest in the capital)
- appointing new trustees.

(The rules for charitable trusts are a little different.)

Individual trustees can delegate to someone else under a power of attorney for a maximum period of 12 months, but remain responsible for the actions of the person they appoint.

Insurance

Trustees may – but do not have to – insure trust property. However, their duty to take reasonable care – see opposite – may require them to arrange insurance.

Investment

In England and Wales, trustees have very wide powers to make any kind of investment but they must take heed of the 'standard investment criteria':

- the investments chosen or retained must be suitable for the trust
- there must be a range of different investments appropriate to that trust.

For example, unless the trust had very short-term aims, it would not be suitable for all its resources to be invested in a building society savings account.

Trustees have a duty to get and consider investment advice when choosing or reviewing investments, unless they can show this would be unnecessary or inappropriate. For example, it might be excessive for a trust with just a few hundred pounds of assets to get investment advice but essential and appropriate for a trust with, say, £50,000.

The Trustee Act 2000 does not apply to Scotland or Northern Ireland. Instead, the earlier Trustee Investments Act 1961 continues to apply. This restricts trusts to a much more limited range of investments unless the trust deed specifically gives the trustees wider investment powers.

Sale

Trustees have extensive powers to sell any trust property and are under a duty to obtain the best price.

Duties of trustees

Conflicts of interest

You should be wary of becoming a trustee if there is or might be a conflict of interest between you and any beneficiary. If a conflict arises after you have taken on the role, you should disclose it to your fellow trustees.

New trustees

You should read the trust documents to make sure you understand the objectives of the trust, the rights of beneficiaries, whether any of those rights have been assigned to someone else, your powers, the nature and whereabouts of any trust property and other assets.

If you are joining an already established trust, you should also check as far as possible that the existing trustees have not committed any breach. Although you cannot be held responsible for the actions of other trustees prior to your joining them, you could be liable if you fail to take reasonable steps to recover any losses their actions caused.

Duty to take reasonable care

In carrying out most of their powers and duties, trustees must exercise reasonable care. This means exercising such care and skill as is reasonable given any special knowledge or experience. Professional trustees – such as solicitors and banks – are under a higher duty than an ordinary, lay trustee. The latter is normally required to act as an ordinary prudent businessman or businesswoman would. This rule must be interpreted within context so, for example, when making investment decisions, a lay trustee is required to act as if he or she was investing for other people whom he or she felt morally obliged to support. Investing in, say, traded options might be prudent for someone investing their own money and given their own circumstances. It would usually not be when the aim was to provide for their children.

Ensure assets are correctly distributed

The trustees must ensure that the right people get the trust assets. In particular, if a beneficiary has assigned an interest to someone else, that other person's claim to the assets should be carefully checked before the assets are handed over to them.

Ensure fairness between beneficiaries

This is especially tricky where some beneficiaries have an interest in income and others in capital. For example, you need to consider how expenses are set off and how to strike the right balance between income-producing investments and those offering capital growth.

Comply with the terms of the trust

You must act in accordance with the trust deed and rules and any legal requirements. In general the rules of a trust can be changed only with the agreement of all the beneficiaries who must all be adults and capable of making such decisions or with the permission of the court.

Provide information and accounts

If they ask, you must provide beneficiaries with information about the trust and its investments, copies of accounts and access to title deeds and any other documents. There is no general requirement to have accounts audited. You are allowed to charge the reasonable cost of producing such documents. You must also allow beneficiaries to inspect the minutes but you are not under any duty to explain the reasons for trustees' decisions.

Duty to act jointly

The law requires that trustees' decisions must be unanimous. However, this can be and often is over-ridden by the individual trust's rules to allow majority voting.

Duties to act without reward and not to profit from the trust

This is the general rule. However, the Trustee Act 2000 gives trustees the power to make reasonable payments to professional trustees (see page 138) and usually the individual trust's rules will include a charging clause.

Duty not to purchase trust property

If you are a trustee, neither you nor your husband or wife (or a company in which either of you has an interest) should buy assets from the trust. Even if you paid a fair price, the beneficiaries can declare the purchase void and require the assets to be resold. The rules of the individual trust may over-ride this rule.

Duty to consult the beneficiaries

If the trust holds land and all the beneficiaries are adults, the trustees should consult the beneficiaries before taking decisions affecting the land.

Choosing the appropriate trust

There are four main types of trust: bare trusts, interest-in-possession trusts, discretionary trusts, and accumulation-and-maintenance trusts (which are in fact a special type of discretionary trust that benefits from favourable IHT treatment as long as special rules are kept). Which type of trust will best suit your needs is dictated in part by the characteristics of each type of trust. Of great importance, however, is your tax position and the tax treatment of the different trusts.

The tax treatment of trusts is undoubtedly complex and there are numerous pitfalls for the unwary. The wording of the trust deed and the powers of the trustees can be crucial in assessing which tax regime applies. You are strongly advised to take advice from a solicitor* before deciding on whether or not to use a trust and which type would be appropriate, and you should ask a solicitor to draw up the trust deed. (In the book and will kit mentioned on page 185, some of the pro forma wills provided include clauses for setting up trusts. Use these only if you are certain that the pro forma will selected reflects your wishes. If in doubt, consult a solicitor. Never try to adapt the wording of one of these wills if it does not quite match your circumstances.)

The main types of trust

Bare trust

How does it work?
Not for kids

This is the simplest type of trust, requiring very little administration. Someone holds assets as nominee for someone else – for example, a parent or some other relative holds investments given by the parent to their child as outlined in Chapter 16. Property is transferred to the bare trustee who holds it for the beneficiary and uses it in accordance with his or her instructions. So, provided the beneficiary is aged 18 or more (or is married if younger), he or she can call for the income and/or capital at any time and the trustee has no right to withhold it. For tax purposes, the beneficiary – not the trustee – is treated as the owner of the trust property.

Pros and cons

A bare trust is not a complex trust to administer. Tax on the trust property will generally be lower than if it were held in, say, an accumulation-and-maintenance trust. Watch out if you are a parent making a gift to your child to be held in a bare trust. Income from any gifts made on or after 9 March 1999 is taxed as yours not the child's, even if it is not paid out, unless it comes to no more than £100 – see Chapter 16. Income from gifts from other sources – for example, from grandparents – counts as that of the child. And any capital gains, whatever the source of the investments, are taxed as the child's. This can make a bare trust more tax-efficient than other trust options in suitable cases. Against this, you must balance the drawbacks. Once the trust is set up, you cannot change the beneficiaries or the shares in which they own the trust property. The settlor has no control at all over the use of the trust property once a child has reached his or her majority. The trust property is part of the beneficiary's estate when he or she dies – if the beneficiary is under the age of 18 at the time of death, he or she would die intestate (see Chapter 12) since he or she would be too young to have made a will.

Possible uses

- Making a gift of property to a child – e.g. a share in a family business – which the child does not yet have the legal capacity to hold because of his or her young age.
- Building up a nest-egg for a child to have on reaching age 18.

EXAMPLE 9.1

Nichola invests £10,000 for her niece, Angela. Although Nichola is the nominal owner of the investments they are held on bare trust for Angela. Income from the investments is treated as Angela's but she pays no tax on it because it falls within her personal allowance. When Angela reaches 18 (or sooner if she gets married), she can demand that the investments are transferred into her own name.

Interest-in-possession trust

Also known as a 'life-interest trust' and a type of 'fixed-interest trust'.

How does it work?

One or more beneficiaries have the right to receive income earned by the assets in the trust as that income arises. Alternatively they have the right to use the assets held by the trust, for example, the right to live in a house. Eventually – for example, on the death of the life interest beneficiaries, at a given date or when a specified event, such as marriage, occurs – the assets in the trust are distributed. The person or people who receive the assets are said to hold the 'reversionary interest'. The beneficiaries who receive the income (or use of the assets) need not be the same as the beneficiaries who have the reversionary interest, though they could be. For example, you might specify in your will that your share of the family home be put into trust, giving your husband or wife a life interest so that he or she could continue living there as long as desired but giving the reversionary interest to your children so that they would inherit on the death of your spouse. See also Example 9.2.

Pros and cons

Interest-in-possession trusts are not as flexible as discretionary trusts or accumulation-and-maintenance trusts. Nevertheless, they have been popular in the past particularly because they enjoyed more advantageous capital gains tax (CGT) treatment than other types of trust. But, from 6 April 1998, the CGT treatment of interest-in-possession trusts was brought into line with the tax treatment of other types of trust – see page 151. You should also be wary if you might want to alter the people who benefit from the trust income or the shares the beneficiaries have in it. Such alterations will usually count as gifts from one beneficiary to another under the IHT rules.

so no adv

Possible uses

- Where you eventually want to pass on assets to one or more people but need to provide for someone else in the interim – see Example 9.2.
- Where you do not want the beneficiary to have full control of the assets in the trust or you want to defer handing over control until a later date.
- If you want to give to children, usually an accumulation-and-maintenance trust would be a better choice. However, you could adapt an interest-in-possession trust to suit gifts to children by, for example, specifying that income should be held for the child(ren) until they reach age 18. In effect, this is combining a bare trust (see page 142) with the interest-in-possession trust.

EXAMPLE 9.2

David's will stipulates that, on his death, a large part of his assets should be placed in trust. The trustees would invest the assets as they saw fit and the income from them (and use of his former share of the family home) should go to his wife during her lifetime. On his wife's death, the assets are to be shared equally between their three children. David has drawn up his will in this way, first, to guard against his widow being short of money during her lifetime and, secondly, to ensure that his children will eventually receive his assets even if his widow remarries.

Discretionary trust

How does it work?

If a trust is not a bare trust or an interest-in-possession trust, it is by default a discretionary trust. That said, the distinguishing features are usually that income can be accumulated within the trust to be paid out later or to be paid out at the discretion of the trustees and that there is usually more than one beneficiary. Often there will be a 'class' of beneficiaries, such as your children or your grandchildren, not all of whom have to be born at the time the trust is set up.

Pros and cons

Although discretionary trusts are very flexible, they are treated less favourably for tax purposes than either interest-in-possession trusts or accumulation-and-maintenance trusts.

Possible uses

- Where you want to be able to alter the people (or bodies) who will benefit under the trust.
- Where you want to be able to alter the proportions in which the beneficiaries share in income and/or capital from the trust.

EXAMPLE 9.3

John had been ill for some time and, knowing that he did not have long to live, he checked his will and brought it up to date. He was a widower and had six sons whose ages ranged from 22 to 30. Two of the sons had good, secure incomes, while three had not settled down to careers yet but had only minor financial problems. The sixth son was generally in financial difficulties – largely of his own making.

John wanted to be fair to all his boys but was not happy with the idea of just sharing out his assets between them. They did not all have the same need and the youngest son in particular would be likely to squander any inheritance. John wanted a solution which would ensure that help was available to all his sons if they needed it but would protect the assets otherwise. He decided to set up a discretionary trust in favour of all the sons. He appointed his own two brothers (the sons' uncles) as trustees and gave them discretion to make payments and loans from the trust fund to the sons if or when, in the trustees' opinion, such help was warranted. After ten years (by which time John felt the boys should all take responsibility for themselves), the remaining trust assets were to be distributed equally among them.

Accumulation-and-maintenance trust

tax shelter
school fees paid
out of income
but total anet a
gift

How does it work?

This is a special type of discretionary trust but, provided certain rules are kept, it escapes the worst of the unfavourable tax treatment normally applying to discretionary trusts. The rules include:

- one or more of the beneficiaries must become entitled to either the income or capital from the trust on or before reaching age 25
- in the run-up to the entitlement above coming into effect, no beneficiary can have an interest in possession. Instead, income from the assets in the trust must be accumulated, except that it can be used to pay for the maintenance, education or other benefit of one or more of the beneficiaries
- the trust can exist for a maximum of 25 years, unless all the beneficiaries have a common grandparent, in which case the life of the trust can be longer (adopted children and stepchildren are treated in the same way as other children of a family for the purpose of this test). Where the 25-year rule applies, the period runs from the date the settlement started or 15 April 1976, whichever is later. Bear in mind that, for those trusts whose clock started in 1978, the end of the 25-year period occurs in 2003 and, if no action is taken, a tax bill will become due (see page 163)
- although the beneficiaries can be a group, such as all your grandchildren, there must be at least one member of the group living at the time the trust is set up. (However, if there is just one member and that person dies before any others are born, the trust can continue.)

Pros and cons

The accumulation-and-maintenance trust is flexible and tax-efficient but only for gifts to children. Unlike a direct gift or a bare trust (see page 142), the trust property is not part of a beneficiary's estate if he or she dies.

Under the anti-avoidance rules, if you are the settlor and income or capital from the trust is used to pay for the maintenance or education of, or to otherwise benefit, your own child who is under age 18 and unmarried, the payments will be taxed as your income unless they come to no more than £100. However, income and gains that remain within the trust to be accumulated are not taxed as the parent's income, so this is a tax-efficient way of building up a nest-egg for your own child. For more information about gifts to children, see Chapter 16.

Possible uses

- Where you want to be able to alter the people who will benefit under the trust, e.g. by allowing for children who are as yet unborn.
- Where you want to be able to alter the proportions in which the beneficiaries share in income and/or capital from the trust.
- Where you want to make gifts as a parent to your child(ren) without income added to the gift being treated as yours (see Chapter 8). But be aware that this advantage is lost if the income is paid out instead of being accumulated within the trust.
- Building up a nest-egg for children and grandchildren.
- Paying school fees.

EXAMPLE 9.4

David set up a trust to accept a gift for his first granddaughter, Jemima. Bearing in mind that there might be more grandchildren to come, he established an accumulation-and-maintenance trust in favour of all his grandchildren. For the present, he has settled £25,000 in the trust but can add more later if he wishes. Jemima is to become entitled to a lump sum from the trust when she reaches age 21. In the meantime, money can be paid out – to pay for school fees, say – at the discretion of the trustees, who are David and his wife, Ruth.

Other special types of trust

Accumulation-and-maintenance trusts are just one type of discretionary trust which qualifies for special treatment. There are others. Most are outside the scope of gift planning (they include, *inter alia*, pension schemes, compensation funds and unit trusts). Two may be of use:

- **charitable trusts**   If you want to give large amounts to a range of charities, setting up your own charitable trust is an option worth considering (see page 52)
- **disabled trusts**   For assets placed in trust on or after 10 March 1981, mainly for the benefit of someone who is incapable of looking after their own property because of mental disorder or someone who is receiving attendance allowance, the disabled person is treated as if he or she has an interest in possession. This means that the more favourable interest-in-possession tax rules apply rather than those for discretionary trusts.

A special type of interest-in-possession trust can also be useful if you want to make a gift to someone but you have real doubts about whether he or she can be trusted to act responsibly. This is a 'protective trust'. Basically, the beneficiary is entitled to the income from, or use of, the trust assets for as long as he or she behaves responsibly. But if a specified event occurs – for example, the beneficiary becomes bankrupt – the interest in possession ceases. The trust then automatically converts into a discretionary trust and the trustees decide how best to use the assets for the maintenance and support of the original beneficiary and/or his or her family.

Chapter 10

Taxation of trusts

The tax treatment of trusts is crucial to any decision regarding the use of a trust as a way of making gifts. Unfortunately, it is also complex. In 1991, the government proposed changes to simplify the income and capital taxation of trusts and to bring it into harmony with the personal tax regime. These proposals were abandoned but then partially reintroduced in the 1995 Finance Act. Further tinkering was made in both the 1998 and 1999 Budgets but the income tax treatment of trusts, in particular, remains detailed and complex. The inheritance tax (IHT) position of trusts was overhauled fairly recently but could be altered further if the government decides at some future date to make substantial changes to the IHT regime.

Bare trusts

Putting a gift into trust

Unless you can use one of the exemptions described in Chapter 5, your gift into a bare trust counts as a potentially exempt transfer (PET), so there is no IHT to pay provided you survive for at least seven years – see page 114. No special rules apply regarding capital gains tax (CGT) – check the ordinary rules in Chapters 5 and 6 to see if any CGT will be payable.

The trust's tax position

The trust does not have a separate tax identity from the beneficiary. Income and gains from the trust property are treated in the same way as if the property were owned directly by the beneficiary. This means that income is taxed at the beneficiary's top rate after taking into account allowances and any other deductions. The exception to this is where the assets in the trust are a gift from a parent to an unmarried child under age 18 and the gift was made on or after 9 March 1999. If such income exceeds £100 a year, it is treated as that of the parent. This applies whether the income is accumulated or paid out. Income from a gift made by a parent before 9 March 1999 is taxed as that of the child provided it is accumulated and not paid out. See Chapter 16 for further details.

Gains are taxed at the beneficiary's top rate after taking account of the yearly tax-free slice.

Payments to beneficiaries

Where, as is usual, tax has already been paid as income and gains arose (see above), there is no further tax to pay when payments are made to the beneficiary or used for his or her benefit.

The exception is where the assets in the trust are a gift from a parent to an unmarried child under age 18 and the gift was made before 9 March 1999. In this case, provided income was accumulated within the trust, it will have been treated as that of the child. But, once paid out to the child, or used for the child's benefit, it becomes taxable as that of the parent if the income exceeds £100. See Chapter 16 for further details.

When the bare trust ends

The trust property has been treated as owned by the beneficiary throughout. Therefore there is no change when the beneficiary takes outright possession of the trust property.

EXAMPLE 10.1

Angela is the beneficiary of a bare trust containing £10,000 capital. This was a gift from her father made before 9 March 1999. The capital has earned approximately £400 a year income and a small amount of capital profit. Both are well within Angela's 2003–4 tax allowances of £4,615 personal allowance against taxable income and £7,900 against chargeable gains. On reaching the age of 18, Angela intends to ask the trustee, Aunt Nichola, to carry on acting as trustee but to advance Angela a regular income to support her while she is at university. This will be taxed in the same way as if it had been accumulated within the trust. On finishing her university course, Angela intends to take outright possession of the trust property. As she is already treated as the outright owner, no transfer takes place and so there is no IHT.

Interest-in-possession trusts

Putting a gift into trust

If you make a gift which is placed in an interest-in-possession trust (and none of the exemptions in Chapter 5 apply), you are treated as if you had made a potentially exempt transfer (PET). No IHT is charged provided you survive for seven years after making the gift (see page 114 for more details). If you die within seven years, the trustees will normally be liable for the tax due. No special rules apply in respect of CGT, so check the ordinary rules to see if tax will be payable (see Chapters 5 and 6).

The trust's tax position

Income from the assets in the trust may be paid either direct to the beneficiaries or first to the trustees who then pass it on to the beneficiaries.

The trustees are responsible for tax on income earned by the trust assets. Tax may be payable at any of three rates, depending on the type of income involved (rates apply to 2003–4):

- on dividends, distributions from share-based unit trusts and similar investments, the rate is 10 per cent
- on savings income (for example, interest from savings accounts or, corporate bonds or distributions from unit trusts investing in bonds), tax is charged at the savings rate of 20 per cent
- on any other income, tax is charged at the basic rate which is 22 per cent.

Example 10.2 on page 154 shows how this can work out in practice.

Until 5 April 1998, an interest-in-possession trust was also liable for CGT on any capital gains but only at the basic rate. No further CGT was payable if capital was paid out to a beneficiary. Therefore, the low rate of CGT on the trust's gains made this form of trust particularly attractive where a beneficiary was a higher-rate taxpayer (who would normally be taxed on gains at a rate of 40 per cent). The government, worried that interest-in-possession trusts were being set up purely for tax-avoidance reasons, closed the loophole. From 6 April 1998 onwards, interest-in-possession trusts have been brought into line with discretionary trusts (including accumulation-and-maintenance trusts): gains realised by all these trusts are now taxable at a uniform special trust rate of 34 per cent. The first slice of gains each tax year is tax-free. The tax-free slice for a trust is usually set at half the rate for an individual – i.e. £3,950 in 2003–4 – but see box opposite.

Payments to beneficiaries

Income paid out to beneficiaries is broadly treated as if it had been received directly by them. This means three different treatments may apply, depending on the type of income:

- dividends and similar income are received net of tax at 10 per cent and accompanied by a tax credit. From 6 April 1999 onwards, non-taxpayers cannot reclaim this tax credit. Starting- and basic-rate taxpayers have no further tax to pay. Higher-rate taxpayers must pay further tax of 22.5 per cent on the grossed-up amount of the dividend – see Example 10.3
- savings income is paid net of tax at 20 per cent. Non-taxpayers can reclaim this. Starting-rate taxpayers can reclaim half the tax deducted. Basic-rate taxpayers have no further tax to pay. Higher-rate taxpayers must pay extra tax of 20 per cent on the grossed-up amount of the interest – see Example 10.3 on page 155
- all other income is paid with tax at the basic rate already deducted. Non-taxpayers can reclaim all the tax deducted and starting-rate taxpayers can reclaim 12 per cent. Higher-rate taxpayers have extra tax of 18 per cent to pay on the grossed-up income. See Example 10.3.

CAPITAL GAINS TAX-FREE SLICE IF YOU SET UP MORE THAN ONE TRUST

Where you put money or assets into more than one trust on or after 7 July 1978, the annual tax-free slice for capital gains is divided between the trusts. But the minimum tax-free slice for each trust is one-fifth. For example, if you set up two trusts, each has a tax-free slice of 1/2 x £3,950 = £1,975 in 2003–4. If you set up five or more trusts, each has 1/5 x £3,950 = £790. In making this adjustment, trusts are included whether or not they are in fact capable of producing any capital gains, but some types of trusts are ignored, for example, trusts for people with disabilities, occupational pension schemes and retirement annuity contracts (but not personal pensions).

There may be arrangements for beneficiaries to receive income direct from the trust investments instead of the income passing through the hands of the trustees. In this case, the beneficiary accounts for tax direct to the Inland Revenue.

If you receive payment of capital from the trust, you cannot reclaim any CGT paid by the trust even if you are a non-taxpayer, starting- or basic-rate taxpayer. Equally there is no extra CGT to pay if you are a higher-rate taxpayer.

When the interest in possession ends

If you have an interest in possession, you are treated, for tax purposes, as owning the assets in the trust – the reversionary interest is ignored. If there is more than one beneficiary, you are treated as owning the trust assets in proportion to your shares in the income from them. When your interest in possession ends, you are deemed to make a gift of the assets to the beneficiary with the reversionary interest (or, if applicable, the beneficiary who takes a subsequent life interest). Provided you are 'giving' the assets to an individual or to an appropriate type of trust, the gift counts as a PET and no tax is payable as long as you survive for seven years (see page 114). If the assets pass, say, to a discretionary trust, the gift counts as chargeable and there may be an immediate IHT bill, depending on your running total of gifts during the last seven years (see page 108).

If, when the trust ends, you become entitled to receive the trust property outright, there is no IHT liability. In most cases there is also no IHT if the property passes back to the settlor (or his or her spouse) when the interest in possession ends.

If a beneficiary's interest in possession ends during his or her lifetime, the beneficiary is deemed to be disposing of the trust assets and there may be CGT to pay. There is no CGT liability when a life interest ends on the death of the beneficiary holding the interest.

A reversionary interest in an interest-in-possession trust counts as 'excluded property' for IHT purposes, which means that it is completely outside the IHT net. This can be useful, since a gift of a reversionary interest cannot create an IHT bill (see Example 10.4) There is no CGT on the gift of a reversionary interest provided you are the beneficiary for whom the interest was created or, if not, you did not buy the interest.

EXAMPLE 10.2

Molly was left a life interest in a trust set up by her husband, Charlie, who died several years ago. The trust holds a mix of investments: some property and various shares and bonds. In 2003–4, the income and tax position of the trust was as follows:

Income

Income from property (before deduction of tax)	£4,000
Dividends from shares (net of 10% tax credit)	£1,800
Interest income (net of 20% savings tax)	£3,200

Tax

Tax at 22% on property income (22% x £4,000)	£880
Tax at 10% already deducted from dividends (10/90 x £1,800)	£200
Tax at 20% already deducted from interest (20/80 x £3,200)	£800
Total tax paid	£1,880
Income after tax (£4,000 – £880 + £1,800 + £3,200)	£8,120

EXAMPLE 10.3

All the income from the trust in Example 10.2 is paid out to Molly in 2003–4. Molly has income from other sources too and is a higher-rate taxpayer. Her trust income is treated for tax as follows:

Income from property Molly receives £3,120 from which tax at 22 per cent has already been deducted. She grosses this up by doing the following sum: 100% / (100% – 22%) x £3,120 = £4,000. Higher-rate tax on this is 40% x £4,000 = £1,600. Tax of £880 has already been paid, so Molly must now pay £1,600 – £880 = £720

Income from shares Molly receives £1,800 in dividends plus a tax credit for £200. She grosses up the dividends by doing the following sum: 100% / (100% – 10%) x £1,800 = £2,000. Higher-rate tax on this is 32.5% x £2,000 = £650. Tax of £200 has already been paid, so Molly must now pay £650 – £200 = £450

Interest income Molly receives £3,200 from which tax at 20 per cent has already been deducted. She grosses this up by doing the following sum: 100% / (100% – 20%) x £3,200 = £4,000. Higher-rate tax on this is 40% x £4,000 = £1,600. Tax of £800 has already been paid, so Molly must now pay £1,600 – £800 = £800.

In total, Molly has further tax of £720 + £450 + £800 = £1,970 to pay on her trust income. This leaves her with a net sum of £8,120 – £1,970 = £6,150.

EXAMPLE 10.4

When Charlie died, he left part of his assets (some £100,000 in total) in trust, giving his wife, Molly, a life interest in the income from the trust and his daughter, Pru, the reversionary interest in the trust property. Pru is in her thirties and has children of her own. Her husband has a well-paid job and the family is financially comfortable. Pru would prefer that her father's assets passed to her children. So she decides to release her reversionary interest in the trust and give it to the children. There is no IHT to pay, because reversionary interests are excluded from the IHT regime.

Discretionary trusts

Putting a gift into trust

A gift put into a discretionary trust counts as a chargeable gift for IHT (unless you can claim one of the exemptions in Chapter 5) and can create an immediate tax bill (see page 108). Whether or not you have to pay any tax depends on whether you can claim an exemption (for example, the yearly tax-free exemption of £3,000) or, if not, on your running total of chargeable gifts during the previous seven years. If the gift when added to your running total is less than your tax-free slice (£255,000 in 2003–4), there will be no immediate IHT bill.

Note that, if you set up other trusts on the same day, they can mean the trust has to pay extra IHT later on – see below. Try to avoid setting up other trusts on the same day as a discretionary trust.

CGT may be due on the gift, if you are giving assets other than cash, but you can claim hold–over relief (see page 100).

The trust's tax position

There is a 'periodic charge' for IHT on the value of the trust property. This charge is made on the tenth anniversary of the setting-up of the trust and at ten–year intervals after that. The amount of tax due is worked out as follows:

- *add* up the value of the trust at the time of the tax charge *and* any gifts made by the settlor (i.e. the person who set up the discretionary trust) to other trusts (apart from charitable trusts) set up on the same day at their value on that day. To this, *add* the value of chargeable gifts made by the settlor in the seven years up to the date of the trust starting
- work out the tax due on that total amount by *deducting* the tax-free slice and *multiplying* by the lifetime rate of 20 per cent (in the 2003–4 tax year)
- *divide* the tax due by the value of everything owned by the discretionary trust. This gives you the 'effective rate of tax'
- take 30 per cent of the effective rate (i.e. *multiply* by 0.3). This gives you the rate at which tax will be charged on the trust property.

This means that the *highest* rate of tax that will have to be paid is 30 per cent of the lifetime rate of 20 per cent – that is, 6 per cent – and the rate could be as low as nothing at all.

If money or assets are paid out of a discretionary trust, an 'interim charge' for IHT is made and must be paid by the trustees. The charge is worked out by multiplying the full ten-year charges by 1/40 for each three-month period during which the property was in the trust since the last periodic charge to IHT. (The procedure is slightly different for payments made before the first ten-year period is up.) This interim charge is also called an 'exit charge'. The tax charge is scaled down similarly in the case of property added to the trust after the start of the relevant ten-year period.

EXAMPLE 10.5

Peter set up a discretionary trust on 1 May 1993, paying £80,000 into it. That day, he also set up an interest-in-possession trust in favour of his daughter and paid £50,000 into that. His cumulative total of chargeable gifts over the seven years before 1 May 1993 was £20,000.

On 1 May 2003, the first ten-year IHT charge becomes payable on the discretionary trust, which is now valued at £230,000. The tax due is worked out as follows:

Current value of discretionary trust	£230,000
plus original value of other trust set up on 1 May 1993	£50,000
plus Peter's seven-year running total up to 30 April 1993	£20,000
	£300,000
less tax-free slice	£255,000
	£45,000
Tax @ 20% on £45,000	£9,000
Effective rate of tax (£9,000 ÷ £230,000)	3.9%
30% x effective rate	1.17%
IHT due on the trust (1.17% x £230,000)	£2,700

EXAMPLE 10.6

In Example 10.5, if Peter had set up the interest-in-possession trust on the day after setting up the discretionary trust, the periodic charge at the discretionary trust's ten-year anniversary would have been lower – in fact, there would have been no charge at all because the value of the trust property and running slice up to the date the trust was created would come to less than the tax-free slice:

Current value of discretionary trust	£230,000
plus Peter's seven-year running total up to 30 April 1993	£20,000
	£250,000
less tax-free slice	£255,000
	£0
Tax @ 20% on £0	£0
Effective rate of tax	0%

The trustees are also responsible for paying income tax on any income received by the trust. This is paid at one of two rates, depending on the type of income involved (rates are for 2003–4):

- on dividends from shares, distributions from share-based unit trusts and similar investments, tax is paid at a rate of 25 per cent
- on other income, tax is paid at 34 per cent.

Example 10.7 on page 160 shows how this can work in practice. These rates are higher than those levied on income from interest-in-possession trusts – see page 151. The reason for this is that beneficiaries of discretionary trusts might have a wide variety of personal tax positions. The tax rates applicable to the discretionary trust are supposed to strike a balance between the basic and higher rates of tax which might apply to beneficiaries.

From 6 April 1999 onwards, trustees must effectively account for extra tax when they pay out dividend income to beneficiaries. This is because the trustees can no longer count the tax credit on dividends the trust has received as part of the tax it deducts from payments to beneficiaries (see below). Where a trust has accumulated funds or other income out of which to pay this extra tax, it might still pass on the full after-tax amount of dividend income. But a trust without alternative funds will be forced to reduce the amount of dividend income it can pass on to beneficiaries. See Example 10.8.

CGT on any taxable capital gains is also payable by the trustees at 34 per cent, though the trust can set a tax-free allowance (usually £3,950 in 2003–4 but see box on page 153) against the first slice of gains.

Payments to beneficiaries

Unlike an interest-in-possession trust (see page 152), income paid out from a discretionary trust is treated in just one way, regardless of the source of income. It is all paid out with tax at a rate of 34 per cent already deducted. As a beneficiary, you receive the net income plus a 34 per cent tax credit. The sum of the two counts as gross income which is taxable but you set the tax credit against your tax bill. In this way, you will normally receive a tax refund if your top rate of tax is lower than 34 per cent. Higher-rate taxpayers have extra tax to pay.

On the face of it, you might think that this opens up a way of reclaiming tax on dividends and similar income from April 1999 onwards (when such tax generally ceased to be reclaimable). In practice, this is not the case. As outlined above, from April 1999 onwards the trustees must effectively pay extra tax when such income is distributed. This means that, unless the trust has other funds available to meet the tax bill, it can afford to pass on to beneficiaries less of the dividend income it receives. So, indirectly, you do feel the impact of tax on dividends ceasing to be reclaimable.

If you receive a payment of capital from the trust, there is no CGT for you to pay and you cannot reclaim any CGT paid by the trust. Note that, once income has been accumulated within the trust, the payment of it to a beneficiary will normally count as a payment of capital.

When the trust ends

When the discretionary trust comes to an end, an 'exit' charge is made on the whole of the trust property as if it were any other payment from the trust (see above).

EXAMPLE 10.7

Some years ago, Jaspar and Anne set up a discretionary trust in favour of their grandchildren. The trust holds a mix of investments: some property and various shares and bonds. In 2003–4, the income and tax position of the trust (before making any payments to beneficiaries) was as follows:

Income

Income from property (before deduction of tax)	£4,000
Dividends from shares (net of 10% tax credit)	£1,800
Interest income (net of 20% savings tax)	£3,200

Tax

Tax at 34% on property income (34% x £4,000)	£1,360
Tax at 10% already deducted from dividends (10/90 x £1,800)	£200
Additional tax on dividends: 25% of grossed-up amount (100/90 x £1,800 = £2,000) less £200 already paid	£300
Tax at 20% already deducted from interest (20/80 x £3,200)	£800
Additional tax on interest: 34% of grossed-up amount (100/80 x £3,200 = £4,000) less £800 already paid	£560
Total tax paid	£3,220
Income after tax (£4,000 – £1,360 + £1,800 – £300 + £3,200 – £560)	£6,780

EXAMPLE 10.8

If the trust in Example 10.7 accumulates its dividend income, the amount available for accumulation in 2003–4 is as follows:

Dividend income received by the trust	£1,800
Non-reclaimable tax credit at 10%	£200
Grossed up dividend	£2,000
Additional tax due: 25% x £2,000 less tax credit	£300
Amount of income available for accumulation (£2,000 – £200 – £300)	£1,500

But further tax may become due if dividend income is paid out to a beneficiary. For example, if the trustees decide to pass on the £1,500 they could otherwise accumulate to a beneficiary, they need to account for the 34 per cent tax credit that would accompany the payment: £1,500 x 34/66 = £772.73. Against this, they can set the £300 tax already paid but not the non-reclaimable £200 tax credit. So, the trustees have to pay the Inland Revenue an extra £472.73. If they do not have, or do not wish to use, other funds to meet this bill, they must reduce the amount they pay to the beneficiary.

If the trustees want to limit the payment to the beneficiary plus the extra tax bill to the amount they could otherwise accumulate, they should pay the beneficiary £1,188. The tax credit on this is 34/66 x £1,188 = £612. The extra tax due is £612 – £300 = £312. This can be paid out of the £1,500 otherwise available for accumulation, leaving £1500 – £312 = £1,188 to fund the distribution to the beneficiary.

EXAMPLE 10.9

The trustees in Example 10.8 decide to use the dividend income to pay out £1,188 plus a tax credit of £612 to one of the beneficiaries, Jenny. Whether she can reclaim tax or has to pay extra depends on her tax situation:

- if Jenny is a non-taxpayer, she can reclaim the full tax credit of £612, bringing the total she receives to £1,800. In other words, she gets the amount of net dividend payment to the trustees but not the non-reclaimable tax credit
- if Jenny is a starting-rate taxpayer (i.e. she pays tax at 10 per cent in 2003–4), she can claim back tax equal to 34% – 10% = 24% of the grossed-up payment of £1,800, which comes to £432. This brings the total she gets to £1,188 + £432 = £1,620. In other words she has paid tax of 10% x £1,800 = £180
- if she is a basic-rate taxpayer (i.e. she pays tax at 22 per cent in 2003–4), Jenny can claim back tax equal to 34% – 22% = 12% of the grossed-up payment of £1,800, which comes to £216. This brings her total receipts to £1,188 + £216 = £1,404. In other words, she has paid tax of 22% x £1,800 = £396

- if she is a higher-rate taxpayer (i.e. she pays tax at 40 per cent in 2003–4), Jenny has extra tax to pay equal to 40% – 34% = 6% of the grossed-up payment of £1,800. This means she pays extra tax of £108 leaving her with net income from the trust of £1,188 – £108 = £1,080.

Accumulation-and-maintenance trusts

Putting a gift into trust

Although accumulation-and-maintenance trusts are a special form of discretionary trust, the tax rules are much more favourable. A payment into an accumulation-and-maintenance trust counts as a PET (see page 114) – assuming none of the exemptions in Chapter 5 apply – and so there is no tax to pay provided you survive for seven years after making the gift.

Normal CGT rules apply to a gift to an accumulation-and-maintenance trust, so you will need to check whether there is any CGT to pay (see Chapters 5 and 6).

The trust's tax position

An accumulation-and-maintenance trust is not subject to the periodic charge regime – that is, there is no IHT to pay on the value of the trust during the lifetime of the trust nor is there any IHT charge when payments are made to beneficiaries.

The income and capital gains tax position of the trust is the same as for other discretionary trusts – see page 158.

Payments to beneficiaries

The rules are the same as for other discretionary trusts (see page 159).

Bear in mind that, if you set up an accumulation-and-maintenance trust for your own child, any income paid out to your child under the age of 18 (and unmarried) or used for his or her benefit will count as your income for tax purposes if it exceeds £100 a year. Any capital paid out will be treated in the same way to the extent that it can be matched against income accumulated within the trust. But you can avoid income being taxed as yours if you leave all the income and capital to accumulate within the trust.

When the trust ends

There is no IHT charge, provided one or more beneficiaries have become entitled to the trust property (or dies before becoming entitled). The trustees may need to pay CGT on any capital gains – this cannot be reclaimed by the beneficiaries. Amounts received by beneficiaries are treated as described under 'Payments to beneficiaries' on page 159.

However, if the income-and-accumulation trust comes to an end in other circumstances – for example, if it simply reaches the end of its 25-year lifespan without any beneficiaries having become entitled to the property, there will normally be an IHT bill. The amount of tax due depends on how long the trust has existed – see Inland Revenue Leaflet IHT16, *Settled property*, for further information. After a full 25 years, the charge would be 21 per cent of the trust property. The charge can be avoided if, before the 25 years are up, you ensure that a beneficiary is given an interest in the trust property – this can either be an interest in possession or to the capital.

Situations when the normal tax rules do not apply

Settlor-interested trusts

A settlor-interested trust is one in which the settlor has a 'retained interest'. If this applies, both income and capital gains made by the trust will be taxed as those of the settlor. Often this will mean a higher tax bill. You will be treated as having a retained interest if you or your husband or wife can in any circumstances benefit from the trust either now or at some future time.

The definition of retained interest is very widely drawn, so you will be caught by the rules not simply if you or your husband or wife is a named beneficiary of the trust, but even if you might become a beneficiary only because of some seemingly unlikely circumstances, for example:

- the trust says your grandchild will become entitled to the trust property provided he or she reaches age 25 but you fail to say what happens if he or she does not reach that age. In that case, the property would automatically revert back to the settlor, so you are a potential beneficiary and have a retained interest
- a trust is set up for your children and remoter issue but the trustees have the power to give the trust property to any other trust that includes the children and remoter issue as beneficiaries. This would not exclude a trust that also included you or your husband or wife as additional beneficiaries, so again you are deemed to have a retained interest.

Note, too, that if you are both the settlor and an actual or potential beneficiary under the trust, the gift with reservation rules apply (see page 118). This means that the trust property continues to count as part of your estate for IHT purposes until you cease to be able to benefit or you die, whichever happens first. Unlike the retained interest rules, the gift with reservation rules do not apply simply because your husband or wife (but not you) is a beneficiary.

Other situations when income from a trust is treated as that of the settlor

If you are the settlor and you or your husband or wife enters into various loan and repayment arrangements with a trust, the income may be treated as yours for tax purposes rather than as income of the trust.

If the income of a trust of which you are the settlor is paid out to, or used for the benefit of, your unmarried children under the age of 18, it is taxed as your income unless it comes to no more than £100 a year. This will also apply to capital from the trust if there is available trust income to match the payment. In the case of a bare trust even undistributed income will be taxed as that of the parent if it exceeds £100 and results from a parental gift into the trust made on or after 9 March 1999.

Table 10.1 Which type of trust?

	Bare Trust	Interest-in-possession	Discretionary	Accumulation-and-maintenance
IHT status of gift when trust set up	PET	PET	Chargeable gift	PET
IHT regime once trust up and running	Does not apply	Favourable	Unfavourable	Favourable
Trust pays tax on income at:[†]	Beneficiary's own rate	22%, 20% and 10%	34% and 25%	34% and 25%
Trust pays tax on gains at:[†]	Beneficiary's own rate	34%	34%	34%
Can build up income within trust	Yes	Not usually	Yes	Yes
Can easily alter who benefits	No	No for income, yes for capital	Yes	Yes
Can easily alter the shares of the beneficiaries	No	No for income, yes for capital	Yes	Yes
Other				Only for minors

[†]2003–4 rates.

Chapter 11

Lifetime gift planning

SKIP THE COUNTRY

'I'd like to give Jake the paddock. The trouble is now that the local council has included it in the development plan, it's worth such a lot. I'll have a massive capital gains tax bill to pay,' groaned Patrick. 'There's only one thing for it,' soothed his wife, Jenny. 'We'll have to flee the country – become tax exiles. But we'll have to stay away for at least five years.' 'Jenny, you're up to something . . .' Patrick had belatedly spied the stack of travel brochures.

If you want to make gifts during your lifetime, most will be free of inheritance tax (IHT) either because of some specific exemption or because they count as potentially exempt transfers (PETs) (and so are tax-free provided you survive for seven years). Therefore your main concern is how to give without triggering an unnecessary capital gains tax (CGT) bill or creating income tax problems. Following the tips in this chapter can help but, if your affairs are complex, it is advisable to get help from an accountant★ or other tax adviser.★

For a detailed look at making gifts of your home or gifts to children, see Chapters 15 and 16, respectively.

Give exempt assets

If you can, give away things which are outside the scope of CGT – for example, cash or personal items worth less than £6,000 – see Chapter 5.

Use your tax-free slice

If you are planning to make a gift within the next few years and it's showing a fairly sizeable gain on which you would face a hefty CGT bill, consider making use of your tax-free slice between now and the year in which you make the gift. You can dispose of a certain amount of chargeable assets, which would otherwise be taxable, each year without having to pay CGT – the tax-free slice for 2003–4 is £7,900.

New-style bed-and-breakfast   *you sell / wife buys !*

Instead of wasting your CGT tax-free slice in years when you are not making any gifts (or other disposals), a widely used ploy used to be to sell assets, most commonly shares, and buy them back again the next day – a practice called 'bed-and-breakfasting'. This realised the gain (or loss) on the asset for tax purposes, using up your tax-free slice for the year (or providing a loss to offset against other gains) and gave a new, higher initial value for calculating future gains on the asset.

However, the 1998 Budget brought traditional bed-and-breakfasting to an abrupt end. From 17 March 1998 onwards, any shares or similar assets which are sold and repurchased within a 30-day period are matched and any gain or loss which would otherwise have been realised is ignored for CGT purposes.

You could still bed-and-breakfast in the old way but leaving more than 30 days between the sale and repurchase. However, this would be a high-risk strategy, since the stock market could move dramatically over a month. Alternative ways to realise gains or losses while keeping your assets largely unchanged include:

- 'bed-and-ISA' your shares. This means selling the shares and immediately buying them back within the shelter of an Individual Savings Account (ISA). An ISA must be taken out through an approved ISA manager (e.g. a stockbroker)
- if you are married, sell your shares and ask your husband or wife to buy the same shares immediately. Ownership has changed but at least the shares are still in the family
- sell your shares and simultaneously buy a 'call traded option' which gives you the right to buy the same company's shares at a fixed price on or before a set future date. This is a relatively

expensive exercise because you must pay a premium for the option

- sell the shares in one company and buy back shares in another company which is expected to perform in a similar manner – usually shares in a company of similar size in the same sector. Deciding which shares are reasonably well-matched could be tricky.

Before attempting new-style bed-and-breakfasting, you would be wise to discuss the various possibilities with a stockbroker.*

Use your husband's or wife's tax-free slice

If your husband or wife does not use his or her tax-free slice (£7,900 in 2003–4) and you have a gift to make on which there is a sizeable gain, you might be able to reduce the CGT bill by first giving part or all of the asset to your husband or wife. Gifts between husband and wife are normally tax-free (see page 99). Note, however, that the gift to your husband or wife must be genuine and you cannot attach any conditions – e.g. insisting that he or she gives away the asset subsequently in accordance with your wishes. Therefore you need to be confident that you and your husband or wife have genuinely similar views and aspirations about making gifts to the recipient.

Skip the country?

In the past, CGT was payable only if you were resident and/or ordinarily resident in the UK during the tax year in which you realised a chargeable gain. However, following changes in the 1998 Budget, you can now still end up with a CGT bill even if you are living abroad.

For anyone who ceases to be resident from 17 March 1998 onwards and for anyone who becomes UK resident again from 6 April 1998 onwards, any gifts or other disposals he or she makes while abroad will be free of CGT only if he or she has been not resident and not ordinarily resident in the UK for five complete tax years or more.

Where your period abroad comes to less than five complete tax years, gains realised in the tax year in which you leave the UK will be taxable in that year. Gains realised while abroad will be taxed in the tax year of your return. However, in February 2003 it was reported that the government might consider tax concessions for non-residents who had unexpectedly returned to the UK on the advice of the UK government because of war with Iraq. Contact your tax office★ for guidance.

The tax statutes say very little about what the terms 'resident' and 'ordinarily resident' mean though, at the time of writing, the government was reviewing this and considering possible changes to the legal definitions of residence and domicile. In the meantime, a body of case law has developed. Under present rules, you will always count as resident for a tax year if you spend 183 days or more in the UK during the tax year and, if you spend fewer days there, you may still count as resident. You will usually count as 'ordinarily resident' if you live in the UK year after year, even if you are away temporarily. The main way in which someone who normally lives in the UK can count as not resident and not ordinarily resident is to go and work full-time abroad, provided the following conditions are met:

- your absence from the UK and your contract of employment both last at least a whole tax year
- you can make visits back home (e.g. for holidays) but the time spent in the UK must not add up to more than 183 days in any one tax year and, over the whole period abroad, must average only 91 days per tax year or less.

By concession, a husband or wife accompanying their spouse while he or she works abroad can also count as resident or non-resident. For more information about residency status, see Inland Revenue booklet IR20, *Residents and non-residents*, available from tax offices.★

Taking a decision to work abroad just so that you can avoid CGT may seem a drastic step. But, looked at from another perspective, if you do find yourself doing a stint working overseas, it would be an excellent time to consider making any gifts which could give rise to a large CGT bill.

EXAMPLE 11.1

Jenny is a fashion designer, working for an international firm. Usually she is based in London but in March 2003 she is posted to the USA. Her husband Patrick decides to go with her. The posting is due to last for a minimum of two years but can be extended thereafter on an annual basis. Jenny will have nine weeks' holiday a year when she can make visits back home. Provided Jenny continues to work abroad for at least five years, this would be an ideal opportunity to give their son, Jake, a piece of land which Patrick owns. The former paddock has been given development land status in the council's local plan which has boosted its value from a few thousand pounds to £150,000. Despite its high value, there is no CGT to pay on the gift, provided Patrick remains non-resident and not ordinarily resident for five whole tax years.

Don't forget hold-over relief

Hold-over relief (see Chapter 6) lets you, in effect, give away your CGT bill along with the asset which is the subject of your gift. One of the circumstances in which you can claim hold-over relief is where the gift counts as a chargeable transfer for IHT. Making your gift to a discretionary trust would fit the bill. Provided you make sure that the gift is covered by one of the IHT exemptions (see Chapter 5) or falls within your tax-free slice (£255,000 for 2003–4), there will be no IHT on the gift. However, make sure that a gift into trust suits your intentions and that you fully understand the tax position of the trust (see Chapter 10). Get advice from a solicitor.★

Gifts to children

It is difficult for a parent to make a gift to his or her child without income paid to the child or used for the benefit of the child counting as the parent's income for tax purposes – see Chapter 16 for ideas on how to avoid this.

Part 3

Inheritance

Whether you are writing your own will or sorting out someone else's will, please note that it is important to consult a legal adviser if substantial sums of money are involved and/or the situation is at all complex.

Chapter 12

Making a will

WILLS ARE IMPORTANT

'Now, Mr Hope' – the solicitor's face became more serious – 'I take it you have made a will?'

'Well, no,' replied Richard, 'but my affairs are very straightforward. Everything would go to my wife – after all, the children are grown up.'

'Precisely, Mr Hope. Without a will, only part of your estate would pass to your wife. Your children would also benefit. Your wife might need to sell the home and there would certainly be a number of unnecessary costs. I would strongly advise you to make a will.'

A will is a legal document which says how your possessions (your *estate*) are to be dealt with when you die. Even if your estate is small and your intentions regarding it extremely simple, you should still make a will. If you do not, a number of problems can arise, as follows:

- your survivors may waste time trying to find out whether or not you did write a will; it may take them a long time to trace all your possessions; and they may have to spend time and money tracing relatives
- if there is no will, it may take longer and cost more to 'prove' the estate (an administrative process which has to be completed before your estate can be 'distributed' – that is, handed on – to your heirs)
- without a will, your next of kin (often a wife or husband) will usually be appointed to sort out your affairs. At the time of bereavement, he or she may prefer not to take on this role and you may, in any case, have friends or relatives who would be more

suited to the task
- the law will dictate how your estate is passed on and this may not coincide with your wishes
- the law may require that various trusts are set up. The terms of these trusts may be overly restrictive and, especially where small sums are involved, unnecessarily large expenses may be incurred
- your heirs may have to pay inheritance tax (or more tax) than would have been the case had you used your will to pass on your possessions tax-efficiently (see Chapter 14).

Apart from avoiding these problems and ensuring that your possessions are given away as you would choose, a will can be used for other purposes too: you can appoint guardians to care for young children; and you can express your preferences about funeral arrangements and any wishes about the use of your body for medical purposes after death.

Note that the rules relating to wills and intestacy in Scotland and Northern Ireland differ in a number of respects from the rules for the rest of the UK – see pages 184 and 185. The rules described here apply to England and Wales.

Definitions

Three types of player are involved in a will:

- **testator/testatrix**   The man or woman whose will it is. You must be aged 18 or over (and of sound mind) to make a valid will
- **beneficiary**   A person or organisation left something ('benefits') under a will
- **personal representative**   The person, people or organisation that sees that your estate is distributed following your death. If you have not made a will, they are your *administrators* and they will distribute your estate in accordance with the law. If you have made a will, they are your *executors* and they will try to ensure that the instructions in your will are carried out.

Dying without a will

If you die without making a will ('intestate') the law dictates how your estate will be passed on (with the exception of joint assets held under a 'joint tenancy' – see page 125 – which pass automatically to the surviving co-owners). The law aims, in the first instance, to protect your immediate family – husband or wife and children. This might coincide with your wishes but, even if it did, it still might not result in your estate being used as you had expected or would have wished. Furthermore, people who are not formally part of your family – for example, an unmarried partner – have no automatic rights under the intestacy laws (though they might still have a claim against your estate – see page 182).

Where part or all of your estate would pass to your spouse under the intestacy rules, this will only happen if he or she survives you by at least 28 days. This 'survivorship provision' (which is a common device used in wills) makes sure that, in cases where you and your spouse die within a short time of one another (for example, as a result of a road traffic accident), the relatives of each of you benefit from your respective estates rather than everything going to the relatives of the second to die. Bear in mind that a person under 18 cannot make a valid will, so the estate of child who dies – including any assets held under a bare trust for the child – would be subject to the intestacy rules.

The intestacy laws assume that all your possessions could be sold by your personal representative to convert your whole estate into cash which would then be distributed according to the rules described below. In practice, the possessions would not necessarily be sold and could be passed on intact but problems can arise where there is a large possession – for example, the family home – if it needs to be split between two or more beneficiaries. The intestacy laws operate as follows.

If you are survived by a husband or wife and no children

Your husband or wife is entitled to all your *personal chattels* (i.e. personal possessions, such as clothes, furniture, jewellery and private cars). If your estate is valued at £200,000 or less, your husband or wife also inherits the whole estate. (See Chapter 13 for guidance on valuing your estate.)

If your estate is valued at more than £200,000, your husband or wife gets the whole lot, provided you had no living parents or brothers or sisters at the time of your death. If you are survived by parents, brothers or sisters, your husband or wife is entitled to a fixed sum of £200,000 (plus interest at a set rate from the date of death until the date the payment is made) plus half of whatever remains. The remainder goes to your parents or, if they are dead, to your brothers and sisters. Chart 12.1 summarises the position.

Chart 12.1 Who inherits if you leave a husband/wife and no children

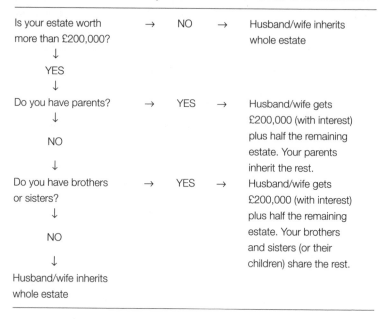

Is your estate worth more than £200,000?	→	NO →	Husband/wife inherits whole estate
↓			
YES			
↓			
Do you have parents?	→	YES →	Husband/wife gets £200,000 (with interest)
↓			plus half the remaining
NO			estate. Your parents inherit the rest.
↓			
Do you have brothers or sisters?	→	YES →	Husband/wife gets £200,000 (with interest) plus half the remaining
↓			estate. Your brothers and sisters (or their
NO			children) share the rest.
↓			
Husband/wife inherits whole estate			

EXAMPLE 12.1

Jeremy and Ali had been married for ten years when tragically Jeremy died in a road accident. He was only 36 and, though he had several times thought about making a will, he had not got around to doing it. His estate was valued at £250,000 and he would have left everything to Ali but under the intestacy laws the estate was divided between Ali and his parents as follows:

Ali's share

Fixed sum	£200,000
plus interest	£4,940
plus half the remaining estate	
(i.e. £250,000 − £204,940) ÷ 2	£22,530
Total	£227,470
Jeremy's parents' share	£22,530

If you are survived by children

If you leave children, but no husband or wife, the inheritance position is simple: your children share your estate equally. Note that 'children' includes offspring from your most recent marriage, any previous marriages, adopted and illegitimate children. However, it does not include stepchildren.

If you are survived by a husband or wife, he or she is entitled to all your personal possessions. And, if your estate is valued at £125,000 or less, he or she also inherits the whole of that.

If your estate is valued at more than £125,000, your husband or wife receives a fixed sum of £125,000 (plus interest at a set rate from the date of death until the date payment is made) and a life interest in half of the remaining estate. A life interest gives him or her the right to the income from that part of the estate (or use of it in the case of, say, a house) but he or she cannot touch the capital. (Note that the husband or wife can decide to take an appropriately calculated lump sum from the estate in place of a life interest.) The rest of the estate passes to your children to be shared equally between them. They also become entitled to the capital bearing the life interest when your husband or wife dies. (Note that children can inherit capital outright only once they reach the age of 18, so they have an income entitlement up to that age.) Chart 12.2 summarises the position.

Chart 12.2 Who inherits if you leave children

Do you have a husband or wife?	→	NO	→	Your children inherit equal shares in the estate
↓				
YES				
↓				
Is your estate worth more than £125,000?	→	NO	→	Husband/wife inherits whole estate
↓				
YES				
↓				

Husband/wife gets £125,000 (with interest) plus life interest in half the remaining estate (which passes eventually to your children). Your children inherit the rest.

EXAMPLE 12.2

Alan died leaving an estate valued at £250,000. Of this amount £200,000 represented his half-share in the family home (which he and his wife, Julia, owned as tenants in common – see page 125). However, he had made no will. Under the intestacy rules Julia and his only child inherited the estate in the following shares:

Julia's share

Capital: fixed sum	£125,000
plus interest	£3,090
Total capital	£128,090
Remaining estate (£250,000 – £128,090)	£121,910

So Julia also gets income/use from half of £121,910 i.e. £60,955

Child's share

Capital now	£60,955
Capital to be set aside for future (Julia has life interest)	£60,955

Unfortunately, Julia's outright inheritance of £128,090 and interest in a further £60,955 come to less than the value of the family home. In order to comply with the intestacy rules requiring capital of £121,910 in total to be set aside for the child, part of the family home must be held in trust for the child.

If you are survived by no near-relatives

If you leave no husband or wife and no children, the intestacy rules rank your heirs in the order in which they will inherit your estate.

Chart 12.3 Who inherits if you leave no near-relatives

Are you survived by your parents?	→	YES	→	Your parents inherit equal shares in your estate
↓				
NO				
↓				
Do you have any brothers or sisters?	→	YES	→	Your brothers and sisters inherit equal shares in your estate[†]
↓				
NO				
↓				
Are you survived by any grandparents?	→	YES	→	Your grandparents inherit the estate in equal shares
↓				
NO				
↓				
Do you have any uncles or aunts?	→	YES	→	Your uncles and aunts inherit the estate in equal shares[‡]
↓				
NO				
↓				
Your estate passes to the Crown				

[†] If a brother or sister has died before you, their offspring, if any, inherit instead. If you have no full brothers or sisters, any half-brothers or half-sisters will share the estate instead.

[‡] If any uncle or aunt has died before you, their offspring inherit instead. If you have no full uncles or aunts, any half-uncles or half-aunts share the estate instead.

If you have no relatives who are eligible to inherit (see Chart 12.3), your estate passes to the Crown in *bona vacantia* (which literally means 'unclaimed goods'). The Crown may make ex gratia payments if your dependants or distant relatives make an application to it. It is important to realise that such claimants have no *right* to receive anything – payments are at the discretion of the Crown. Applicants who are most likely to succeed include the following:

* someone who had a long, close association with you: for example, an unmarried partner or someone who lived with you as a child
* someone whom you clearly intended to benefit under a will that was invalid for some reason.

EXAMPLE 12.3

Harold died aged 89 without making a will. He was an only child. His wife and parents died before him and he himself had no children. But his Uncle Jack (who died long ago) had two children, Jean and Richard, who are both still living. They each inherit half of Harold's estate.

Partial intestacy

Your will should cover all your assets. If you do not specify how part of your estate is to be used, that part will be subject to the intestacy rules even though the rest of your estate is disposed of in accordance with the will.

Problems caused by intestacy

The main problems of intestacy arise where you are survived by a partner (either married or not) and/or you have children. Unless you make a will, you cannot be certain that they will be adequately provided for in the event of your death.

If you are not married to your partner, he or she has no automatic right of inheritance in the event of your death. However, he or she will be able to claim a share of your estate under the Inheritance (Provision for Family and Dependants) Act 1975 if they lived with you as husband or wife throughout the two years prior to your death. If that condition does not apply and if they can show that they were being partly or wholly maintained by you when you were alive, they may still be able to claim support from your estate. In either case, a claim must usually be made within six months of permission being granted to distribute the estate. It will then be considered by the courts, which is generally a lengthy and often costly procedure.

If you are married, there is a tendency to assume that your husband or wife will automatically inherit everything. The foregoing sections have shown that this is by no means certain. And, even if you are happy for your husband or wife and children to share your assets, the practical application of the intestacy rules may be very distressing to your survivors. Where the estate must be shared between husband or wife and children, or husband or wife and other relatives, your husband or wife has the right to claim the family home as part or all of his or her inheritance (provided he or she lived there with you prior to your death). If the home is worth more than the amount he or she is entitled to inherit, your husband or wife can 'buy' the excess from the estate. But if he or she does not have sufficient resources to be able to do this, the home may have to be sold so that the cash raised can be split as required by the intestacy provisions.

Minors cannot inherit directly under the intestacy laws, so any assets passing to these children must be held in trust. The trustees will be required to invest the assets in accordance with the Trustee Act 2000 (see page 137) assuming the law of England and Wales applies. Fortunately, this gives the trustees very wide investment powers. They may be required to obtain professional advice. This could be unduly costly if only a relatively small sum is involved. In Scotland and Northern Ireland, the more restrictive investment rules of the Trustee Investments Act 1961 apply. This could mean an unduly high proportion of the trust fund being held as deposits, gilts and other bonds, and the trustees will be required to get investment advice unless they stick to a narrow range of investments largely made up of National Savings & Investments products.

Assets continue to be held in trust until the child reaches age 18, at which point he or she takes over direct ownership of the assets. This might be earlier than you would have wished – in a will, you could require assets to be held in trust until a later age.

Tax and intestacy

Although intestacy might mean your estate is not passed on as you would have wished, it does in fact impose a certain amount of tax-efficiency. This is because the rules require a share of your estate above the fixed amounts to be passed to people other than your husband or wife, so using up some or all of your inheritance tax-free slice. This can save up to £102,000 inheritance tax (in 2003–4) on the subsequent death of your husband or wife – see page 216.

Intestacy in Scotland

The law in Scotland works differently for those who die without making a will, as follows.

- **If you were married with no children** Your husband or wife has 'prior rights' to the family home (provided it is in Scotland) up to a value of £130,000, furniture and household effects up to £22,000 and a cash sum up to £58,000. He or she also has 'legal rights' to half the remaining 'moveable estate' (i.e. excluding land and buildings). See below for the remaining estate.
- **If you were married with children** Your husband or wife has prior rights to the family home up to £130,000, furniture and effects up to £22,000 and a cash sum up to £35,000 plus legal rights to share one-third of the remaining moveable estate. The children also have legal rights to share one-third of the moveable estate between them. See below for the remaining estate.
- **If you had children but no husband or wife** The children have legal rights to half the moveable estate.
- **The remaining estate** Whatever remains after meeting the prior rights, the legal rights and, in the case of partial intestacy, bequests under a will is known as 'the dead's part' and is distributed in the following order of priority:

  - children
  - if there are both parents and brothers and sisters, half the remainder goes to the parents, half to the brothers and sisters
  - brothers and sisters, if there are no parents
  - parents, if there are no brothers and sisters

- husband or wife
- uncles and aunts (or, if they have died, their children)
- grandparents
- brothers and sisters of grandparents (or, if they have died, their children)
- remoter ancestors, going back one generation at a time
- the Crown.

Intestacy in Northern Ireland

The law is also different in Northern Ireland for those who die without making a will.

- **If you were married with no children** Your husband or wife inherits all your personal effects plus the first £200,000 of your estate and half of any residue. The remainder passes to parent(s) or brother(s) and sister(s) if there are no parents still living. If there are no children, no parents and no brothers or sisters (or nephews or nieces), then your spouse inherits your whole estate.
- **If you were married with children** Your husband or wife inherits all your personal effects plus the first £125,000 of your estate plus half of any residue if there is one child, or one-third of the residue, if there are two or more children. The remainder of the estate passes to the child(ren) – in trust if they are aged under 18.
- **If you had children but no husband or wife** The estate is divided equally between the children.
- **If you had no children and no husband or wife** Your estate goes to your relatives, starting with parents but extending to very distant relatives if no closer ones survive you.

Drawing up a will

In many people's minds, making a will is inextricably linked with using a solicitor but this need not be so. Provided your personal circumstances are not overly complicated and you understand what you are doing, there is no reason why you should not write your own will. A number of books and kits are available to help you do this: for example, *Wills and Probate* or *Make Your Own Will* Action Pack available from Which? Books.★ The main advantage of writing your own will is, of course, the saving in solicitors' fees. But a simple will, for example involving only personal (no business) assets in the UK, with everything left to your husband or wife, need not cost much even if you do go to a professional. If your affairs are more complex, you should be wary of the DIY route.

A will, to fulfil its purpose, must record your intentions clearly and unambiguously and should include contingency plans to cover the possibility, for example, of a beneficiary dying before you. There are also various pitfalls to be avoided – some that would invalidate the will and leave your estate subject to the intestacy laws and others which would not invalidate the will but would interfere with the intentions expressed in it. For example, a valid will must be signed by two or more witnesses, who may not also be beneficiaries (or the husbands or wives of beneficiaries) under the will; so, if you are leaving anything to your husband or wife, say, do not ask him or her to be a witness – the will would be valid but your spouse would not be allowed to inherit under it.

If your affairs are complicated – e.g. you run your own business, you have been divorced or you have step-children – or you do not feel confident about your knowledge of the law relating to wills, you would be wise to employ a professional rather than trying to draw up a will yourself. Lawyers claim to make more money from sorting out defective DIY wills than from writing wills themselves.

The traditional source of help drawing up a will is a solicitor. Most high street firms can draw up a simple will – leaving, say, everything to your husband or wife – and charges often start as low as £50. If you and your husband or wife draw up similar wills at the same time (often called 'reciprocal wills', 'mirror wills' or 'back-to-back wills'), you might get a special rate of, say, £70 or £80 the pair. But prices vary greatly and, even for a simple will, some solicitors charge in the region of £100 to £150. If your affairs are complicated, the charge will depend on the time the solicitor needs to devote to your case and so you should expect to pay more. Always check the expected price before going ahead.

Solicitors must pass exams, go through rigorous post-graduate training and continue to update their skills through continuous professional development. But dealing with estates is a specialist area, so you may prefer to choose a member of the Society of Trust and Estate Practitioners (STEP).★ Solicitors must belong to a professional body – one of the Law Societies⋆ – that lays down strict rules of business conduct backed up by disciplinary procedures and ensures that you have access to an independent complaints body – the Office for the Supervision of Solicitors⋆ – if things go wrong.

Will-writing services are an alternative to a solicitor. These are often small firms working under a franchise or as agents of a larger company. Most work by gathering the necessary details from you and feeding these into a computer which produces your will. Unlike solicitors, people running, or working for, will-writing firms are not required to have any formal legal qualifications, though they will probably have received some initial training and the computer software they are using will have been developed using legal experts; these firms may also use a solicitor to draw up complex wills. In the past, problems have arisen with some of these services: a number of firms have gone bust and, in one case, it was found that a potentially large number of the wills written contained a flaw and might not be valid. However, the will-writers' industry has been developing over the years and now many practitioners voluntarily belong to one of the trade/regulatory bodies operating in this area. The Society of Will Writers (SWW)⋆ and the Institute of Professional Willwriters (IPW)⋆ aim to promote the professionalism of their members in the following ways:

- **training** Members of the SWW who have passed examinations relevant to will writing or can display competence in some other way can become fellows of the society and be able to use the initials FSWW. But other members (using the initials ASWW or MSWW) will not normally have the relevant training. All members of the IPW must have passed an exam before being admitted to membership

- **code of conduct** Members of both the SWW and IPW are required to follow the *Code of Conduct and Practice for the Will Writing Profession*. The code sets out rules of good business practice, including: disclosing fees and charges to customers before taking on their business, not taking on work beyond the member's competence, advising customers to seek legal advice if their affairs are beyond the will-writer's competence, having professional indemnity insurance and operating a proper written complaints system.

In the event of a complaint, you should first take the matter to the will-writing firm but, if not satisfied with the response, you can take the complaint to the SWW's or IPW's conciliation service. If conciliation fails, the case can be referred to arbitration. Though there is a fee for this, it is refundable if you win the case. As an alternative to conciliation and arbitration, you could take a complaint to any other relevant body, such as your local Trading Standards Office,★ or you could take court action.

Will-writers generally charge a flat fee – say, £45 to £50 for a single will or £70 to £80 for mirror wills. Not surprisingly, their wills tend to have a standardised format – if your affairs are complex, a solicitor will normally be the better choice.

A third source of will-writing is banks, building societies and life insurance companies. These offer a will-preparation service but some insist that you agree to them also acting as executors of the will (which is not generally a good idea – see below). You have an interview with the bank, society or company either at their offices or in your home. The interviewer you meet is not usually the person who actually draws up the will. If a bank or building society writes the will and you have a complaint, you can go to the Financial Ombudsman Service (FOS).★ The FOS does not cover insurance companies drafting wills.

Many charities also offer will-writing services. As discussed on page 50, make sure that the solicitor or other will-writer is acting for you alone and that you do not feel under any pressure to make a bequest to the charity in your will.

In addition to writing your will, a solicitor or other will-writing service might offer extras, such as storing your will, drawing up a 'living will' (also called an 'advance directive') or severing a joint tenancy to create a tenancy in common (see page 125). Do not feel pressurised into taking up any of these services unless you want to. Bear the following points in mind:

- **will storage** Most important is that your executors will be able to find your will and can be confident that it is your most recent will. If you are known to have a family solicitor, storing your will with the firm could be a good idea. You do not necessarily have to pay anything for this – some firms will store your will free of charge (because they hope to be employed later in executing your will). If you do not have an ongoing relationship with a solicitor, that might not be the best place to store your will. Other options include a bank safe-deposit box or a safe or strong box at home. Whatever you decide, it is a good idea to give your executors a sealed copy of the will

- **living will**   This typically sets out in advance your wishes regarding healthcare – especially refusal of medical treatment – if you become incapacitated by a terminal illness or degenerative disease. In general, medical practitioners are required to give whatever treatment they deem necessary but a patient has the right to refuse treatment. Clearly an unconscious patient cannot do this but refusal can still be effective even if it was given in advance of becoming unconscious. There has been much debate about the legal status in the UK of living wills, but it seems that, provided the document states your intentions clearly and reflects your *informed* decision, a living will is likely to be legally binding. A good place to store a living will would be with your medical records

- **severance of joint tenancy**   As discussed on page 125, if you want to transfer ownership of something – such as your home – from a joint tenancy to a tenancy in common, you do not need a formal deed drawn up by a solicitor. Notice in writing from one owner to the other is all that is required. Of course, your notice should clearly identify the property concerned, the action you are taking and the date from which it is effective. If you do not feel confident about getting the detail right, you might prefer a solicitor to draw up a notice for you.

Appointing executors

You have a choice when it comes to deciding who will sort out your affairs for you in accordance with your will: you can appoint a professional as your executor – e.g. a solicitor or your bank – or you can appoint friends or relatives. In general, professionals often charge more and if problems arise, such as long delays, the beneficiaries can do little because they do not themselves have a contract with the executor, so have little access to information and limited power to challenge the executor's actions. If, instead, you appoint relatives or friends, they always have the option to employ a solicitor direct if they need help.

You can choose anyone you like to act as executor (provided they are aged 18 or over when they apply for probate) and it is common to appoint the main beneficiary. Normally, you should appoint two executors, just in case one dies before you or refuses to act. Make sure you ask the people concerned whether they would be willing to take on the role.

Bear in mind that being an executor is a demanding task. Your executors will need to locate your will and personal papers, track all your assets and establish their value, establish what gifts you have made during the last seven years, deal with debts and funeral expenses, trace and contact beneficiaries, handle paperwork, deliver an account to the Inland Revenue and ensure any tax is paid. As tax will depend not just on the estate you leave but also on gifts made within the seven years up to death, your executors will be expected actively to try to trace gifts. This may mean trawling through old bank and building society statements and making enquiries among family members. Make sure you choose someone who has the time, energy and confidence to deal with officials and form-filling.

You can make your executors' lives easier if you lodge a record of your assets, their location and any gifts you have made along with your will or personal papers.

Reviewing your will

You should not view making a will as a task once done to be forgotten. As your circumstances alter, so your will needs to be updated. In some situations – for example, if you marry or remarry – any will made before the marriage will automatically be invalidated (unless it was a will made specifically in contemplation of the marriage). All bequests and references to your ex-husband or ex-wife are automatically revoked by divorce and the appointment of your 'ex' as guardian of any children will be revoked, unless you have made clear that this is still your intention. In other respects, the rest of your will stands. The same is not true of separation – the whole will including bequests to your spouse is still valid; in that situation, you should review the terms of your will.

Other circumstances in which you might want to revise your will are the birth or adoption of a child or if you decide that you would like to leave a legacy to a charity. It is wise to read through your will every two years, say, as a matter of course, to check that it reflects your current wishes.

If you do decide to alter a will – even slightly – it is better to draw up a new will containing the revisions than to add an amendment (a 'codicil'). The trouble with codicils is that they can easily become detached from the will and lost. Beware of stapling, clipping or pinning anything other than a codicil to a will. It is quite likely that any other note or document would be detached before the will was sent for probate and the marks left on the will might then raise doubts about whether there had been a codicil attached that has become lost. Enquiries into the non-existent codicil could delay proceedings.

A new will should always start with a clause revoking any previous wills; this automatically invalidates any earlier wills. (Interestingly, if a will is not automatically revoked – by, say, a later will or marriage – the law requires that you *physically* destroy your will if it is to be revoked. Simply putting a cross through it and scribbling 'cancelled' or 'revoked' across it is not enough.)

Making gifts in your will

In your will, you can give away anything you own. There are different types of gift. The distinction between them is important both for tax reasons (see Chapter 13) and because of the order in which they can be redirected to meet expenses and settle debts that you leave at the time of your death. The main types of gift are described as follows.

Specific gift

This can be a named or identifiable possession such as a piece of furniture, an item of jewellery or a particular car. It may be a specific possession that you own *at the time you write the will*. If you later sell the item the beneficiary who was to have received it will get nothing after all.

Alternatively, you might leave a more general type of specific gift. This would be the gift of a possession but not restricted to a specific item that you own at the time of drawing up the will. For example, you might give away 'the car I own at the time of my death', which would take into account the possibility that you might change your car from time to time.

A specific gift might be even more widely defined: for example, simply 'a car'. In this latter case, the executors of your will would have a duty to make sure that the beneficiary received a car – either one that you owned at the time of death or, if you had none, one bought specifically to fulfil the terms of the will – or, alternatively, the trustees would have to pay over an equivalent sum of money.

Legacies

A 'pecuniary legacy' is a particular type of specific gift which is a straightforward gift of money: for example, '£1,000 to my niece, Claire'.

A 'demonstrative legacy' can be either a general gift or a pecuniary legacy which is to be paid from a specific fund: for example, 'a violin to be paid for out of my account with Barclays Bank' or '£1,000 from my account with the Halifax'. If there was not enough money in the account, the shortfall would have to be met by using other assets in the estate.

On the whole, it is best to keep bequests of particular items or demonstrative gifts to a minimum. Particularly where your will is made a long time before death, there can be many changes to your possessions and the accounts and investments you hold.

Your personal representative(s) have wide powers (called the power of appropriation) to use any part of your estate to satisfy legacies. For example, if you leave £1,000 to your niece, the executors could give, say, shares worth £1,000 rather than selling the shares and giving her the proceeds from the sale.

Residuary gift

A will which assigned every part of your estate as a particular gift or legacy would be out of date almost immediately, because the value of your estate fluctuates even in the course of your daily transactions and will alter more widely during the course of time. Therefore, it is usual to leave whatever remains of your estate, after all your debts, expenses and various gifts as listed above have been paid, as a 'residuary gift' or 'residue'. You may intend your residue to be a substantial gift or it may be a small amount with, say, the bulk of your estate given away through pecuniary gifts.

To meet debts and expenses, any intestate part of your estate will be used up first, followed by the residue.

EXAMPLE 12.4

Daisy died at the ripe old age of 92. Her sole survivor, Albert, had expected to inherit a sizeable sum. However, Daisy had already given Hadley Hall to Albert and clearly considered that was enough, because out of the £750,000 estate that she left, she gave £600,000 to a spread of charities. After deducting outstanding debts, funeral expenses and a small tax bill, Albert inherited the residue of only £20,000.

Gifts you do not want to make

By omission, your will can also express your intention not to leave anything (or only very little) to people who might have expected to inherit from you. However, if these people were dependent on you (or you had a partner who had lived with you for at least two years as husband or wife without necessarily being dependent), they have the right to make a claim through the courts under the Inheritance (Provision for Family and Dependants) Act 1975 for reasonable provision out of your estate. The main people who are entitled to make such a claim are as follows:

- your husband or wife
- a former husband or wife, provided he or she has not remarried (and is not precluded from making a claim under the divorce settlement)
- a child of yours (whether legitimate, illegitimate or adopted)
- a child of your family (i.e. a stepchild or foster child)
- an unmarried partner.

An application under the Act must usually be made within six months of the personal representatives being given permission to dispose of the estate, though the court can extend this time limit. The court decides whether or not the applicant is entitled to financial support from the estate and, if it decides in favour of the applicant, it can order the payment of either a lump sum or income (or both).

You might seek to anticipate and thwart such a claim by giving away as much of your estate as possible but this strategy will not work. The court has the power to revoke such gifts in order to ensure that enough funds are available to meet the needs of your surviving dependants.

You can include in your will a statement setting out your reasons for excluding your dependants and the court will take this into account. It would be worth seeking advice from a solicitor about the most effective wording to use.

In Scotland, you cannot disinherit your husband, wife or children, who can claim their 'legal rights' to part of your estate. For more information see *Wills and Probate* available from Which? Books.*

Chapter 13

Tax at the time of death

NOT JUST A RICH MAN'S TAX

'When I die, my will is very simple,' said Percy, draining his glass. 'I haven't so very much to leave behind, but I'll give my son a bit to help him with his business. Then, I'll just split what's left between the wife and Rose.'

'You should watch out,' replied his friend as he got up to buy another round. 'If there is any tax to pay, it will probably come out of Rose's share – she might end up with a lot less than you expect.'

When you die, you are deemed to make a gift of all your possessions just before death. There is no capital gains tax (CGT) on your estate, but there might be inheritance tax (IHT) on the estate and there could be extra tax due on gifts which you had made in the seven years before death.

Tax on gifts made before death

Chapter 7 looked at the immediate tax position of gifts made during your lifetime. In the case of potentially exempt transfers (PETs) there was no tax to pay at the time of the gift but, if you die within seven years of making a PET, the gift becomes a 'chargeable transfer' and tax is due. The effective rate of tax ranges from 8 per cent up to 40 per cent, depending on the time that has elapsed since you originally made the gift (see page 115).

Similarly, a chargeable transfer – on which tax may have been paid at the time of the gift but at the lower lifetime IHT rate of 20 per cent – will be reassessed and there may be further tax to pay if you die within seven years of making the gift (see page 113).

The reassessment of these earlier gifts and the payment of any tax which becomes due on them is entirely separate from the calculation of tax on your estate. However, if you made PETs within seven years of dying, the fact that they have been reassessed as chargeable gifts will increase your running total up to the time of death and that could create an IHT bill, or increase the amount of IHT payable, on your estate. What is more, there is no 'taper relief' (see page 115) on any extra tax payable on the estate due to the reassessment of PETs. This is a constant source of confusion but taper relief can apply only to tax on the reassessed PETs themselves; taper relief has no impact whatsoever on extra tax on the estate.

Tax on your estate

On your death, IHT is due on the value of your estate plus your running total of gifts made in the seven years before death if they come to more than the tax-free slice. The tax-free slice for 2003–4 is £255,000. See Chapter 7 for previous years' figures. This may seem a large sum but £255,000 can soon be swallowed up, especially if you own your own home. Your estate is made up of:

- the value of all your possessions at the time of death, including your home, car, personal belongings, cash and investments
- *plus* any gifts with reservation (see page 118) that you made
- *plus* the proceeds of any insurance policies which are paid to your estate
- *less* your debts
- *less* reasonable funeral expenses.

This total is called your 'free estate' and it is the amount that is available for giving away. For the purpose of calculating any IHT, you can deduct from the free estate any gifts made in your will that count as tax-free gifts (see below). But you must *add* all the PETs and other taxable gifts which you made in the seven years before death to find the relevant running total. If the running total comes to more than the tax-free slice, inheritance tax at a rate of 40 per cent is payable.

Gifts under your will

If the value of your estate plus taxable gifts in the seven years before death comes to less than the tax-free slice, making gifts under your will is fairly straightforward. Assuming that the estate is sufficiently large (after paying off debts and expenses), the recipients will receive the amounts that you specify in your will.

However, if there is inheritance tax due on the estate, matters are not always so simple. To work out how much the recipients will actually receive, you need to know how tax will be allocated between the various gifts. For IHT purposes, there are three types of gift which you can leave in a will:

- **tax-free gifts** (see above and Chapter 5)   There is no tax at all on these
- **free-of-tax gifts** (not to be confused with tax-free gifts)   The recipient gets the amount you specify and any tax due is paid out of the residue of the estate
- **gifts which bear their own tax**   With these, the amount you give is treated as a gross gift *out of which* the recipient must pay any tax due.

In general, a specific gift under your will is automatically treated as a free-of-tax gift unless it is tax-free or you have explicitly stated that the gift should bear its own tax. But, to avoid confusion, it is a good idea to state for every gift whether it is 'free-of-tax' or 'to bear its own tax'. Beware of specifying that a gift of a thing – for example, a piece of jewellery, furniture, painting or other heirloom – should bear its own tax, unless you are confident that the recipient has other resources from which to pay the tax. Otherwise, the gift you have made may need to be sold in order to pay the tax due.

Whatever is left of your estate after deducting specific gifts is called the 'residue' or 'residuary gift'. The residue can be either a tax-free gift or taxable, in which case it bears its own tax. The residue may be split, with part counting as a tax-free gift and part as a taxable one.

The fun starts when you try to calculate how much tax will be deducted either from the residue of the estate or from the specific gifts. The calculations vary depending on the mix of gifts which you are making. The following sections describe the main possibilities.

If you find the calculations that follow daunting, do not despair – you can ask your solicitor or accountant to work out for you the tax position of various gifts that you are considering as part of your will. The most important point is that you should be aware that tax can affect the gifts in different ways.

If all your gifts are tax-free

This is the simplest case. As with lifetime gifts, some gifts from your estate are free of IHT, in particular: gifts of any amount to your husband or wife, gifts to charities, gifts of national heritage property, gifts to political parties and gifts to Housing Associations (see Chapter 5 for more details).

So, for example, you might make a gift to charity and leave the residue to your husband or wife. Since both types of gift are tax-free, there is no inheritance tax at all.

EXAMPLE 13.1

When Connie dies in October 2003, she leaves an estate made up as follows:

Cottage	£65,000
Personal possessions	£21,500
Cash in bank	£496
Investments	£331,204
Gross value of estate	£418,200
less various small debts	£500
less funeral expenses, administration costs, etc.	£2,700
Net value of 'free estate'	£415,000

Connie had made no gifts during the previous seven years. Since the value of the estate exceeds the tax-free slice, you might expect IHT to have been payable. In fact, it was not because Connie used the whole of the 'free estate' to make tax-free gifts. She left a legacy of £100,000 to charity and the residue to her husband.

If all your specific gifts bear their own tax

Again, this is a relatively simple case. The amount of tax on each gift is in proportion to the values of chargeable gifts. This is done by working out the tax due on the whole of the chargeable estate and then expressing this as a percentage of the chargeable estate – this gives you an 'effective' IHT rate. The effective rate is then applied to each gift that is to bear its own tax to find out the amount of tax due on the gift. Example 13.2 should make this clear.

EXAMPLE 13.2

Jim dies in July 2003 leaving an estate of £500,000. He makes two specific gifts bearing their own tax: £100,000 to his friend Ben and £180,000 to his cousin Gerald. He leaves the residue to his wife. Jim made no PETs or chargeable transfers in the seven years before he died. The tax position is worked out as follows:

Tax position of the estate

Value of free estate	£500,000
less tax-free gifts (i.e. residue to his wife)	£220,000
Chargeable part of estate	£280,000
less tax-free slice	£255,000
	£25,000
Tax on £25,000 @ 40%	£10,000
Effective tax rate ([£10,000 ÷ £280,000] x 100)	3.571%

WHO GETS WHAT

Tax on Ben's gift @ 3.571%	£3,571
Net amount Ben receives	£96,429
Tax on Gerald's gift @ 3.571%	£6,429
Net amount Gerald receives	£173,571
Amount left to wife	£220,000

If all your specific gifts are free of tax

The main complication in this situation is that, when the estate pays the tax due (out of the residue), it is deemed to be making a gift of the tax as well. To take account of this, all the free-of-tax gifts must be 'grossed up', which simply means that you find the total that equals the amount of the actual gifts plus the tax on them. The tax is then deducted from the residue.

EXAMPLE 13.3

Alec also dies in July 2003 leaving an estate of £500,000. He makes two specific gifts which are free of tax: £100,000 to his friend Douglas and £180,000 to his friend Annette. He leaves the residue to his wife. Alec made no PETs or chargeable transfers in the seven years before he died. The tax position is worked out as follows:

GROSSING UP THE GIFTS

[1]*Add together* all free-of-tax gifts (£100,000 + £180,000)	£280,000
[2]*less* tax-free slice	£255,000
	£25,000

[3]gross up (see page 263) at the 40% tax rate
(i.e. divide by $1 - 0.4 = 0.6$)   £41,667

The grossed-up value of the gifts is
£41,667 + £255,000   £296,667

TAX POSITION OF THE ESTATE

[4]Value of estate   £500,000
less tax-free part of the estate
(£500,000 – £296,667)   £203,333

[5]Chargeable estate   £296,667
less tax-free slice   £255,000

                                                                £41,667

[6]Tax on £41,667 @ 40%   £16,667

WHO GETS WHAT

Net amount Douglas receives   £100,000
Net amount Annette receives   £180,000

Amount left to wife
[7](£500,000 – £100,000 – £180,000 – £16,667)   £203,333

Notes
1   The free-of-tax gifts are added together. This is not their taxable value, because they need first to be grossed up. Note that, at this stage, we do not know what part of the estate is tax-free, because we do not know yet how much tax must be deducted before the residue passes to Alec's wife.
2   We do not gross up the whole of the free-of-tax gifts, because some fall within the tax-free slice. Therefore, at this step, we deduct the tax-free slice to leave just the (net) value of the gifts which are to be taxed.
3   The gifts are grossed up at the death rate and the tax-free slice is added back to give the full grossed-up value of the free-of-tax gifts.
4   We now have the information to find the tax-free part of the estate. (The arithmetic seems circular in this example, but using this method allows us to deal with more complicated examples later on.)
5   The value of the estate less the tax-free part leaves the chargeable estate.
6   Tax is due on the chargeable estate less the tax-free slice at the death rate of 40 per cent.
7   There is, of course, no tax deducted from the free-of-tax gifts. All the tax is paid out of the residue, so the amount left to Alec's wife is the value of his estate less the gifts to other people less the tax bill.

If you leave a mixture of free-of-tax gifts and other types of taxable gift

This is the most complex situation. Problems arise because the free-of-tax gifts must be grossed up by the IHT rate. Initially the appropriate rate is not known because it is worked out in relation to the *whole* chargeable estate (which includes the gifts bearing their own tax as well). The problem is solved by splitting the calculation into two stages.

First, the free-of-tax gifts are grossed up by the full death rate of 40 per cent. The rest of the chargeable estate is added and IHT worked out in the normal way – but the result is only a notional amount of IHT. If notional IHT is divided by the size of the chargeable estate, this gives an assumed notional rate of IHT.

Now the second stage of the calculation can proceed. The notional rate of IHT is used to re-gross up the free-of-tax gifts. As before, the rest of the chargeable estate is added and tax is worked out in the normal way (using the 40 per cent death rate). Dividing the tax bill by the total chargeable estate gives the 'final estate rate' which is used to apportion the tax between the different chargeable gifts. See Example 13.4.

You will need to do the same sort of calculation if, in addition to leaving free-of-tax gifts, you also divide the residue so that part is tax-free and part is taxable – this would be the position, for example, if you divided the residue between your children and your husband or wife. The taxable part of the residue is treated as if it is a gross gift bearing its own tax, so it does not need to be grossed up. See Example 13.5.

EXAMPLE 13.4

Suppose, in Example 13.3, Alec left £100,000 free of tax to Douglas and £180,000 free of tax to Annette, as before, but also left a gift of £10,000 to bear its own tax to his daughter Judy. He leaves the residue to his wife. The tax position is as follows:

STAGE 1
GROSSING UP THE GIFTS

[1]*Add together* all free-of-tax gifts (£100,000 + £180,000)	£280,000
[2]*less* tax-free slice	£255,000
	£25,000
[3]gross up at the 40% tax rate (i.e. divide by 0.6)	£41,667
The grossed-up value of the gifts is £41,667 + £255,000	£296,667

TAX POSITION OF THE ESTATE

[4]Value of estate	£500,000
less tax-free part of estate (£500,000 − £296,667 − £10,000)	£193,333
[5]Chargeable estate	£306,667
less tax-free slice	£255,000
	£51,667
[6]Tax on £51,667 @ 40%	£20,667
[7]Notional rate of IHT ([£20,667 ÷ £306,667] x 100)	6.739%

STAGE 2
[8]RE-GROSSING UP THE GIFTS

Total free-of-tax gifts	£280,000
gross up at the notional IHT rate (i.e. divide by 1 − 0.06739 = 0.933)	
Re-grossed-up value of free-of-tax gifts	£300,107

REVISED TAX POSITION OF THE ESTATE

[9]Value of estate	£500,000
less tax-free part of estate (£500,000 – £300,107 – £10,000)	£189,893
New total for chargeable estate	£310,107
less tax-free slice	£255,000
	£55,107
[10]Tax @ 40% on £55,107	£22,043
Final estate rate ([£22,043 ÷ £310,107] x 100)	7.108%

WHO GETS WHAT

[11]Tax on Judy's gift @ 7.108%	£711
Net amount Judy receives	£9,289
[12]Net amount Douglas receives	£100,000
Net amount Annette receives	£180,000
[13]Tax to be deducted from residue (£22,043 – £711)	£21,332
[14]Amount left to wife (£500,000 – £100,000 – £180,000 – £10,000 – £21,332)	£188,668

Notes

1   The free-of-tax gifts are added together. This is not their taxable value, because they need to be grossed up.

2   We do not gross up the whole of the free-of-tax gifts, because some fall within the tax-free slice. Therefore, at this step, we deduct the tax-free slice to leave just the (net) value of the gifts which are to be taxed. This is a simplification, because there is another taxable gift which should benefit from the tax-free slice.

3   The free-of-tax gifts are grossed up at the death rate (40%) and the tax-free slice is added back to give the full grossed-up value of the free-of-tax gifts. This is a first approximation, because we have yet to take account of the other taxable gift which will derive some benefit from the tax-free slice.

4   We now have the information to make a first approximation of the tax-free part of the estate. This is the value of the estate less the grossed-up free-of-tax gifts less the gift bearing its own tax.

5   The value of the estate less the tax-free part leaves our estimate of the chargeable estate.

6   Tax is worked out on this first approximation of the chargeable estate at the death rate of 40 per cent after deducting the tax-free slice.

7   Dividing the amount of tax by the value of the chargeable estate gives us the rate of IHT on the chargeable estate, called the 'notional rate'.

8   We can now get a more accurate figure for the gross value of the free-of-tax gifts by grossing them up at the notional rate of IHT.

9   The estate can now more accurately be divided into its elements: the tax-free part and the chargeable part.

10 Tax at the death rate can now be calculated on the chargeable part. This gives the actual tax bill to be divided between the various bequests. The rate of tax to be applied to each gift is found by dividing the tax bill by the value of the chargeable estate.

11 Judy's gift bears its own tax, so the amount she receives is reduced by the tax due.

12 The free-of-tax gifts are intact with tax on them being borne by the residue.

13 Tax to be deducted from the residue is the total tax bill less any tax being borne by particular bequests.

14 The residue is the value of the estate less the value of the bequests less the tax on the free-of-tax gifts. There is, of course, no tax deducted from the free-of-tax gifts. All the tax is paid out of the residue, so the amount left to the wife is the value of the estate less the gifts to other people less the tax bill.

EXAMPLE 13.5

Percy dies in October 2003 leaving an estate of £750,000. He makes a specific free-of-tax gift of £300,000 to his son, Harold, and leaves the residue equally to his wife and his daughter, Rose. Percy made no PETs or chargeable transfers in the seven years before he died. The tax position is worked out as follows:

STAGE 1
GROSSING UP THE GIFTS

¹*Add together* all free-of-tax gifts	£300,000
²*less* tax-free slice	£255,000
	£45,000
³gross up at 40% tax rate (i.e. divide by 1 − 0.4 = 0.6)	£75,000
The grossed-up value of the gift is £75,000 + £255,000	£330,000

TAX POSITION OF THE ESTATE

[4]Value of estate	£750,000
less tax-free part of the estate (£750,000 – £330,000 – [residue ÷ 2])	£210,000
[5]Chargeable estate	£540,000
less tax-free slice	£255,000
	£285,000
[6]Tax on £285,000 @ 40%	£114,000
[7]Notional rate of IHT ([£114,000 ÷ £540,000] x 100)	21.111%

STAGE 2

[8]RE-GROSSING UP THE GIFTS

Free-of-tax gift	£300,000
gross up at the notional IHT rate (i.e. divide by [1 – 0.21111] = 0.78889)	
Re-grossed up value of free-of-tax gift	£380,281

REVISED TAX POSITION OF THE ESTATE

[9]Value of estate	£750,000
less tax-free part of estate (£750,000 – £380,281 — [residue ÷ 2])	£184,860
New total for chargeable estate	£565,140
less tax-free slice	£255,000
	£310,140

[10]Tax @ 40% on £310,140 £124,056

Final estate rate ([£124,056 ÷ £565,140] x 100) 21.951%

WHO GETS WHAT

[11]Harold receives £300,000

Tax on Harold's legacy @ 21.951% of £380,281
(to be borne by estate) £83,475

[12]Residue (£750,000 – £300,000 – £83,475) £366,525

[13]Wife receives ($\frac{1}{2}$ x £366,525) £183,263

[14]Tax on Rose's share of the residue
@ 21.951% x £183,263 £40,228

Rose receives (£183,263 – £40,228) £143,035

Notes
1   The free-of-tax gifts are added together. This is not their taxable value, because they need to be grossed up.
2   We do not gross up the whole of the free-of-tax gifts, because some fall within the tax-free slice. Therefore, at this step, we deduct the tax-free slice to leave just the (net) value of the gifts which are to be taxed. This is a simplification, because another taxable gift (in this case, part of the residue) should benefit from the tax-free slice.
3   The free-of-tax gifts are grossed up at the death rate and the tax-free slice is added back to give the full grossed-up value of the free-of-tax gifts. This is a first approximation, because we have yet to take account of the other taxable gift which will derive some benefit from the tax-free slice.
4   We now have the information to make a first approximation of the tax-free part of the estate. This is the value of the estate less the grossed-up free-of-tax gift (£330,000) less half of what remains ([£750,000 – £330,000] ÷ 2), which will be a gift bearing its own tax.
5   The value of the estate less the tax-free part leaves our estimate of the chargeable estate.
6   Tax is worked out on this first approximation of the chargeable estate at the death rate of 40 per cent after deducting the tax-free slice.
7   Dividing the amount of tax by the value of the chargeable estate gives us the rate of IHT on the chargeable estate, called the 'notional rate'.
8   We can now get a more accurate figure for the gross value of the free-of-tax gifts by grossing them up at the notional rate of IHT.
9   The estate can now more accurately be divided into its elements: the tax-free part and the chargeable part. This latter comprises the re-grossed up gifts (£380,281) *plus* the taxable part of the residue ([£750,000 – £380,281] ÷ 2).
10 Tax at the death rate can now be calculated on the chargeable part. This gives the actual tax bill to be divided between the various bequests. The rate of tax to be applied to each gift is found by dividing the tax bill by the value of the chargeable estate.
11 The free-of-tax gift to Harold is intact with tax on it being borne by the residue.
12 The residue is the value of the estate less the value of the free-of-tax bequest less the tax on the free-of-tax gift (calculated at the final estate rate).
13 The wife receives half the residue as specified in the will.
14 The remaining half of the residue goes to Rose, but this is a taxable bequest. Tax is found by multiplying her half of the residue by the final estate rate. This substantially reduces Rose's share of the residue.

Quick-succession relief

If you left a substantial gift in your will to someone – for example, a son or daughter – who then died shortly after you, there could be two IHT bills on the same assets in a short space of time. To guard against this, a claim can be made for 'quick-succession relief'. This is available where the person inheriting the assets dies within five years of the assets becoming part of that person's estate (even if the assets are then sold or given away before the recipient's death). The relief is tapered: full relief is given if the recipient's death occurs within one year of the gift; a reduced rate applies if a longer time elapses (see Table 13.1).

Quick-succession relief is also available where the original gift was a lifetime gift and the recipient dies within five years. However, the amount of tax due, if any, on the original gift will not be known until seven years have passed since the gift was made, so there will be a delay before the amount of any relief can be calculated.

Table 13.1 Quick-succession relief

Years between first and second death	Tax relief on second death as a percentage of tax applicable to the original gift[†]
Up to 1	100
More than 1 and up to 2	80
More than 2 and up to 3	60
More than 3 and up to 4	40
More than 4 and up to 5	20
More than 5	no tax relief

[†]The percentage is multiplied by the formula:

$$\frac{G - T}{G} \times T$$

where
G = the gross amount of the original gift
T = the tax paid on the original gift.

EXAMPLE 13.6

In February 2000 Ahmed gives his nephew, Jagdish, £30,000. The gift is a PET but sadly Ahmed dies two years later. The PET is reassessed as a chargeable gift (see page 114) and Jagdish pays £9,600 tax that then becomes due.

Tragically, Jagdish is killed in a car crash in November 2003. His estate of £450,000 passes to his partner. They were not married and IHT of £78,000 is charged on the estate. However, this is reduced by quick-succession relief in respect of the gift from Ahmed. The gift was made more than three but less than four years before Jagdish's death so the quick-succession relief percentage is 40 per cent. The relief is worked out as follows:

$$40\% \times [(£30,000 - £9,600) / £30,000] \times £9,600 = £2,612$$

Tax on Jagdish's estate becomes £78,000 - £2,612 = £75,388.

Passing on your business

Handing on your business is a complex matter. There are many different ways of arranging the transfer, and which is appropriate for you will depend very much on your particular circumstances. You would be unwise to make plans without seeking professional advice from your accountant and a solicitor. Business planning is outside the scope of this book but it is worth pointing out here the important reliefs against IHT that may be available to you and your heirs.

Business property relief

If, on death, your business passes to someone else, your personal representatives may be able to claim 'business property relief' which will reduce the value of the transfer of the business for IHT purposes and thus reduce or eliminate any IHT otherwise payable. To be eligible, you must have been in business for at least two years. Only 'qualifying' business assets attract relief; these are assets which are either

- used wholly or mainly for the purpose of your business, *or*
- are required for future use by the business.

Assuming you operate your business as a sole trader or as a partner in a partnership, business property relief will be given at the higher rate of 100 per cent – that is, it could completely eliminate an IHT charge.

EXAMPLE 13.7

Gerald dies leaving a greengrocery valued at £500,000 which he has run for the last ten years. In his will, he hands the business to his son, Paul. He also leaves £250,000 to his wife. The IHT position is as follows:

Value of free estate	£750,000
less tax-free gift to wife	£250,000
Value of grocery business	£500,000
less 100% business property relief	£500,000
Chargeable part of the estate	£0

Relief of 100 per cent is also available if you pass on a holding of shares in an unquoted company – which includes shares traded on the Alternative Investment Market (AIM).

A lower rate of business property relief – set at 50 per cent – is available to set against transfers of a *controlling* holding (i.e. 5 per cent or more) in a fully quoted company.

Business property relief is intended to take most hand-overs of family companies outside the IHT net. However, even 100 per cent relief will not necessarily entirely mitigate an IHT bill. In particular, you should note that, if the business property is subject to a binding contract for sale, relief will not normally be given. This might be the case where, say, a partnership has arranged that the surviving partners will buy out the share of a partner who dies; the deceased partner's share of the business would not qualify for relief in this situation. This sort of problem can be avoided with some advance planning – for example, by giving surviving partners the option but not the obligation to buy – so it is very important that you get advice from an accountant★ or other tax adviser★ at the time you draw up the partnership agreement.

Most types of business can qualify for business property relief. The only exception is businesses whose sole or main activity is dealing in stocks, shares, land or various other investments. Letting out property does not normally count as a business and so does not usually qualify for business property relief.

Any IHT due after business property relief has been given can be paid by interest-free instalments over a period of ten years.

Agricultural property relief

Agricultural property relief – which is similar to business property relief – is available when a farm is handed on. The relief, which is given automatically and does not have to be claimed, is given against the agricultural value of the land and buildings. The equipment and stock do not qualify for agricultural property relief but they may qualify for business property relief (see above). Note that the agricultural value of the farm may be lower than the market value if, say, the land has development value – the excess will not qualify for agricultural property relief, though it may be eligible for business property relief.

To qualify for agricultural property relief, you must either have occupied the farm, or a share of it, for the purpose of farming for at least two years, or you must have owned the farm, or a share in it, for at least seven years. If you farmed the land yourself, relief is given at the higher rate of 100 per cent. If you let the land to someone else to farm, relief is restricted to the lower rate of 50 per cent.

As with business property relief, agricultural property relief is also not available if the farm is subject to a binding contract for sale (see above).

Any IHT due after relief has been given can be paid by interest-free instalments over a period of ten years.

Paying the tax

In England, Wales and Northern Ireland, your personal representatives are responsible for delivering an account (**form IHT200**) to the Probate Registry★ together with any tax due before the grant of probate can be made (or letter of administration in the case of intestacy). In Scotland, the account, called an inventory, must be delivered to the Sheriff Clerk★ with the tax due before confirmation can be granted. If you fail to deliver the account on time, penalties are charged – see Inland Revenue leaflet IHT13.

The account sets out all the assets, liabilities, reliefs and gifts within the seven years before death on which the tax bill is based. The requirement to deliver an account is waived where the total value of the estate and pre-death gifts comes to no more than £220,000 for deaths from 6 April 2002 onwards and certain other conditions are met. These estates are known as 'excepted estates' and, since their value is below the inheritance tax-free slice, there is no tax to pay. From 2002, the excepted estate rules are largely the same for Scotland and England, Wales and Northern Ireland. Other changes were also introduced to allow many more estates to qualify as excepted – for example, an estate including an interest in possession in a single trust up to the value of £100,000 may now qualify whereas before an estate involving any trust property could not be excepted. For more information, see Inland Revenue leaflet IHT12 (or IHT12(S) for Scotland).

The time limit for delivering the account or inventory is 12 months from the end of the month in which death occurred (or, if later, within three months of the personal representative starting to act). However, the time limit for paying inheritance tax is within six months of the end of the month in which death occurred or, if earlier, on delivery of the account. This means you may initially need to pay tax on the basis of an estimated account. Once the account is finalised, you pay any extra tax due or reclaim any overpayment. Interest is charged on late tax and paid on refunds.

As a personal representative you may well find yourself having to pay the tax before having access to the estate assets (because probate/confirmation has not yet been granted). In this situation, you might need to take out a temporary bank loan to cover the tax bill. However, you are allowed to use certain estate assets prior to probate/confirmation purely to pay the IHT due. These assets are most National Savings & Investments products and gilts. In January 2003, the Inland Revenue announced that in future (the date was yet to be announced at the time of writing) personal representatives would also be able to use estate money held in bank and building society accounts for this purpose. If you do have to take out a loan to pay inheritance tax, you can claim income tax relief on the interest you pay.

Where tax is due in respect of land, buildings, shares that gave the deceased a controlling interest in a company (whether listed or unlisted) or certain unquoted shares, you can apply to pay the tax in ten equal yearly instalments. Interest is charged on the amount outstanding.

The Inland Revenue can agree to accept heritage property in lieu of some or all of the IHT due. Eligible property includes pictures, prints, books, manuscripts, works of art and scientific objects, provided they are 'pre-eminent' for their national, scientific, historic or artistic interest. Buildings and land of outstanding scenic, historic or scientific interest and items associated with them are also eligible.

Personal representatives may find the following Inland Revenue leaflets, available from Capital Taxes Offices,★ particularly helpful:

- IHT3 *Inheritance tax. An introduction*
- IHT4 *Notes on informal calculation of inheritance tax*
- IHT11 (or IHT11(S) for Scotland) *Payment of inheritance tax from National Savings or from British Government Stock on the Bank of England Register*
- IHT12 (or IHT12(S) for Scotland) *When is an excepted estate grant appropriate?*
- IHT14 *Inheritance tax. The personal representatives' responsibilities*
- IHT15 *Inheritance tax. How to calculate the liability*
- IHT17 *Inheritance tax. Businesses, farms and woodlands*
- IHT210 *How to fill in form IHT200.*

Chapter 14

Inheritance planning

IT'S NEVER TOO LATE, BUT ...

'So you mean that we can, in effect, rewrite Dad's will to swap the gifts around and cut the tax bill?'

'Precisely, Miss Cale. The law does currently allow this,' said the solicitor, somewhat ponderously. 'However, I should point out that matters would have been a great deal simpler and cheaper had Mr Cale made satisfactory arrangements *before* his death. There would have been considerably greater scope for minimising – or even eliminating – the inheritance tax bill had he done so.'

This chapter draws together a number of points discussed in earlier chapters and introduces some new ones to show what you can do to plan your giving through inheritance more precisely and tax-efficiently.

The particular strategies you adopt will depend largely on your personal intentions and circumstances. Although many of the points given below can be applied simply and with a minimum of paperwork, others are not so straightforward and may hide potential pitfalls that you should take into account. Always seek advice from, for example, a solicitor★ or accountant★ if you are in any doubt about a proposed course of action. And, if you are giving away large sums, get advice first.

There are two main aims to planning inheritance:

- to make sure that your estate is divided as you had wished
- to minimise the amount of tax to be paid on the estate.

Clearly, the two aims are interlinked since a lower inheritance tax (IHT) bill means that more of your estate is left to give to your family and friends. Strategies to meet either or both aims are discussed below.

Gifts when you die

Make tax-free gifts in your will

Some gifts you make on death are always free of IHT, for example, bequests to charity and whatever you leave to your husband or wife (provided they are UK-domiciled – otherwise there is a limit of £55,000). In addition to these and other gifts that are always tax-free whether made on death or during your lifetime (see page 70), there are a few gifts that are specifically tax-free on death only:

- lump sum from a pension scheme, provided the trustees had discretion to decide who would receive it (though in practice they generally follow any nomination made by you). The lump sum by-passes your estate altogether and goes straight from the scheme to the recipient
- similarly the proceeds of a life insurance policy that was written in trust for the recipient. The proceeds by-pass the estate, going straight from the life insurance company to the recipient
- the whole estate if the person died from a wound, accident or disease acquired or exacerbated while on active service against an enemy. To claim this exemption, the personal representatives need a certificate from the Ministry of Defence
- £10,000 received by the deceased as an ex-gratia payment to the survivors (or spouses of survivors) who were prisoners of war held by the Japanese during the Second World War
- amounts received by the victim (or his or her spouse) from specified schemes that provide compensation to people (such as Holocaust victims) for wrongs suffered during the Second World War.

Use your tax-free slice

Try to make use of your tax-free slice (which covers the first £255,000 of chargeable transfers in the 2003–4 tax year), and bear in mind that some gifts – for example, to your husband or wife or to charity – are always tax-free.

It may be tempting simply to leave everything tax-free to your husband or wife but this can mean an unnecessarily large tax bill when he or she dies (see Example 14.1). Planning instead to use your tax-free slice can save as much as 40% x £255,000 = £102,000 in tax in 2003–4.

EXAMPLE 14.1

Sam dies and leaves his whole estate of £200,000 to his wife, Harriet. Since this is a tax-free gift, there is no IHT to pay. When Harriet dies her free estate is valued at £300,000 and is left completely to their only child, Phyllis. There is IHT to pay on the estate calculated as follows:

Value of free estate	£300,000
less tax-free slice	£255,000
	£45,000
Tax on £45,000 @ 40%	£18,000

However, suppose instead that Sam had left £100,000 to Phyllis (on which no IHT would be payable because it would be covered by the tax-free slice) and the remaining £100,000 to Harriet. On Harriet's death, her estate would have been valued at £200,000. Giving this to Phyllis would have been completely covered by Harriet's tax-free slice, so no IHT would be payable. Straightforward planning to make use of Sam's tax-free slice would save £18,000 in tax.

If you and your husband or wife intend to leave something to your children, it may be best to draw up your wills so that whoever dies first leaves part of the estate directly to the children. This will ensure that at least some use is made of the available tax-free slice. The remainder of the estate can be left to the surviving spouse. If you can, arrange the wills so that both of you can make maximum use of your tax-free slices but take care to ensure that the surviving spouse will have enough to meet financial needs.

Be aware of how gifts are taxed

Examples 13.2 and 13.3 in Chapter 13 are intentionally identical, except that in one the gifts bear their own tax and in the other the gifts are free-of-tax. The outcomes highlight two important points which you should bear in mind when planning gifts under your will:

- a gift which bears its own tax will generally be smaller than a gift of the same size which is free of tax
- leaving free-of-tax gifts reduces the size of the residue. If you leave a lot of free-of-tax gifts, the residue may be reduced to a trivial amount (or nothing at all).

Consider will trusts

There are several situations in which setting up a trust in your will can be particularly useful. The first is where you want to give some of your assets to the next generation but your wife or husband will carry on needing the income from, or use of, those assets. One way around this is to leave the assets in trust, giving your spouse an interest in possession during his or her lifetime, with your children (or perhaps their children) holding the reversionary interest (see page 143). But note that, while this ensures that your assets are used largely as you would wish, it does not have any IHT advantage. This is because, under IHT, a person with an interest in possession is deemed to own the underlying trust assets and to give them away when the interest ends. So there could be a large IHT bill at the time of the second death. You could avoid this problem by using a discretionary trust instead, with both your spouse and your children named as beneficiaries. This would be tax-efficient provided the transfer of assets into the trust was covered by your tax-free slice or one of the other exemptions.

However, an interest-in-possession trust can be useful for IHT planning if assets are being passed to subsequent generations. This is because a reversionary interest does not count as part of a person's estate and so there is no IHT liability if it is transferred to someone else. If your children held the reversionary interest in a trust, they could easily transfer this interest to their own children if they wished to do so, without incurring any IHT liability.

Under IHT law, you can use your will to set up a discretionary trust and, provided the trust property is distributed within two years of your death, the gifts from the trust are treated for IHT purposes as if they had been bequests under your will. This can be a useful device if, say, you hope to use your tax-free slice as described on page 216 but you are not sure at present whether your husband or wife would be able to manage without the assets. Your will could direct that an amount up to the tax-fee slice be left in trust with, say, your children and surviving spouse as potential beneficiaries. The trustees could then distribute the trust property taking into account the needs of your spouse at that time.

Another important planning use of will trusts is where you are passing on your business. Rather than pass total control to, for example, a relatively inexperienced son or daughter, or to a spouse who is not involved in the business, it may make sense to put the land or property used by the business into trust. Provided the owner qualifies for business property relief or agricultural property relief, the trust will also qualify (see page 209). This is a complex area and you should seek the advice of your accountant★ and/or solicitor.★

A trust set up under your will is deemed to start on the date of death.

Using lifetime gifts

One way to reduce the IHT payable on your death is to reduce the size of your estate by making gifts during your lifetime. However, before going down this road, you must consider your own financial needs. Any IHT payable on your estate is not really your problem; it will simply reduce the amount by which others benefit from your estate. It is not worth jeopardising your financial security in order to reduce the IHT bill of your heirs. So the first planning point is: do not give away more than you can afford to do without.

Assuming that you can afford to make a number of gifts during your lifetime, you will obviously want to ensure that they do not themselves give rise to a large tax bill. Chapter 5 lists the gifts which you can make during your lifetime which are tax-free.

It is not enough to look only at the IHT position of lifetime gifts. You must also consider the capital gains tax (CGT) position (see Chapters 5, 6 and 11). Taking the two taxes together, the 'best' gifts to make will tend to be the following:

- cash gifts (always free of CGT) that qualify for an IHT exemption
- cash gifts that count as PETs (see page 114) for IHT purposes
- business assets that qualify for hold-over relief from CGT (see page 100) and count as PETs for IHT or qualify for business property relief
- other gifts that are exempt from IHT or that count as PETs and for which the CGT bill is relatively small due to unused CGT allowance, indexation allowance or CGT taper relief (see Chapter 6).

Anti-avoidance rules

In an ideal world, you would be able to make tax-efficient lifetime gifts to reduce the eventual tax on death but in the meantime continue either to have the use of the assets you give away or to get an income from them. Not surprisingly, the tax authorities do not recognise this as a genuine gift. As described in Chapter 7, if you give something away but continue to benefit from it, you fall foul of the IHT gift with reservation rule. This works by continuing to include the value of the gift as part of your estate either until you cease to benefit or until you die, whichever happens first. However, a variety of complicated schemes are available which aim to exploit legitimate loopholes in the legislation to let you both reduce the size of your estate and continue to receive an income from the gifted assets – see page 225–230 for an outline of some of the more common schemes.

If you are attracted to complicated tax planning, always get professional advice and bear in mind the following points:

- arranging your tax affairs within the rules so as to pay as little tax as possible is usually legitimate tax avoidance. But going against the rules is illegal tax evasion for which there are heavy penalties including the possibility of a prison term
- the courts are wise to 'shams' – in other words, attempts to dress up illegal tax arrangements to look like legal ones
- even where an arrangement seems to be within the law it may fall foul of the 'associated operations' rules. These have built up through case law and mean that a series of transactions can be looked at as a whole. If they do not have a bona fide commercial

motive and have been devised primarily as a way of saving tax, they can be deemed to be an artificial tax-avoidance scheme and the tax-saving effects nullified
- the Inland Revenue takes an aggressive approach towards tax-avoidance schemes. It is prepared to challenge schemes through the Inland Revenue Commissioners and subsequently the courts, so there is no guarantee that a complicated scheme that you thought would save tax actually will do so at the end of the day. In addition, you may run the risk of becoming involved in lengthy and costly legal disputes
- even if the taxpayer wins a case against the Inland Revenue, the government can change the law to close loopholes and ban schemes, though such changes are seldom retrospective.

Make tax-free lifetime gifts

Particularly important for IHT purposes is your yearly tax-free exemption (see page 74), which lets you give away up to £3,000 each year without incurring any IHT liability. If you choose cash gifts, there will be no CGT either.

Another very useful gift which is free of IHT is normal expenditure out of income – this can be particularly handy when used in conjunction with an insurance policy (see pages 72 and 224).

For tax purposes alone, it is not generally worth making, in your lifetime, a gift which would in any case be tax-free on your death: for example, a gift to charity. A safer course would be to retain the assets in case you need to draw on them and make the desired gift in your will.

Give assets whose value will rise

If your aim is to reduce the value of your estate at the time you die, then it makes sense to give away assets whose value you expect to increase. In that way the increase will accrue to the recipient of the gift and will be outside your estate.

Consider lifetime gifts to a trust

Generally, you cannot be a beneficiary or potential beneficiary of a trust you set up without the assets you put into it counting as a gift with reservation. However, your husband or wife can benefit under the trust without triggering these rules *provided* that you yourself in no way benefit from your spouse's interest in the trust. Even in the latter case, however, the income tax and CGT rules may make this type of arrangement unattractive (see page 163).

A further exception to the gift with reservation rules is that if you retain a reversionary interest (see page 143) in a trust to which you have given assets, the gift does not count as one with reservation.

Beware of setting up more than one trust on the same day, if one of them is a discretionary trust. If you do, it may increase the periodic charge on the discretionary trust.

If you yourself inherit money or assets which are surplus to your needs, you might consider putting them into trust straight away to benefit your children or grandchildren – this is a practice known as 'generation-skipping'. The transfer can often be made tax-efficiently through a 'deed of variation' or possibly a 'disclaimer' (see page 232).

Make loans

One way to 'freeze' the value of part of your estate is to make an interest-free loan to someone and leave him or her to keep the proceeds from investing the loan. A condition of the loan would normally be that it is repayable on demand. From your point of view, this is more secure than making an outright gift and can be a useful arrangement if you are unsure whether or not you will need the money back at some time in the future.

Of course, there is little point demanding repayment of a loan if the borrower simply does not have the money available to repay you. An even more secure route would be to make the loan to a discretionary trust and to name the intended recipient as a potential beneficiary under the trust.

Using life insurance

There are three straightforward ways in which life insurance can be a useful inheritance planning tool:

- covering the potential tax bill on a PET
- making a gift which builds up outside your estate
- covering an expected tax bill on your estate.

These are discussed in turn below. All rely on making use of two factors:

- **Tax-free gifts** Taking out insurance for the benefit of someone else means that the premiums count as gifts. You can ensure that there is no possibility of IHT on these premiums if you make sure they count as tax-free gifts. The most commonly used exemptions are to make the premiums as normal expenditure out of your income or to ensure that they fall within your yearly tax-free exemption of £3,000.

- **Trust status** If the proceeds of an insurance policy are payable to you, the payout will be added to your estate when you die, which will increase the size of your estate and will cause delay before your beneficiaries have access to the payout. Therefore, it is important that the policy proceeds are paid direct to the intended beneficiary. You make sure this happens by 'writing' the insurance policy 'in trust', which means that the policy is held in trust for the benefit of whomever you name and the proceeds are the property of that person rather than of you or your estate. Insurance companies will generally write a policy in trust for you at no extra charge (since they are able, in most cases, to use standard documents).

The cost of insurance increases with the likelihood of the insurance company having to pay out. So, if you are in poor health, or very old, buying life insurance may be very expensive.

PETs and insurance

If you make a gift which counts as a PET, you may want to be absolutely sure that any IHT bill which subsequently arises could be paid. (Similarly, you might want to ensure that any extra tax on a chargeable gift arising on death could be paid.) One way of ensuring this would be to take out a 'term insurance' policy. Term insurance pays out if you die within a specified time – in this case, seven years; should you survive the specified period, it pays out nothing. Since the liability for IHT on a PET decreases as the years go by, the cover you need can also reduce – in other words, you want 'decreasing term insurance'. See Example 14.2 overleaf.

EXAMPLE 14.2

In 2003–4 Jeremy gives his niece, Penny, a gift of £10,000. It counts as a PET, so there is no tax to pay at the time of the gift. However, Jeremy's running total exceeds £255,000 and, if he were to die within seven years of making the gift, Penny would face a demand for tax on the gift. The potential tax liability would be as follows:

Years between gift and death	% Rate of tax on the gift (at 2003–4 tax rates)	Potential tax bill (£s)
Up to 3	40	4,000
More than 3 and up to 4	32	3,200
More than 4 and up to 5	24	2,400
More than 5 and up to 6	16	1,600
More than 6 up to 7	8	800
More than 7	no tax	0

Jeremy takes out a seven-year term insurance which would pay Penny £4,000 if he died within the first three years and a reducing sum thereafter to cover the tax bill which would arise.

Reducing the size of your estate

You could use life insurance to build up a gift which does not count as part of your estate. For example, you might use the full £3,000 yearly tax-free exemption to pay the premiums for an investment-type life insurance policy (see box on page 226) that will pay out to the recipient either after some specified period (in which case, you need an 'endowment policy' – see Glossary) or when you die (in which case, you need a 'whole-life policy' – see Glossary).

In choosing this strategy, you will need to weigh it against alternative strategies: for example, setting up a trust which could invest in a wide range of assets. The 'up-front' costs of setting up your own trust will be higher but the ongoing costs could work out to be less than for a life insurance policy. If you have relatively small sums to give, the insurance route would be more appropriate.

Since April 2001, you can use personal stakeholder pension

schemes in a similar way by making regular contributions to a scheme for someone else (see example on page 73). The charges for stakeholder schemes are capped at a modest 1 per cent a year of the amount in the pension fund.

Paying IHT when you die

You could take out a whole-life policy (which pays out *whenever* you die) to provide a lump sum to meet an expected IHT bill on your estate. In essence, this is no different from using insurance as a way of making a gift on death as already discussed but the factors to consider are slightly different: you could save in your own investment fund (either within your estate or within a trust) to meet a potential IHT bill but it would take time to build up the full amount needed. If you died in the meantime, your investment would be insufficient to cover the IHT. Taking out a whole-life insurance policy removes that risk because (provided you have bought the appropriate level of cover) it would pay out the full amount needed whether you die sooner or later.

If you have made a PET and die within seven years, the PET will use up some of the tax-free slice available at the time of death. This could cause extra tax to be due on the estate. Therefore, in addition to a whole-life policy to cover the main tax on the estate, it may be worth taking out a seven-year level term insurance policy to cover the extra tax bill on the estate if you die within seven years of making a PET. This is quite separate from a decreasing term insurance policy to cover possible tax on the PET itself (see above).

More complicated IHT planning

Life insurance is at the heart of many schemes that aim to let you reduce your estate through lifetime gifts yet retain an income from the gifted assets without triggering the gift with reservation rules. There are two reasons why life insurance is particularly suitable for these schemes:

- policies can easily be written in trust
- special tax rules allow you to make regular withdrawals of capital from an insurance policy – see box overleaf – which can be used to provide an 'income' stream.

A very brief outline of some of the main schemes is given here, but you should always get advice either from the life insurance company concerned or an independent professional before deciding to use such a scheme. Each basic scheme often varies in detail from one company to another and may be given a variety of names, so make sure you understand what type of scheme you are being offered and how it fits with your planning objectives. Bear in mind that complicated tax-saving schemes may be challenged by the Inland Revenue (see page 220).

SPECIAL TAX RULES FOR LIFE INSURANCE

There are two types of life insurance: term insurance which provides protection only by paying out if you die within a specified period but lapsing without any payout if you survive; and investment-type life insurance where your premiums are invested and the policy builds up a cash value. Investment-type life insurance usually also has some protection element (paying out on death either within a specified period or whenever it occurs) though often the amount of protection is small.

With investment-type policies, the insurance company usually pays tax on income and gains from the underlying investments. If the policy is a 'qualifying' one, there is no more tax for you to pay when you receive a payout from the policy.

With a 'non-qualifying policy', when the policy pays out, there may be some income tax for you to pay, but only if you are a higher-rate taxpayer. However, a special facility lets you draw an 'income' each year up to one-twentieth (5 per cent) of the premium(s) you have paid without any tax being due at the time. Tax is deferred – for example, until the policy comes to an end – and is then charged with reference to your tax position at that time.

Gift and loan plans

You make a small gift to start up a discretionary trust – for example, a gift of £3,000 using your yearly tax-free exemption (see page 74). The beneficiaries are whoever you want eventually to receive your gift.

You then make a much larger interest-free loan to the trust. Under the terms of the loan it will normally be repaid in annual instalments but the whole amount is repayable on demand or in the event of your death. The annual loan repayments provide you with 'income'.

The trust invests the gift and the loan. Any growth-oriented investment could be used but often a single-premium life insurance bond is chosen. Five-per-cent withdrawals can then be made from the bond under the special tax rules for life policies (see box opposite) and these fund the loan repayments.

On your death, the trust repays the loan to your estate and the remaining trust property – which is outside your estate – passes to the beneficiaries. The longer the trust has run, the larger the amount that has built up outside your estate will normally be.

EXAMPLE 14.3

Adam makes a gift of £3,000 to a trust in favour of his children. Subsequently he lends the trust £97,000 repayable on demand or on death. The trust uses the £100,000 to buy a single-premium insurance bond. It withdraws 5 per cent of the premium – in other words 5% x £100,000 = £5,000 – each year to pay to Adam in part-repayment of the loan. This provides Adam with his income.

Ten years later, Adam dies. The value of the bond stands at £102,500, and 10 x £5,000 = £50,000 of the original loan has been repaid, so the trustees must now repay the remaining £97,000 – £50,000 = £47,000. This leaves £102,500 – £47,000 = £55,500 to pass IHT-free to the children.

Back-to-back plans

You use a lump sum to buy an annuity that pays out an income for the rest of your life. Your estate is immediately reduced by the amount you pay for the annuity. This is because the annuity will automatically stop when you die and therefore has no capital value to be included in your estate.

You also take out a whole-life insurance policy written in trust for the benefit of whoever you want to receive your eventual gift. This is an investment-type insurance that builds up a cash value. The policy has annual premiums and these are funded using part of each annuity payment. The remaining annuity payment provides you with income.

The premiums for the whole-life policy are gifts to the beneficiary but should qualify for the normal expenditure out of income exemption (see page 72).

When you die, the whole-life policy pays out the greater of its cash value or the sum assured to the beneficiaries, by-passing your estate.

There is a risk that a back-to-back plan could be caught by the 'associated operations' rules – see page 220 – in which case you might be treated as making a gift of, say, the whole lump sum put into the plan instead of just the premiums paid for the whole-life policy. This risk is thought to be avoided if you buy the annuity and the whole-life policy from two separate life companies.

Discounted gift plans

These plans also aim to reduce the value of your estate but give you a continuing income from the gifted assets. There are several variations on the theme and one example is described below.

You use a lump sum to buy a series of single-premium endowment policies. These are investment-type insurance policies that pay out if you die within a set period or pay out a lump sum at the end of the period if you survive. The payout both on death and on maturity depends on investment growth.

Each policy is written under an interest-in-possession trust (see Chapter 9), so that if you die, it pays out, by-passing your estate, to the beneficiary you have named, but if the policy reaches maturity the proceeds are paid to you – in other words you have a reversionary interest. There is no IHT charge when property in trust reverts to the original settlor. The reversionary interest is treated as a quite separate asset from the interest the beneficiaries have, and the Inland Revenue has said that the retention by the settlor of the reversionary interest does not trigger the gift with reservation rules.

The policies are designed so that one matures each year up to your reaching, say, age 100. The maturing policies provide you with an income – this will be variable because it depends on investment growth.

At the time you set up the plan, you are treated as having made a

PET to the beneficiary which is tax-free provided you survive seven years. The amount of the PET is the original lump sum less the estimated value today of the income you will get from the maturing policies. Because the income is uncertain (you may die before all the policies mature) and accrues in the future (when its buying power may have fallen), the value of the income is discounted (reduced). The amount of discount depends on your age and health. The larger the discount, the more efficient the gift, but the Inland Revenue would challenge an unrealistic valuation.

EXAMPLE 14.4

Haseena, aged 80, invests £100,000 in a discounted gift plan. This buys her 20 single-premium bonds of £5,000 each with one maturing each year until she reaches age 100. The bonds are written in trust, so that on maturity each one pays out to her but if she dies before a bond matures it pays out to her niece, Amanda. The insurance company works out that the discounted value of the plan is £75,000 – this is the value of the PET Haseena has made.

Ten years later, Haseena dies. There is no tax on the PET because Haseena survived seven years. She has received an increasing income each year from the maturing bonds. Ten of the bonds remain in force and the proceeds of these are paid IHT-free to Amanda.

Retained interest trusts

Again, the aim is to give away assets but continue to receive income. This time, you use a lump sum to buy a single-premium insurance bond (an investment-type policy). The bond is split into two separate parts: a 'retained interest' which is yours and the gifted part which is held on trust for the beneficiary you name.

Under the special tax rules for life insurance (see box on page 226), you can take a tax-efficient 'income' up to 5 per cent a year of the premium you paid for the bond. This is 5 per cent of the whole premium regardless of the subsequent split of the bond into two parts. However, the income is actually paid only from the retained part. The retained part does benefit from any investment growth, but nevertheless is progressively eroded as you draw out the income. If you survive long enough to use up the retained part completely, the income has to stop.

Meanwhile, the gifted part of the bond grows outside your estate as investment growth is added and on your death passes IHT-free to the beneficiary.

At the time you set up the trust, you are deemed to have made a PET equal to the premium paid for the bond less the value of the part you have retained.

Family wealth trusts

This type of arrangement enables you to reduce the value of your estate but still have the option to recover some or all of your money if circumstances change later on.

You make a gift to a flexible trust (see page 136) which initially is set up to give your husband or wife a life interest. The trustees later on use their discretion to revoke the life interest in favour of a group of beneficiaries including, say, your children but also you and your husband or wife. Your spouse, who loses the life interest, is treated as making a PET of the trust property to the new beneficiaries, so this gift is free of IHT provided he or she survives seven years.

This type of arrangement is a settlor-interested trust (see page 163) but the gift with reservation rules should not apply because initially you are making a gift of the life interest to your husband or wife. The gift to your spouse is exempt (see page 71), which means the reservation rules do not apply.

The Inland Revenue has tried challenging this type of arrangement but the courts found in favour of the taxpayer. As a result there is a strong possibility that the law might be changed in future to outlaw these schemes.

Using long-term care insurance

The longer you live, the greater the chance that you may suffer some infirmity in your old age. If you then need a carer to help you with day-to-day living or have to move into a residential or nursing home, this will inevitably be expensive. In England and Wales, if your capital comes to less than £19,000 (limit applying from 8 April 2002) and your income is low, the state will pay some or all of the costs for you. If your capital is greater than this, you will have to pay out of your own pocket until the stage at which your capital has been run down to less than £19,000. However, since October 2001 the cost of nursing care up to limits (but not any of the cost of personal care or bed and board) is covered by the state whatever your income and capital.

If you had to move into a residential or nursing home and your husband or wife or a dependant would be left at home, the value of your house should not be included in the assessment of how much capital you own. But, if you had been living alone, your home would normally count as part of your capital and might have to be sold to cover the care fees.

You could consider long-term care insurance as a way of protecting your capital and, thus, the inheritance you want to pass on to your heirs. In brief, long-term care insurance pays out a regular sum towards the cost of care either in your own home or in a residential or nursing home if you can no longer carry out a given number of specified 'activities of daily living' (ADLs) for yourself.

Long-term care insurance is costly and so buying a policy makes a large dent in your assets. But you can view this as a damage-limitation strategy because the policy will pay out however long you need care. Without this type of protection, a prolonged spell in a nursing or residential home would quickly and progressively eat up your capital. A care home easily charges around £400 to £500 a week – in other words, about £20,000 to £26,000 a year.

In Scotland, the cost of both nursing and personal care are borne by the state regardless of your means, so there is less need to consider long-term care insurance.

For a detailed look at long-term care policies, see *The Which? Guide to Insurance* or *Be Your Own Financial Adviser*, both available from Which? Books.★

Gifts from the deathbed

If, say, you are seriously ill and do not expect to live for long, you might make a gift in contemplation of your death – known as a *donatio mortis causa*. Such a gift does not take effect until your death and it lapses completely if you do not die after all (or if the recipient dies before you).

In a situation as described above, should your intention be to make an outright gift to someone that is not conditional on your dying, it would be wise to set down your intention in writing – in, say, a signed letter to the recipient – to safeguard against the gift being mistakenly treated as a *donatio mortis causa* (and thus being treated as part of your estate if you survive).

A further point to watch out for is that a gift which is made by cheque is not made until the cheque has been *cleared* against the giver's account. If death takes place before then, the gift would become invalid.

Altering a will after death

Oddly enough, your will is not the final word in regard to your estate. Following death, there is a two-year period during which the will can be varied – in effect, rewritten – and your gifts reallocated. The allocation of the estate can also be varied where a person dies intestate (see Chapter 12).

The variation must be agreed by all the beneficiaries named under the will and is made by one or more of them who must complete a written deed. No beneficiary may receive any payment either in cash or kind in return for benefits given up due to the variation.

A variation can affect part, or the whole, of an estate, except that the amount an infant child would receive cannot be reduced without the consent of the court, and the way in which assets put into trust are left may not be varied.

Where the variation was intended to affect the IHT payable on the estate (or CGT payable on the assets since death), you used to have to make an election to the Inland Revenue within a set time limit. Since 1 August 2002, this is now no longer necessary. Instead you should ensure that the wording of the deed of variation makes clear whether tax is to be affected. You do not automatically send the deed to the Inland Revenue, but you should keep it in a safe place in case you are asked to produce it. If, as a result of the variation, extra IHT is payable, you must declare the tax within six months of the date of the deed.

There are, in fact, two ways in which the passing on of an estate can be varied: by deed of variation or by 'disclaimer'. The main difference between the two methods is that, under a deed of variation, who is to receive various assets can be changed from one person to another. Under a disclaimer, the named beneficiary in the will merely says he or she does not want the gift, in which case the assets are reallocated according to the terms of the will (for example, they might simply be added to the residue) or to the rules of intestacy. It follows from this that a disclaimer can only increase the share of the estate going to some or all of the other beneficiaries. By contrast, a deed of variation can be used to make gifts to people who did not originally stand to benefit from the will or intestacy.

Note that a disclaimer cannot be made if the original beneficiary has already received some benefit from the inherited assets that he or she intends to disclaim.

In considering whether or not to vary the way an estate is left, and the form that any variation should take, all the normal planning considerations come into play: for example, making sure the tax-free slice is used, choosing whether gifts should be free of tax or bear their own tax, creating or renouncing life interests. See Example 14.5.

In the 1989 Budget, the government of the day announced its intention to restrict severely the possibilities for using deeds of variation (but not disclaimers). In the event, the proposal was dropped from the subsequent Finance Bill after concerns that, without the ability to vary wills, unwelcome pressure would tend to be brought to bear on people, when they were already under stress due to illness or old age, to sort out their affairs efficiently. Nevertheless, the then Conservative government said it would keep the matter under review and the current Labour government is more, rather than less, likely to tighten up the IHT regime, so there may be further attempts to reduce the use of deeds of variation. The message is clear: plan ahead so that variation is unnecessary.

For more information, see Inland Revenue leaflet IHT8, *Alterations to an inheritance following a death*, available from Capital Taxes Offices.★

EXAMPLE 14.5

When Fred died, his will revealed that he had left £500,000 to his wife, Betty, and the residue of his estate to his daughter, Linda. His daughter's share was £50,000 on which no tax was due, because Fred's taxable estate plus a couple of PETs made in the last seven years came to a running total of only £60,000.

Betty intends, when she dies, to leave everything to Linda but this will mean a large IHT bill on an estate made up of Betty's own £20,000 and the £500,000 left to her by Fred. Assuming she had made no chargeable gifts in the seven years before death, tax of [£520,000 – £255,000 = £265,000] x 40% = £106,000 would be payable (based on 2003–4 rates). But this bill could be reduced if some changes are made to Fred's will.

Betty does not need the whole £500,000, so she and Linda make a deed of variation directing that Fred's estate of £550,000 be split as follows: £245,000 to Linda – which, with the earlier PETs, uses up the whole of Fred's tax-free slice – and the residue of £305,000 to his wife. There is still no IHT to pay on Fred's estate and the potential bill when Betty dies is reduced to [£305,000 + £20,000 – £255,000 = £70,000] x 40% = £28,000. This is a saving of £78,000.

Part 4

Special situations

Chapter 15

Your home as a gift

A ROOF OVER YOUR HEAD

'If we gave the house to you now, Becky, it would mean a lot less tax to pay at the end of the day,' explained Joan. 'But where would you and Dad live? You surely wouldn't want to stay here with all our children around you?' quizzed Becky, trying hard to take in the whole idea. 'Good grief, no!' laughed Joan. 'That might not achieve the tax savings we had in mind anyway. No, Dad and I were planning on moving to the cottage. After all, we don't need to be in town these days. Well, what do you think?'

In essence, your home is no different from any other asset which you own. It can form part of your estate and can be the subject of a gift in much the same way as any other possession you own. As such, the bulk of this book applies to your home as much as to any other asset. However, because your home is likely to be your most valuable possession, it is worth drawing together here some of the points which should be borne in mind if you are contemplating making a gift of your home either as a lifetime gift or at the time of death.

Who owns what?

If you own your home jointly with someone else, it is important to think about how you own it. As discussed in Chapter 8, there are two forms of joint ownership (in England and Wales): joint tenancy and tenants in common.

If you own your own home as a joint tenant with someone else, you each have equal shares in the home and have identical rights to enjoy the whole home. On death, the share of the owner who dies passes automatically to the remaining co-owner(s). This is very simple and convenient and can be the best arrangement for married couples and other partners in stable relationships, especially if the value of their estates taken together is no more than the tax-free slice for inheritance tax (i.e. £255,000 in 2003–4).

However, owning the home as tenants in common gives you greater flexibility and better scope for tax planning. Tenants in common still have the right to enjoy the whole home but you each have distinct shares in the home which need not be equal and do not pass automatically to the other owner(s) on death. Instead, the share of the home is passed on in accordance with your will or, if you had not made a will, the rules of intestacy.

We have already seen in Example 14.1 how failing to use the tax-free slice when the first partner of a married couple dies can result in an unnecessarily large tax bill when the second spouse dies. With ownership of the home arranged as tenants in common, it becomes possible for each spouse to arrange to use their tax-free slice by, for example, passing their share of the home on to their children instead of to their wife or husband. This can save inheritance tax (IHT) overall but is worth doing only if you can be sure that the surviving spouse will continue to have a secure home – for example, by giving him or her the protection of a formal tenancy agreement.

The importance of a will

Chapter 12 described the problems which can arise if you die intestate – i.e. without having made a will. These can be especially acute if your home is the main asset in your estate.

If you die without a will and you are survived by children or other relatives, your husband or wife inherits outright only a certain part of your estate. He or she does have the right to opt to take his or her share of your estate in the form of the home rather than other assets. But what if that share of your estate is worth less than the home? The husband or wife may well find that part of the home has to be put into trust for the benefit of young children, say, or that older offspring or more distant relatives insist on the sale of the home in order to release their own inheritance as cash.

The position of an unmarried partner is even worse. He or she may have no automatic right to share in your estate. If he or she has been your partner throughout the two years up to death or has been financially dependent on you, he or she can apply to the courts under the Inheritance (Provision for Family and Dependants) Act 1975. But the court can only make awards of income (which can be rolled up as a lump sum); it cannot direct that capital assets are distributed in one way or another.

Therefore, if the home is jointly held as tenants in common, it is essential that you make a will specifying how your share of the home is to be passed on.

Your home as a lifetime gift

If you expect your estate at death to exceed the tax-free slice, it would be very convenient if you could give away your home now in your lifetime. Making a gift of your home to your children, say, would count as a potentially exempt transfer (PET). There would be no IHT to pay at the time you made the gift and, provided you survived seven years, no IHT at all. There is, however, a small snag: if you give away your home, where do you intend to live? If you mean to stay in the home, the gift will not work for IHT purposes, because it will count as a gift with reservation (see page 118).

There are a couple of ways around this problem, though neither is very satisfactory. First, you could share the home with the people to whom you give it. Provided you all live together and share the running costs of the home, the gift should not count as one with reservation. But, if the recipients subsequently move out, the gift will become a gift with reservation – so make sure you do not fall out!

The second solution relies on the caveat that a gift is not a gift with reservation if you give full consideration in money or money's worth for the use you continue to make of the gift. For example, you could give away your house but pay the full market rent to live there under a tenancy agreement or licence. Or you could buy a lease at the full market rate which lets you live in it for some specified period – for example, long enough to cover your expected remaining years, plus a few extra years to be on the safe side. Alternatively, you might offer your services as, for example, a housekeeper or gardener, provided the value of your work was equivalent to the market rent for the property you continue to occupy.

239

Other promising ideas tend to fall foul of the rules governing associated operations (see page 220) or fail to save tax by unwittingly creating an interest in possession so that the home continues to be treated as owned by the beneficiary rather than transferred to, say, a discretionary trust (see Chapter 9). Tax experts, from time to time, come up with other complicated schemes. But their legal status is often unclear and the Inland Revenue is quick to lay a challenge. If you want to explore this area further, get professional advice from an accountant★ or other tax adviser.★

Benefits which should not trigger the gift with reservation rules

The IHT legislation says that a gift with reservation occurs if the recipient of a gift does not enjoy the gifted assets 'virtually to the entire exclusion of the donor and of any benefit to him'. These words are not defined but the Inland Revenue has provided some guidance on benefits you might still enjoy without triggering the reservation rules. In relation to a home you have given away, they include:

- you stay in the home in the absence of the recipient for no more than two weeks a year
- you go to stay in the home with the recipient but for no more than a month a year
- you are invited to make social visits that do not include overnight stays, provided you visit the recipient no more often than you would have done if the gift had not been made
- you stay temporarily with the recipient for a special reason, such as while you or the recipient is convalescing or your home is being redecorated
- you visit the home in order to babysit or for some other domestic reason.

Change of plan

The only satisfactory way of giving your home as a lifetime gift is if you genuinely do have somewhere else to live – for example, a retirement cottage or moving in with friends or relatives. But suppose your circumstances change and you move back into the home you had previously given away? This could trigger the gift with reservation rules. However, if you become unable to maintain yourself because of old age, infirmity or some other reason and your moving back into your old home is a reasonable way for the recipient of the gift – who would have to be your relation or spouse – to provide care for you, the gift with reservation rule will not apply.

Watch out for CGT

Giving away your home does not normally trigger a capital gains tax (CGT) bill, because any gain on your only or main home is generally exempt. In some situations, however, there will be a CGT bill. These arise where:

- you have lived away from home for a time
- you have let out all or part of the home
- part of the home has been used exclusively for your work
- the garden was greater than the normal size for a home of that type (usually taken to be greater than half a hectare).

Keep your options open

Do not be in too much of a hurry to give away your home. People are tending to live longer but increasingly need some degree of professional care in their later years. This is very expensive and many people are surprised to find that the state foots the bill only if their income and assets are very low – see page 230. Taking out long-term care insurance, as described on page 231, might be a solution. If not, the home which you had expected to pass on to your children might in the end be needed to fund nursing or residential home costs. Your home can also be a valuable source of additional income if your resources become tight in later old age. Taking out a home income plan (usually a mortgage linked to an annuity) or home 'reversion scheme' (selling part of your home to raise a lump sum or buy an annuity) enables you to convert the capital in your home into a lifetime income.

Chapter 16

Giving to children

A NICE LITTLE NEST-EGG

'She is just beautiful,' crooned Yuen, falling instantly in love with his first grandchild. 'Now, Mum, I want to invest a little nest-egg for young Lily here. It will help her when she goes to university.' Lily's Mum smiled: 'Yuen, she is far too small for us to worry about that sort of thing now.' 'No, my mind is made up – if I invest £3,000 now, it could be worth three or four times that amount by the time she reaches 18.'

There are many reasons for wanting to make a gift to a child. You might want to build up a nest-egg that the child can draw on when, say, he or she goes to university or buys his or her first home. Alternatively, you might want the money to be available sooner to help with education costs or as a tool to help the child learn how to handle money.

There are two main concerns when considering gifts to children:

- the tax-avoidance rules that may affect gifts from a parent to a child
- how to arrange the gift, given that the child may be too young to hold an investment or to use the gift wisely.

In the 2003 Budget, the government announced that every child born from September 2002 onwards will qualify for a cash gift from the government under the new child trust fund scheme – see page 248 for details.

Gifts from a parent to a child

Every person, however young, is within the tax system and so benefits from the basic tax allowances, in particular the personal allowance for income tax ($£4,615$ in 2003–4) and yearly tax-free slice for capital gains tax ($£7,900$ in 2003–4). In theory, families could save tax by spreading their income and assets across all family members including the children. But in the case of income tax there are rules to prevent this.

If a parent makes a gift to a child who is under the age of 18 and unmarried, and the gift produces more than $£100$ a year income, the whole of the income (not just the excess over $£100$) is taxed as that of the parent who made the gift. The $£100$ limit applies to each parent and each child, so two parents could jointly make gifts to each child, which would produce up to $£200$ a year income without triggering the anti-avoidance rule.

EXAMPLE 16.1

Andy and Rebekah have jointly invested £5,000 for each of their two daughters in building society accounts. At present, each account earns 3.5 per cent a year interest and produces £175 a year in income. This is less than the limit of 2 x £100 = £200 (a double limit applies here because the gift is from both parents) at which the anti-avoidance rules kick in. Therefore, the income each daughter gets is treated as that of the child and is tax-free because it is covered by each daughter's personal allowance.

However, Andy and Rebekah should keep an eye on their daughters' investments. If interest rates rise the income each daughter gets could quickly exceed the £200 limit, in which case all of the income would be taxed as that of the parents. Because it was a joint gift, half would be taxed as Andy's income and half as that of Rebekah.

The anti-avoidance rules do not apply to capital gains produced by a gift from a parent, nor do they apply to some types of tax-free income. So by choosing the investments carefully you can still make some tax-efficient gifts to your child – see below.

The rules apply in only a limited way to accumulation-and-maintenance trusts (see page 162), so these can be a good way of tax-efficiently building up a nest-egg for your child if you have a reasonably large sum to invest. (The costs of setting up and running a trust make it uneconomic for small sums.) But you will run into the anti-avoidance rules if you want to draw the income out of the trust either to give direct to the child or to use for his or her benefit (for example, by paying school fees). See Chapters 9 and 10 for more information.

Investing for a tax-free income

If you invest a gift you have made to your own child and it produces tax-free income, in most cases the anti-avoidance rules do not apply so it will not matter if the gift produces more than £100 income. The exception here is mini cash individual savings accounts (ISAs).

Mini cash ISAs are not an option for most children because you have to be aged at least 16 to be eligible (and 18 for stocks and shares ISAs and insurance ISAs). There is no tax on income from an ISA so you might think there would be no problem if parental gifts to a teenager were invested in cash ISAs. But, unusually for tax-free income, the anti-avoidance rules specifically apply to cash ISAs so, if the income from the parental gifts exceeded £100 it would be taxed as that of the parent.

The main investments that parents can make for their children without being taxed on the income are National Savings & Investments (NS&I) children's bonus bonds, friendly society tax-free savings plans and stakeholder pensions – see 'Investments for children' on page 249 for details.

Investing for gains instead of income

Since the anti-avoidance rules apply only to income from parental gifts, you can get around them by giving your child investments that are expected to produce capital gains instead. Suitable gifts might be growth-oriented unit trusts and open-ended investment companies (OEICs), and capital shares in split-capital investment trusts – see 'Investments for children' on page 249 for details. You could also consider collectors' items such as paintings and antiques.

Gifts from other people

The anti-avoidance rules apply only to parental gifts. They do not affect gifts from grandparents, uncles, aunts, friends of the family or anyone else. To avoid confusion with the Inland Revenue you should be able to distinguish these gifts from any parental gifts. It would be sensible to invest the two types of gifts separately – for example, you could put small parental gifts in a building society account and gifts from other people in another account. It is also a good idea to ask people who give money to your child to accompany it with a brief note stating the amount of the gift and who it is from. Keep such notes and letters in a safe place in case the Inland Revenue needs to see them.

Where a child is young, money is often given to the parents to invest or use on the child's behalf rather than being given directly to the child. This may in effect create a trust with the parent as the trustee who is obligated to use the money as instructed by the person who made the gift. Even though the parent may then open an investment in the child's name, the gift should not count as a parental gift and so should not be caught by the anti-avoidance rules.

Deciding how to arrange your gift

Before deciding which investments to choose for a child, you first need to decide how to arrange your gift.

You could invest money now in your own name and later on give the proceeds to the child. This has the advantage of flexibility because you choose the precise timing of the gift and in the meantime you have the freedom to change your mind, for example, if you run short of money or the child turns out to be a spendthrift. If you are not already making full use of your yearly ISA allowance, you could use this to invest for a tax-free return. The main drawback of this approach is the failure to make use of the child's own tax allowances. In addition, the investment remains part of your estate until the gift is finally made. So if you die before handing over the gift, there could be inheritance tax (IHT) to pay.

It is usually more tax-efficient to make an immediate gift to the child. Often this means asking the child's parents (if you are not yourself the parent) to manage the investment on his or her behalf, but children can operate their own bank and building society accounts and NS&I investment accounts. They can also hold tax-free friendly society plans in their own names.

Instead of making a gift direct to a child, you could put it in trust. The simplest option is a bare trust (see page 142). If you hold something on bare trust for, say, your grandchild, the child is treated as the owner of the asset for tax purposes, but he or she can also take possession as soon as he or she reaches age 18 (or marries if younger). Another possibility that gives you more control over the gift is an accumulation-and-maintenance trust. This will be appropriate only if you are giving a relatively large sum (say, £50,000 or more). A big advantage of this type of trust is flexibility – for example, you could set one up to benefit all your grandchildren, even those who are not yet born, and you can delay the point at which the investments pass to a child until age 25. In the meantime, the income from the trust can be used for the child's or children's maintenance, education or other benefit.

Investment-type insurance policies (such as endowment policies or investment bonds) can be written in trust so that any benefits payable on surrender, maturity or your death are paid direct to a child (or children). However, the insurance company pays tax on income and gains from investments held through an insurance policy. This tax can't be reclaimed by the policyholder, so insurance-based investments tend to be suitable only for higher-rate taxpayers or if you are involved in complicated IHT planning (see Chapter 14).

EXAMPLE 16.2

Yuen has just become a grandparent and wants to invest £3,000 for his granddaughter, Lily, to build up a lump sum to help her when she reaches adulthood. The gift falls within Yuen's yearly tax-free allowance for inheritance tax. He decides to put the money into a unit trust. Yuen is the legal owner of the units but the account is designated as 'Yuen Chan a/c Lily Chan'. This effectively creates a bare trust with Yuen holding the units as nominee for Lily. For tax purposes, Lily is the recipient of any income and gains from the units, and can set her allowances against them. To make doubly sure the bare trust is recognised, Yuen could write to his tax office saying that he has made this investment on behalf of Lily.

Child trust funds

In the 2003 Budget, the government announced that it was introducing child trust funds. Under this new scheme, every child born from September 2002 onwards qualifies at birth for a cash sum from the government of £250, or £500 if the child's family is relatively poor (measured as qualifying for the full child tax credit).

The cash will be invested in a child trust fund where it will grow until the child reaches the age of 18. At that time, the young person can withdraw the money in the fund to use for any purpose or roll the money into some other form of savings vehicle. There is no access to the fund before age 18.

The government is still considering whether it might add further sums to each child's fund, for example, on starting primary school and again on starting secondary education.

Parents, other relatives and friends will also be able to add to the child's fund. Additions from all non-government sources will be capped at £1,000 a year.

The child trust fund will have to be invested in a special account. Private businesses – for example, banks and building societies – will be invited to set up these accounts. The government expects them to be up and running by 2005 and the accounts will then be backdated to the birth of eligible children.

At the time of writing, further information was not available. The government was planning to issue a document in summer 2003 setting out the details, including how the trust fund would be treated for tax (it is expected to grow tax-free), whether there would be tax incentives to encourage family and friends to add to the fund, and any constraints on how the fund is invested.

The philosophy behind child trust funds is that equality cannot be addressed simply through income measures. The potential to take advantage of life's opportunities – for example, regarding higher education and training – depends also on access to some capital. Poorer families in particular tend to have very low levels of savings and so their children are likely to lack this capital base. The child trust fund will both provide some capital to draw on from age 18 and hopefully trigger further saving by parents and others on behalf of the child.

Investments for children

The investments you choose to give a child depend largely on the purpose of the investment, the amount involved and whether you want to invest on a regular basis or as a single lump sum, how long you want to invest, the amount of risk you are comfortable taking, and how the investment is taxed. Table 16.1 suggests some suitable investments depending on the purpose you have in mind.

Table 16.1 Investments for children

Aim of the gift	Suitable investments
Teach the child money management skills	Bank or building society account Cash ISA (if child is age 16 or over)
Encourage the child to learn how to save	Bank or building society account NS&I investment account Cash ISA (if child is aged 16 or over)
Build up a nest-egg	NS&I children's bonus bonds NS&I premium bonds Friendly society tax-free plan Unit trusts and OEICs Investment trusts
Build up a pension	Stakeholder pension

To encourage money-management skills, cash gifts direct to the child are likely to be best. These can be paid into a bank or building society account. Many providers offer accounts specifically for children with free gifts, regular magazines and so on. It is important that the child has ready access to the account, so check out banks and building societies that have branches near the child's home.

If your main aim is to build up a nest-egg over the medium to long term (five to ten years or more), share-based investments are likely to be more suitable. In the past, share-based investments have tended to produce higher returns than bank and building society accounts. But share-based investments involve capital risk. If you are not comfortable with this risk, stick to the safer investments such as savings accounts or NS&I children's bonus bonds.

A middling-risk option would be a friendly society tax-free plan (sometimes marketed as 'baby bonds') invested on a with-profits basis. However, government rules limit the maximum investment in these plans to £25 per month or £270 per year per person. With such a small amount, any flat-rate charges can eat heavily into the investment, so check the impact of charges carefully before you invest.

This leaves unit and investment trusts as the main choice for long-term growth. A child can't hold these direct, however you can make the investment in your name but 'designated' for the child. This is normally enough to ensure that a bare trust is created, though to be sure you could write to your tax office stating your intention that the investment be treated as belonging to the child.

Finally, if you are thinking very long term indeed, you can pay up to £2,808 a year into a stakeholder pension scheme for a child. This limit applies per recipient, so if you want to make gifts to several children you could pay in up to £2,808 a year for each of them. The child will not usually be able to take any proceeds from the scheme until he or she has reached at least age 50 under current rules (and 55 if proposed changes to the pension rules go ahead).

If you are not sure which investments to choose, get advice from an independent financial adviser (IFA).*

The investments in detail

Bank and building society children's accounts

Description/suitable for Accounts especially for children, usually offering introductory gifts, magazines and so on. Useful as a way of teaching children how to manage money and getting them into the savings habit.

Return and charges Interest, usually variable, on the amount invested. No explicit charges.

Risk No capital risk (see box opposite).

How long you invest Usually these are instant access accounts.

Minimum investment Usually £1.

Maximum investment Usually none.

Tax Interest usually paid with income tax at the savings rate already deducted. Higher-rate taxpayers have extra to pay. Starting-rate taxpayers can reclaim some tax. Non-taxpayers should either reclaim the tax or arrange to be paid gross interest. Usually the interest counts as the child's income (but see 'Gifts from parents' on page 244) and the child is likely to be a non-taxpayer.

How to invest Contact relevant bank or building society.

Mini cash ISAs

Description/suitable for   Savings account that pays tax-free interest. Many are instant access accounts. Must be aged at least 16.

Return and charges   Interest on the amount invested. This is often variable, but occasionally fixed. Interest rates may be tiered with higher rates paid on larger balances. No explicit charges.

Risk   No capital risk (but see box below).

How long you invest   For instant access accounts there is no set period. For other types of accounts, check the conditions.

Minimum investment   Often £1.

Maximum investment   £3,000 a year – this is the limit set in the tax rules.

Tax   Tax-free interest.

How to invest   Contact provider which may be a bank, building society or NS&I.★ You cannot hold an ISA on behalf of someone else (such as a child).

Capital risk

In this section, unless specifically mentioned, we have assumed that the risk of your losing capital because the provider goes out of business is minimal. In the event that this does happen, you might be eligible for compensation from the Financial Services Compensation Scheme.★ The compensation limits are shown in Table 16.2.

Table 16.2 Financial Services Compensation Scheme limits on compensation

Type of savings or investment	Level of cover	Maximum pay-out
Deposits (e.g. bank and building society accounts)	100% of the first £2,000 90% of next £33,000 0% of anything more	£31,700
Non-insurance investments (e.g. unit trusts and OEICs) and bad investment advice	100% of first £30,000 90% of next £20,000 0% of anything more	£48,000
Insurance-based investments (e.g. insurance bonds, personal pensions)	100% of first £2,000 Up to 90% of remainder	Unlimited

NS&I children's bonus bonds

Description/suitable for Bonds that can be bought by anyone aged 16 and over for someone aged 16 or less. Useful as a way of giving a small nest-egg to a child.

Return and charges Fixed return made up of interest and bonus added at end of term. No explicit charges.

Risk No capital risk. NS&I issues investments on behalf of the government which is very unlikely to default. Locking into a fixed return means the child would miss out if competing interest rates rose.

How long you invest Five-year term. The child can have the money back early, but then loses interest. At the end of five years, you can reinvest for a new fixed return over five years, provided the child is still under age 16. Bonds must be cashed by age 21.

Minimum investment £25.

Maximum investment £1,000 per issue per child.

Tax Interest is tax-free, even if the child becomes a taxpayer. Treated as child's income even if the bond is a gift from a parent (see page 244).

How to invest NS&I★ or through post offices.

NS&I premium bonds

Description/suitable for Bonds that give you the chance to win prizes by, in effect, gambling with the interest you would otherwise have earned.

Return and charges Prizes ranging from £50 up to £1 million. Random prize draw is held every month. Each £1 invested counts as a separate bond and has a chance to win. From June 2003, the yearly prize fund as a percentage of the total invested is 2.25 per cent. No explicit charges.

Risk No capital risk. NS&I issues investments on behalf of the government which is very unlikely to default. From June 2003, the chance of winning any prize with a single bond was 1 in 30,000. If winnings are not reinvested, or winnings are small, your capital is vulnerable to inflation risk.

How long you invest No set period.

Minimum investment £100.

Maximum investment £20,000 plus reinvested prizes.

Tax Prizes are tax-free.

How to invest NS&I★ or through post offices. Bonds can be bought on behalf of children by parents and grandparents.

Friendly society plans

Description/suitable for Friendly societies are similar to insurance companies and generally offer similar types of product. But friendly societies are able to offer small savings plans that give you a completely tax-free return (in contrast to most insurance policies where the insurance company has already paid tax on the return from the underlying investments). Useful as a way of building up a small nest-egg. Some of these plans are specifically marketed as investments for children.

Return and charges The plan usually pays out a lump sum after a set number of years, for example ten years. Usually, there is an administration fee when you invest. If the plan is invested on a unit-linked basis (similar to a unit trust), there is usually an initial charge (up to, say, 5 per cent) and an annual management charge (for example, 1.5 per cent a year of the value of the investment fund) with other costs charged direct to the fund. If the plan is invested on a with-profits basis (see box overleaf), charges influence the level of bonuses.

Risk Capital risk varies depending on the underlying investments.

How long you invest Usually you must invest for at least ten years. If you cash in your investment early, surrender charges reduce the amount you get back – perhaps to even less than you had invested.

Minimum investment Varies from one society to another.

Maximum investment £25 a month or £270 a year.

Tax The return is tax-free. Treated as child's income even if plan is a gift from a parent (see page 244).

How to invest Through direct contact with friendly societies or via an IFA.★

Share-based unit trusts and OEICs

Description/suitable for   You buy 'units' in a unit trust (or shares in an OEIC) which give you a stake in an investment fund. The fund is a ready-made portfolio of many different shares. You can choose funds that aim to produce income and/or growth.

Return and charges   The return takes the form of income distributions usually paid/credited every six months and/or, if you sell your units for more than you paid, a capital gain. You can choose growth funds that pay low or no distributions. There is usually an up-front charge (up to 5 per cent or so of the amount you invest) and an annual management charge (usually around 1 to 1.5 per cent a year of the value of your investment). Other charges are deducted direct from the investment fund.

With-profits investments

Your savings grow through the addition of yearly bonuses which, once added, can't usually be taken back. The size of bonuses depends largely on the growth of an underlying investment fund which is typically invested in shares, gilts, corporate bonds, property and cash, but also on the overall profitability of the provider's business. Bonuses are smoothed by keeping back in reserve some growth from good years to top up your return in poor years. An extra 'terminal' bonus is also added when the policy matures.

The broad spread of investments in the investment fund and the fact that bonuses once added cannot normally be taken away reduces capital risk, making the with-profits basis a medium-risk approach to investing. However, you are not totally protected from stock market swings. If you cash in your policy early and investment returns have been poor, the provider can levy a 'market value reduction' (MVR) on top of any surrender charges and this effectively claws back some of the bonuses that had already been credited to your policy. Note that the level of future bonuses is not normally guaranteed. A company which is financially strong – for example, with a high level of reserves – is generally more likely to maintain its bonuses in future.

Risk The price of your units can fall as well as rise, so you are exposed to capital risk. However, investing in a broad spread of different shares reduces risk by reducing your exposure to the misfortunes of any one company. Over the long term, share-based investments have tended to rise at least in line with inflation and in line with the growth of the economy as a whole.

How long you invest No set period but because the value of the investment fund can fall as well as rise you should normally aim to invest for the long term (more than five years).

Minimum investment Varies from, say, £500 or more as a lump sum and £50 per month for regular savings.

Maximum investment None.

Tax Distributions are paid with tax at 10 per cent already deducted. Non-taxpayers cannot reclaim this tax. There is no further tax to pay for starting-rate and basic-rate taxpayers. Higher-rate taxpayers must pay extra. Capital gains are taxable, however if you have unused allowance there may be no tax to pay.

How to invest You can go to the provider direct, but you'll often pay less in charges if you go to a discount broker★ or fund supermarket.★ You can also invest through most IFAs★ and many stockbrokers.★

Investment trusts

Description/suitable for These give you a stake in an investment fund and so are an alternative to investing in unit trusts or OEICs, however they work in a different way. An investment trust is a company whose business is running an investment fund. The fund might specialise in shares, gilts, bonds, property and so on. You invest indirectly in the fund by buying the shares of the investment trust company. The share price is heavily influenced by the value of the investments in the trust but is also affected by other factors, such as whether the company has large borrowings and the balance of supply and demand for the company's shares.

Return and charges In a conventional investment trust, your return is in the form of dividends, usually paid out twice a year and, if you sell the shares for more than you paid, a capital gain. A 'split capital trust' is different. It has a set date on which the company will be wound up. There are two main types of shares: 'capital shares' which receive no income but get most of the proceeds of selling the investment fund at wind up; and 'income shares' which receive all the income from the fund in the form of dividends and only a small share of the fund at wind up. You incur dealing costs when you buy and sell investment trust shares, and there is stamp duty to pay on purchases. In addition, the trust company levies an explicit annual management charge, often in the region of 1 per cent of the value of the fund. Other charges are deducted from the fund.

Risk The price of your shares can fall as well as rise, so you are exposed to capital risk. However, the broad spread of different shares in the investment fund reduces your exposure to the misfortunes of any one company. Over the long term, share-based investments have tended to rise at least in line with inflation and in line with the growth of the economy as a whole. The potential returns and also the risks increase if the trust borrows money to invest (a process called 'gearing'). Some, but not all, investment trusts have invested in each other's shares. This practice also increases risk because if one investment trust performs badly this also affects the performance of the other trusts that have bought its shares. It is important to check the extent of borrowing and cross-holdings before you invest.

How long you invest No set period but, because the value of the investment fund can fall as well as rise, you should normally aim to invest for the long term (more than five years).

Minimum investment Most investment trusts run their own savings schemes through which you can invest, say, £500 or more as a lump sum or £50 or more a month as regular savings. If instead you buy shares through a broker, dealing costs make transactions below, say, £1,000 to £1,500 uneconomic.

Maximum investment None.

Tax Dividends are paid with tax at 10 per cent already deducted. Non-taxpayers cannot reclaim this tax. There is no further tax to pay for starting-rate and basic-rate taxpayers. Higher-rate taxpayers must pay extra. Capital gains are taxable, however if you have unused allowance there may be no tax to pay.

How to invest Through the trust company's own savings scheme or a stockbroker.* Some fund supermarkets* offer investment trusts which can be relatively cheap way to invest.

Stakeholder pension schemes

Description/suitable for A way of saving for retirement. Anyone – even a child – can have a scheme. Other people can invest in your scheme on your behalf. Money invested early in life has a long time to grow so makes a particularly valuable contribution towards retirement savings.

Return and charges Your money can be invested either on a unit-linked basis (similar to unit trusts) or a with-profits basis (see box on page 254).

Risk Capital risk varies depending on the underlying investments.

How long you invest Until at least age 50 under current rules (55 if proposed changes go ahead).

Minimum investment £20 whether this is a regular contribution or a lump sum.

Maximum investment Under current rules, £2,808 a year (unless you have earnings in which case you may be able to invest more).

Tax The government adds basic-rate tax relief to your contributions (even if you are not a taxpayer). Gains and some of the income from investing the contributions are tax-free. You can take part of the proceeds as a tax-free lump sum; the rest must be taken as taxable pension.

How to invest Through direct contact with pension providers or via an IFA.★

Glossary

A word or phrase shown in *italics* has a separate entry in the Glossary.

accumulation-and-maintenance trust A type of *discretionary trust* which enjoys special tax treatment: gifts to the trust count as *potentially exempt transfers*; there is no *inheritance tax* on the property within the trust nor when property is paid out to *beneficiaries*. The special treatment is only granted provided certain rules are kept: for example, at least one beneficiary must become entitled to part or all of the trust property by the age of 25. These trusts are especially useful as a way of giving to one or more young children, for example, grandchildren.

administrator The *personal representative* who settles the affairs of someone who has died without leaving a will. He or she is appointed by the court and will often be the husband or wife of the deceased person.

affinity card another name for *donation card*.

allowable business expense Spending you make in the course of running your business that can be set against the income of the business when working out the profits for income tax purposes. Generally, to count as allowable, the spending must have been made 'wholly and exclusively' for the purpose of the business.

Alternative Investment Market (AIM) A stock market for fledgling companies which want to raise money by issuing shares to the public but at lower cost and with fewer restrictions than a listing on the main stock market would involve. Opened in 1995, it replaced the Unlisted Securities Market (USM) which is now closed to new entrants.

asset Anything which you own: for example, your home, car, personal possessions, money and investments.

bare trust   Arrangement whereby someone holds property as nominee for someone else. For tax purposes, the ultimate beneficiary is treated as owning the property outright.

beneficiary   A person who may receive property from a trust, or who has been left something in a will.

bequest   A gift to someone in a will. Also called a legacy.

CAF   Abbreviation for the *Charities Aid Foundation*.

capital gains tax (CGT)   Tax on gains that you make from selling an *asset* for more than it was worth when you first started to own it. If you give the asset away, you are deemed to have made a gain if the asset has risen in value over the time you have owned it. In practice, there is often no tax to pay on a gain because you are allowed to make various deductions in calculating the gain for tax purposes. The most important deductions are *indexation allowance,* CGT *taper relief* and the 'tax-free slice'. The tax-free slice enables you to make a given amount of otherwise taxable gains free of CGT. The rates at which tax is levied on taxable gains are 10 per cent, 20 per cent and 40 per cent in 2003–4.

CGT   Abbreviation for *capital gains tax*.

CGT taper relief   Reduction in the value of capital gains on which tax is charged. The reduction is given according to the number of complete years since 5 April 1998 you have held the asset on which the gain is realised.

chargeable transfer   A gift that is not a *potentially exempt transfer* and that is not tax-free for another reason (for example, if it were a gift between husband and wife), and on which there may be an *inheritance tax* bill.

charitable trust   A type of *trust* whose aims and purposes meet the requirements for charitable status. This means that there is no *income tax*, *capital gains tax* or *inheritance tax* on the trust property or payments from it provided they are used for charitable ends. (From 1999, however, charitable trusts have been unable to claim tax deducted from dividends on shares.) In addition, income tax relief is given on gifts to the trust provided they are made through one of the special schemes available – such as through *payroll giving* or *gift aid*.

Charities Aid Foundation (CAF)   A charity whose aim is to promote and assist other charities. It is a rich source of information about charities and operates a Charity Account which provides individuals (and companies) with a tax-efficient and flexible method of giving to charity.

Charity Commission   The government department responsible for registering charities, investigating abuse of charitable status and helping charities to run efficiently and within the charity laws.

chattels   A tax term for those of your possessions which are physical and portable things: for example, jewellery, furniture, cars, antiques. Technically they are referred to as 'tangible movable property'.

children   This may be defined in various ways for the purpose of specific pieces of legislation. For example, under the *intestacy* rules, 'children' means children of your current marriage, children of any former marriage(s), illegitimate children and adopted children, but it does not include stepchildren. Under the *income tax* rules, 'children' is more widely defined and does include stepchildren.

child tax credit   State benefit available from 2003–4 to all but the wealthiest families with children. The amount you can get depends broadly on your income for tax purposes and so is influenced by, for example, gift aid donations you make. The full tax credit is available only to poorer families and increases the amount of money to be paid into the children's child trust fund.

child trust fund   New government scheme by which every child born from September 2002 onwards qualifies at birth for cash from the government. Other sums may be added to the fund which must be left invested until the child reaches age 18.

codicil   An amendment to a *will* to be considered in conjunction with the will. If the amendments are many or complicated, it will usually be better to rewrite the will rather than use a codicil.

covenant   A legally binding agreement to make regular payments of income to a person or organisation. Before 15 March 1988, gifts to people and charities under a covenant could attract relief from *income tax* but, from that date onwards, tax relief is restricted to covenanted gifts to charities. From 6 April 2000 onwards, tax relief for covenanted payments to charity is given through the *gift aid* scheme.

deed of variation   See *variation*.

demonstrative legacy   A gift of money or things made under a *will* and to be provided out of a specified part of the deceased person's *estate*.

disabled trust   A type of *discretionary trust*, qualifying for special tax treatment, for the maintenance or other benefit of a mentally disabled person. Gifts to the trust by the disabled person are free of *inheritance tax* and gifts by other people to the trust count as *potentially exempt transfers (PETs)*; property held within the trust is free of *inheritance tax*, as are payments to the disabled person. The disabled person is treated as owning the trust property and thus if he or she gives it away the gift counts as a PET.

disclaimer   The voluntary giving up of a gift made to you under a *will* following the death of the giver. The gift is then distributed according to the other terms of the will (for example, it might increase the value of the *residue*).

discretionary trust   A *trust* in which none of the beneficiaries has an *interest in possession* and the distribution of trust property or income from it is at the discretion of the *trustees*. The tax treatment of this type of trust is not as favourable as the regime for other trusts: gifts to a discretionary trust count as *chargeable transfers*; the trust fund is subject to *income tax*, *capital gains tax* and *inheritance tax (IHT)* with IHT being levied every ten years according to a complex formula; there is also IHT to pay on payments from the trust to the beneficiaries.

domicile   The country or state which is considered to be your permanent home in the sense that it is the place where you would expect to end your days. It is not necessarily the place where you live at present. In some circumstances, you can be deemed to be UK domiciled for inheritance tax purposes even if your legal domicile for other purposes is elsewhere.

donation card   A credit card which, when used, generates donations to charity. The card-issuing company usually agrees to make a donation when you first take out a card and then further donations each time you use it. In other respects, the card is like a normal credit card.

endowment policy   A type of life insurance policy which builds up an investment value over a specified term (the 'endowment' period). At the end of the term, the policy matures and the investment can be cashed in. Earlier encashment is possible, but returns may be low.

Enterprise Investment Scheme (EIS)   A tax-efficient scheme for investing in the shares of new unquoted companies (including *Alternative Investment Market* companies). Various reliefs from income tax and capital gains tax are given, provided certain conditions are met.

estate   All a person's possessions – home, car, money, investments and chattels – less their debts.

excluded property   Possessions and assets which are outside the scope of *inheritance tax*, for example, a *reversionary interest* in trust property (in most cases), certain government stocks if you are *domiciled* and *resident* outside the UK.

executor   The *personal representative* who sorts out the affairs of someone who has died in accordance with his or her *will* (and any subsequent *variation* to it). The executor will normally be a person (or company) appointed by the deceased person in his or her will.

family provision claim A claim by someone who, in the first instance, does not benefit from your *estate*, either under the terms of your *will* or under the *intestacy* rules, for financial support from the estate. The claimant will need to show that he or she was dependent on you during your lifetime or that he or she was an unmarried partner living with you as husband or wife throughout the two years prior to your death.

fixed-interest trust Another name for an *interest-in-possession trust*.

friendly society plans A type of investment, basically the same as some investment-type life insurance but which qualifies for special tax treatment. You pay premiums to the society that are invested for a given time, after which you receive a pay-out. There is no *income tax* or *capital gains tax* on the investment fund and there is no tax on the pay-out. The sum you can invest in these plans is restricted to a relatively low amount.

gift aid Tax-efficient scheme for making donations to charity. From 6 April 2000 onwards, the scheme applies to gifts of any amount, whether one-off or part of a series of gifts, provided you give basic personal details to the charity. You get tax relief at your top rate of income tax.

gift with reservation This occurs when you give away something but retain the right to use or enjoy the thing: for example, you might give away your home but continue to live there, or give away a piece of furniture but continue to keep it in your home. For *inheritance tax* purposes, a gift with reservation does not count as a gift at the time it is made but continues to be part of your estate. Tax becomes due (if payable) at the time the reservation stops: for example, on death. It is possible to make an outright gift and for the reservation to arise some time after the gift is made (for example, if you move back into a home you gave away).

gilts A type of investment issued by the government which generally pays a regular income and a capital sum after a specified period of time. (Some stocks do not offer the capital sum, only income.) When you buy a gilt, you are, in effect, making a loan to the government. These are considered to be very secure investments because of the very low risk that the government would be unable to repay you.

gross Used in the context of tax computations to mean 'before tax'.

gross covenant A legally binding agreement to make annual payments to a person or body – e.g. a charity. Under the agreement, the person or body receives a fixed sum – i.e. if the payments are to a charity and so qualify for tax relief, the sum you pay will vary if the tax rate varies.

'grossing up' The process of finding out the before-tax amount of a payment from the *net* amount. The 'grossed up' value is the sum of the net value plus the amount of tax which has been paid (or deemed to have been paid). Grossing up is carried out by dividing the net sum by (100% – tax rate). For example, take net income of £78 which has been taxed at the basic rate of *income tax* of 22 per cent. The grossed up value is: £78 ÷ (100% – 22%) = £78 ÷ 78% = £78 ÷ 0.78 = £100. In other words, tax of £22 has been paid and the grossed up value is the sum of £78 + £22.

hold-over relief   The process of deferring a *capital gains tax* bill due at the time a gift is made by passing the liability to the recipient of the gift. This is done by deducting from the recipient's initial value of the gift the amount of tax otherwise payable.

IHT   Abbreviation for *inheritance tax*.

income tax   Tax payable on most types of income: for example, earnings from a job, interest on investments, and so on. Everyone has a personal allowance (£4,615 in the 2003–4 tax year), which means that income of up to that amount is tax-free. Other allowances and deductions may also apply. Tax is charged at a lower rate of 10 per cent, a basic rate of 22 per cent and a higher rate of 40 per cent in the 2003–4 tax year. A special savings rate of 20 per cent applies to interest and similar income from many types of savings and investments. Dividends and similar income are taxed at 10 per cent or, if you are a higher-rate taxpayer, 32.5 per cent.

independent taxation   System of taxing married couples introduced from 6 April 1990 under which husband and wife are treated as separate units for *income tax* and *capital gains tax* purposes. This means, for example, that they each have their own personal allowance and starting- and basic-rate tax bands. (Under the earlier system, income and gains of the wife were generally treated for tax as being those of the husband.)

indexation allowance   That part of a capital gain on an *asset* that is judged to be due to the asset's value keeping pace with inflation (either since you first owned it or since March 1982, whichever date is later). This part of the gain is not liable for *capital gains tax (CGT)* and is deducted from the capital gain in calculating any CGT liability. Indexation allowance is available only for periods up to April 1998. After that time, it is replaced by *CGT taper relief*.

Individual Savings Account (ISA)   Tax-efficient savings scheme introduced from 6 April 1999 through which you can invest in, for example, bank and building society accounts, shares, unit trusts and life insurance products.

inheritance tax (IHT)   Tax due on a *chargeable transfer* either in your lifetime or when your *estate* is passed on at the time of death. Tax is worked out by looking at the running total of all such transfers over the last seven years. If this total comes to more than the tax-free slice (of

£255,000 in the 2003–4 tax year), tax will be payable. IHT is charged at a rate of 20 per cent on chargeable transfers made during your life (though extra tax may be due if you die within seven years) and at a rate of 40 per cent on transfers at the time of death.

interest in possession   The right to receive income from trust property. You may also have the right to receive the capital at some specified time or this may pass then to someone else.

interest-in-possession trust   A type of *trust* where one or more *beneficiaries* have the right to receive the income from the trust property at the time the income arises (called an *interest in possession*). The same person or someone else may have the right to the trust property when the trust comes to an end (called the *reversionary interest*). The tax treatment of this type of trust is fairly favourable: gifts paid into the trust count as *potentially exempt transfers (PETs)*; there is no *inheritance tax* on the trust property or on the income payments from it; the person holding the interest in possession is treated as owning the trust property so, when the trust comes to an end, that person is deemed to make a PET.

intestacy   Dying without having made a *will*. Your *estate* is distributed according to the rules of intestacy. These rules aim to protect your husband or wife up to a certain degree and your children. But the application of the rules can cause problems with, for example, part of your estate going to relatives outside the immediate family or an unmarried partner being left nothing (though he or she would be eligible to make a *family provision claim*).

investment trust   A type of investment where you buy shares in a company whose business is investing in other companies and/or other assets.

ISA   Abbreviation for *Individual Savings Account*.

joint tenancy   A way of sharing the ownership of an *asset*. You and the other joint tenant(s) have equal shares in the property and the same rights to enjoy the use of the whole asset. You cannot sell or give away your share of the asset independently of the other joint tenant(s) and on death your share automatically passes to them.

life interest   The right to receive the income from an *asset* for as long as you live but not the asset itself. On your death, the asset passes to whoever has the *reversionary interest*.

long-term care insurance   Insurance which pays out if you are unable to care for yourself. It helps you meet the cost of outside care either in your own home or in a residential or nursing home and is useful as a way of protecting capital which you hope to pass on as an inheritance.

millennium gift aid   Temporary scheme to encourage giving to charities which support education and poverty-aid programmes in the world's poorest countries. From 31 July 1998 to 31 December 2000, tax relief at your top rate was available on such gifts of £100 or more (or a series of gifts together totalling £100 or more). However, the millennium gift aid tax reliefs became redundant from 6 April 2000 with the opening up of *gift aid* to gifts of any amount.

National Savings & Investments (NS&I) products   A group of 'deposit-type' investments that are issued by the government. You invest and either receive a tax-free return or receive an income paid before the deduction of income tax. They include: NS&I Investment Accounts, NS&I Certificates, the Children's Bonus Bonds and NS&I Income Bonds.

net   Used in the context of tax computations to mean 'after tax has been deducted'.

net assets   Your *assets* less your debts and outstanding expenses.

net covenant   A legally binding agreement to make annual payments to a person or body – e.g. a charity. Under the agreement, you agree to pay a fixed sum – i.e. if the payments are to a charity and so qualify for tax relief, the overall sum the charity receives will vary if the tax rate varies.

Payroll deduction   Another name for *payroll giving*.

Payroll giving   A special scheme for making gifts to charity directly out of your earnings from a job. The gifts qualify for relief from *income tax* at your top rate.

pecuniary legacy   A gift in a *will* of a specified sum of money.

PEP   Abbreviation for *personal equity plan*.

personal equity plan (PEP)   An investment in shares, unit trusts, investment trusts and/or some types of bonds where the income and gains are free of *income tax* and *capital gains tax*, respectively, as long as the investments remain in the PEP. No new PEPs can be taken out after 5 April 1999.

personal representative   The person (or company) who sorts out the *estate* of someone who has died. There are two types of representative: the *administrator* who acts when there is no *will* and the *executor* who acts when there is a will.

PET   Abbreviation for *potentially exempt transfer*.

potentially exempt transfer (PET)   A gift between individuals or a gift between an individual and a *trust*, other than a *discretionary trust*, made during the lifetime of the giver. There is no *inheritance tax* charge on the gift provided the giver survives for seven years. If they do not, the PET is reassessed as a *chargeable transfer* and tax may then be due after all.

purchased life annuity   An investment whereby you hand over a lump sum to an insurer, which then pays you an income for life. You cannot get back your investment in the form of a lump sum but part of each regular payment to you is deemed to be return of your capital – the rest is deemed to be income. The capital element of each payment does not count as income for tax purposes, so there is no *income tax* on that part and it cannot be used to make 'regular payments out of income' under the inheritance tax rules.

registered charity   A charity listed on the Register of Charities kept by the *Charity Commission*. Registration tells you that the charity met the criteria for charitable status at the time it applied for registration, but should not be regarded as a 'seal of approval'.

residence   The country or state which you currently make your home. 'Ordinarily resident' means that you make your home there year after year. 'Resident' may refer to a shorter-term home, e.g. while you are posted abroad. The terms are imprecise and are not defined in any Act of Parliament.

residuary gift   The gift under your *will* of whatever is left after all the *specific gifts* have been made, and debts and expenses (including tax) paid.

residue   Whatever is left after all the *specific gifts* have been made, and debts and expenses (including tax) paid.

Retail Prices Index   The government index which tracks the general cost of living. Changes in the index give a widely used measure of inflation.

reversionary interest   The right to the property in a *trust* at some specified time or on a specified occurrence, but not the right to income from or use of the property before that time.

settlor   The person who sets up a *trust* and puts money or *assets* into it.

single-premium life insurance bond   A type of investment whereby you use a lump sum to buy an insurance policy. The life-cover element is low and the main aim of the policy is to provide investment growth. Special tax rules enable you to withdraw money periodically from the bond but to defer any liability for *income tax* on the withdrawals until later. These withdrawals do not count as income for the purpose of the 'regular payments out of income' exemption from *inheritance tax* on gifts.

specific gift   Gifts of money or things under a *will*. The gifts can be of various types: for example, a named item, a type of *asset*, a *pecuniary legacy*, a *demonstrative legacy*.

survivorship destination   An arrangement under Scottish law which ensures that, on the death of a joint owner of property, his or her share of the property passes automatically to the surviving co-owner(s), even if the deceased person's *will* specifies otherwise.

taper relief   Tax relief which reduces the amount of *inheritance tax* due on a *potentially exempt transfer* (*PET*) or *chargeable transfer* which is reassessed following the death of the giver within seven years of making the gift. The size of the relief increases with the elapse of time from the making of the gift. Taper relief *does not* reduce extra tax due on an *estate* as a result of PETs being reassessed. (This form of taper relief should not be confused with *CGT taper relief*.)

tenancy in common   A method of jointly owning an *asset*, where you and the other owners have specified shares of the asset which you can sell or give away without the agreement of the other owners. On death, your share is given away in accordance with your *will* or the rules of *intestacy*.

testator   The person (strictly, a man) who makes a *will*.

testatrix   A woman who makes a *will*.

trust   A legal arrangement whereby property is held by *trustees* on behalf of one or more *beneficiaries* to be used in accordance with the rules of the trust and trust law. Trusts can be very useful when making gifts as a way of giving *assets* but retaining some control over the way in which the assets are used; they are also useful if you wish to split the income and capital of assets and give each to a different person (or group of people).

trustee   A person who is responsible for investing and distributing *trust* property in accordance with the rules of the trust and trust law. The trustees of a trust are the owners of the trust property but they hold it for the benefit of the *beneficiaries* and not their own use.

variation   The process of changing the gifts made under a *will* after the *testator/testatrix* has died. This is achieved by a 'deed of variation' drawn up by one or more of the *beneficiaries*.

Venture Capital Trust (VCT)   A tax-efficient scheme for investing in a *trust* company whose purpose is to invest in the shares or securities of unquoted companies. Various reliefs from *income tax* and *capital gains tax* are given, provided certain conditions are met.

whole-life policy   A type of life insurance policy designed to pay out on the death of the policyholder whenever that might occur. Policies can also cover more than one person with payment due on either the first or second death.

will   A legal document specifying how your *estate* is to be distributed and to whom at the time of death.

Addresses

Accountant – to find one

Association of Chartered Certified Accountants
29 Lincoln's Inn Fields
London WC2A 3EE
Tel: 020-7396 7000
Fax: 020-7396 7070
Email: info@accaglobal.com
Website: www.acca.co.uk

Institute of Chartered Accountants in England and Wales
PO Box 433
Chartered Accountants' Hall
Moorgate Place
London EC2P 2BJ
Tel: 020-7920 8100
Fax: 020-7920 0547
Email:
generalenquiries@icaew.co.uk
Website: www.icaew.co.uk

Institute of Chartered Accountants in Ireland
Chartered Accountants' House
87–89 Pembroke Road
Ballsbridge
Dublin 4
Republic of Ireland
Tel: (00 353) 1637 7200
Fax: (00 353) 1668 0842
Email: ca@icai.ie
Website: www.icai.ie

Institute of Chartered Accountants of Scotland
CA House
21 Haymarket Yards
Edinburgh EH12 5BH
Tel: 0131-347 0100
Fax: 0131-347 0105
Email: enquiries@icas.org.uk
Website: www.icas.org.uk

CAF Charity Account
Kings Hill
West Malling
Kent ME19 4TA
Tel: (01732) 520055
Fax: (01732) 520001
Email:
charityaccounts@CAFonline.org
Website: www.allaboutgiving.org

Capital Taxes Office (Inland Revenue)
Helpline: (0845) 302 0900
Forms orderline: (0845) 234 1000
Fax: (0845) 234 1010
Email: ir.purchasing@gtnet.gov.uk
Website:
www.inlandrevenue.gov.uk/cto

England and Wales
Ferrers House
PO Box 38
Castle Meadow Road
Nottingham NG2 1BB

Northern Ireland
Level 3
Dorchester House
52–58 Great Victoria Street
Belfast BT2 7QL

Scotland
Meldrum House
15 Drumsheugh Gardens
Edinburgh EH3 7UG

Central Register of Charities
See *Charity Commission* below for
regional offices
Website:
www.charitycommission.gov.uk

**Charities Aid Foundation
(CAF)**
Kings Hill
West Malling
Kent ME19 4TA
Tel: (01732) 520000
Fax: (01732) 520001
Email: enquiries@CAFonline.org
Website: www.caf.org.uk

Charity Commission
Tel: (0870) 333 0123
Email: enquiries@charitycommission.
gsi.gov.uk
Website:
www.charitycommission.gov.uk

Liverpool
20 Kings Parade
Queen's Dock
Liverpool L3 4DQ
Central register open 9am–4.30pm

London
Harmsworth
13–15 Bouverie Street
London EC4Y 8DP
Central register open 9am–5pm

Taunton
Woodfield House
Tangier
Taunton
Somerset TA1 4BL
Central register open 9.30am–4pm

**Department for Social
Development** (Northern Ireland)
Churchill House
Victoria Square
Belfast BT1 4SD
Tel: 028-9056 9100
Website: www.dsdni.gov.uk

**Discount broker – some
examples**

Chase de Vere Investments plc
Eastcheap Court
11 Philpot Lane
London EC3M 8AE
Tel: (0845) 609 2009
Fax: 020-7618 0400
Email:
enquiry@chasedevere.co.uk
Website: www.chasedevere.co.uk

Hargreaves Lansdown
Kendal House
4 Brighton Mews
Clifton
Bristol BS8 2NX
Tel: (0117) 900 9000
Fax: (0117) 980 9915
Email:
helpdesk@hargreaveslansdown.co.uk
Website:
www.hargreaveslansdown.co.uk

Financial Ombudsman Service
South Quay Plaza
183 Marsh Wall
London E14 9SR
Tel: (0845) 080 1800
Fax: 020-7964 1001
Email: complaint.info@financial-ombudsman.org.uk
Website:
www.financial-ombudsman.org.uk

Financial Services Compensation Scheme
7th Floor
Lloyds Chambers
1 Portsoken Street
London E1 8BN
Tel: 020-7892 7300
Fax: 020-7892 7301
Email: enquiries@fscs.org.uk
Website: www.fscs.org.uk

Fund supermarket – some examples
www.charcolonline.co.uk
www.chasedevere.co.uk
www.egg.com
www.fidelity.co.uk (Funds Network)
www.hargreaveslansdown.co.uk
www.tqonline.co.uk

Independent Financial Adviser – to find one

IFA Promotion
17–19 Emery Road
Brislington
Bristol BS4 5PX
Tel: (0800) 085 3250
Fax: (0117) 972 4509
Website: www.unbiased.co.uk
Contact the telephone number above for a list of IFAs in your area

The Institute of Financial Planning
Whitefriars Centre
Lewins Mead
Bristol BS1 2NT
Tel: (0117) 9345 2470
Website:
www.financialplanning.org.uk

Matrix Data UK IFA Directory
Website:
www.ukifadirectory.co.uk

Money Management National Register of Fee-based Advisers
Matrix-Data Ltd
New London House
172 Drury Lane
London WC2B 5QR
Tel: 020-7074 1200
Fax: 020-7074 1201
Email: info@matrix-data.co.uk

Society of Financial Advisers (SOFA)
20 Aldermanbury
London EC2V 7HY
Tel: 020-7417 4442
Website: www.sofa.org
Can provide a list of independent financial advisers who have more than just the basic qualifications

Inland Revenue
See also *Capital Taxes Office* above.
For local tax enquiry centres look in
The Phone Book under 'Inland
Revenue'. For your local tax office,
check your tax return, other tax
correspondence or check with your
employer
Website: www.inlandrevenue.gov.uk

Inland Revenue (Charities Division)
Applications – in writing only – for
information about charitable status of
non-registered charities. For
registered charities, contact the
Charity Commission above
Tel: (0845) 302 0203
Fax: 0151-472 6060
Website:
www.inlandrevenue.gov.uk/charities

England, Wales and Northern Ireland
St John's House
Merton Road
Bootle
Merseyside L69 9BB

Scotland
Meldrum House
15 Drumsheugh Gardens
Edinburgh EH5 7UL

Institute of Professional Will Writers
Midland House
New Road
Halesowen
West Midlands B63 3HY
Tel: (0845) 644 2042
Fax: (0845) 644 2043
Email: ipw@whsmithnet.co.uk
Website: www.ipw.org.uk

Insurance broker – to find one

British Insurance Brokers' Association (BIBA)
14 Bevis Marks
London EC3A 7NT
Tel: 020-7623 9043
Fax: 020-7626 9676
Email: enquiries@biba.org.uk
Website: www.biba.org.uk
Can provide a list of brokers in your area

Law Societies

The Law Society (England and Wales)
113 Chancery Lane
London WC2A 1PL
Tel: (0870) 606 6575
Fax: 020-7320 5964
Email:
info.services@lawsociety.org.uk
Websites: www.lawsociety.co.uk,
www.solicitors-online.com

The Law Society of Northern Ireland
Law Society House
98 Victoria Street
Belfast BT1 3JZ
Tel: 028-9023 1614
Fax: 028-9023 2606
Email: info@lawsoc-ni.org
Website: www.lawsoc-ni.org

The Law Society of Scotland
26 Drumsheugh Gardens
Edinburgh EH3 7YR
Tel: 0131-476 8137
Fax: 0131-225 2934
Email: cro@lawscot.org.uk
Website: www.lawscot.org.uk

National Council for Voluntary Organisations (NCVO)
Regent's Wharf
8 All Saints Street
London N1 9RL
Tel: 020-7713 6161
Fax: 020-7713 6300
Email: ncvo@ncvo-vol.org.uk
Website: www.ncvo-vol.org.uk

National Savings & Investments (NS&I)
Tel: (0845) 964 5000
Minicom: (0800) 056 0585
Email:
customerenquiries@nsandi.com
Website: www.nsandi.com

Cash mini ISAs
National Savings & Investments
Durham DH99 1NS
Fax: 0191-374 5603

Children's bonus bonds, investment accounts
National Savings & Investments
Glasgow G58 1SB
Fax: 0141-636 8724

Premium Bonds
National Savings & Investments
Blackpool FY3 9XP
Fax: (01253) 693182

Northern Ireland Council for Voluntary Action (NICVA)
61 Duncairn Gardens
Belfast BT15 2GB
Tel: 028-9087 7777
Fax: 028-9087 7799
Email: info@nicva.org
Website: www.nicva.org

Office for the Supervision of Solicitors

Victoria Court
8 Dormer Place
Leamington Spa
Warwickshire CV32 5AE
Helpline: (0845) 608 6565
Minicom: (0870) 600 1565
Fax: (01926) 431435
Email:
enquiries@lawsociety.org.uk
Website:
www.oss.lawsociety.org.uk

Probate Registry

For Scotland, see *Sheriff Clerk* below

England & Wales

Principal Probate Registry
First Avenue House
42–49 High Holborn
London WC1V 6NP
Tel: 020-7947 7000
Fax: 020-7947 6946
Minicom: 020-7842 7602
Website: www.courtservice.gov.
uk/you_courts/probate/directory/
index.htm

Northern Ireland

Probate and Matrimonial Office
Royal Courts of Justice (Northern Ireland)
Chichester Street
Belfast BT1 3JF
Tel: 028-9023 5111
Fax: 028-9031 0568
Email: probate&matrimonial@
courtsni.gov.uk
Website: www.courtsni.gov.uk

Scottish Charities Office

25 Chambers Street
Edinburgh EH1 1LA
Tel: 0131-226 2626
Fax: 0131-226 6912
Email: scottishcharitiesoffice@
copfs.gsi.gov.uk
Website: www.crownoffice.gov.uk/
departmental/Scottish_charities.htm

Scottish Council for Voluntary Organisations (SCVO)

The Mansfield
Traquair Centre
15 Mansfield Place
Edinburgh EH3 6BB
Tel: 0131-556 3882
Fax: 0131-556 0279
Textphone: 0131-557 6483
Email: enquiries@scvo.org.uk
Website: www.scvo.org.uk

Sheriff Clerk
HM Commissary Office
27 Chamber Street
Edinburgh EH1 1LB
Tel: 0131-247 2850
Website: www.scotcourts.gov.uk

Society of Trust and Estate Practitioners (STEP)
26 Dover Street
London W1S 4LY
Tel: 020-7763 7152
Fax: 020-7763 7252
Email: step@step.org
Website: www.step.org

Society of Will Writers
First Floor Chambers
Roe House
Boundary Lane
South Hykeham
Lincoln LN6 9NQ
Tel: (01522) 687888
Fax: (01522) 696919
Email:
society.willwriters@virgin.net
Website:
www.thesocietyofwillwriters.co.uk

Solicitor – to find one
Contact the *Law Societies* or *Society of Trust and Estate Practitioners* above for a list of members

Stockbroker – to find one

Association of Private Client Investment Managers and Stockbrokers (APCIMS)
112 Middlesex Street
London E1 7HY
Tel: 020-7247 7080
Fax: 020-7377 0939
Email: info@apcims.co.uk
Website: www.apcims.co.uk

London Stock Exchange
Old Broad Street
London EC2N 1HP
Tel: 020-7797 1000
Email: enquiries@londonstock
exchange.com
Website:
www.londonstockexchange.com

Tax adviser – to find one

The Chartered Institute of Taxation
12 Upper Belgrave Street
London SW1X 8BB
Tel: 020-7235 9381
Fax: 020-7235 2562
Email: info@ciot.org.uk
Website: www.tax.org.uk

Tax enquiry centre
See *Inland Revenue* above

Tax office
See *Inland Revenue* above

Trading Standards Office
This is a department of your local
council. Look in The Phone Book
under 'Councils' or the relevant
council's name
Website:
www.tradingstandards.gov.uk

**Wales Council for Voluntary
Action (WCVA)**
Baltic House
Mount Stuart Square
Cardiff CF10 5FH
Tel: 029-2043 1700
Fax: 029-2043 1701
Minicom: 029-2043 1702
Email: enquiries@wcva.org.uk
Website: www.wcva.org.uk

Which? Books
Castlemead
Gascoyne Way
Hertford X
SG14 1LH
Tel: (0800) 252100
Website: www.which.net

Index

Page references in **bold type** indicate an entry in the Glossary

abroad, residence
  and CGT 169–71
  domicile 71, 74, **262**
  and gifts between husband and
    wife 71
  and hold-over relief 101
  making gifts if you move abroad
    70
  'resident' and 'ordinarily resident'
    169, 170
  tax concessions for returnees 170
accumulation-and-maintenance
  trusts 141, 144, 146–7, 165,
  244–5, **259**
  maximum lifespan 146
  tax treatment 100, 162–3
active service, death on 216
affinity cards *see* donation cards
age allowance, gift aid and 36–8
agricultural property relief 102, 121,
  211, 219
allowable business expense 55, **259**
  charity donation as 55
Alternative Investment Market
  (AIM) 103, 210, **259**
annuities 68, 227, 228, 241
  purchased life annuity 73, **267**
anti-avoidance rules 128–9, 147,
  220–1, 243, 244, 245
Arts Councils 58, 60
assets 65–6, **259**

bed-and-breakfasting 79, 92,
  168–9
business assets 80, 95, 102–5, 209,
  220
for CGT purposes 66
disposal 65, 66
giving to charity 49
held in trust 183, 218
intangible assets 68
jointly-owned assets 125–8, 177,
  237–8, **265**
life interest 179, **265**
rearranging 124, 125–8
rising value 221
scope of 66
in Scotland 128
survivorship destination 128, **268**
tax on disposal of 65–6, 70, 80
tenancy in common 125, 126,
  127, 238, **268**
associated operations 220–1, 228,
  240
Awards for All 59, 60

baby bonds 245, 249–50
back-to-back insurance plans 227–8
bank and building society accounts
  for children 247, 249, 250
banks, building societies and
  insurance companies, will drafting
  by 188

bare trusts 135, 141, 142–3, 144, 164, 165, 177, 247, **260**
  tax treatment 142, 149–51
bed-and-breakfasting 79, 92, 168–9
bequests *see* legacies
birthday presents 75
bonds 68
  Children's Bonus Bonds 245, 249, 252
  Premium Bonds 68, 249, 252–3
Business Expansion Scheme (BES) 68
business property relief 121, 209–11, 219, 220
  qualifying business assets 209
  qualifying businesses 102–3, 210
businesses
  allowable business expense 55, **259**
  assets 80, 95, 102–5, 209, 220
  gifts from 55–7
  gifts to 75
  giving away 101–5, 121
  passing on 209–11, 219
  putting land or property into trust 219

capital gains tax (CGT) 16, 65–70, 79–106, **260**
  calculation of liability 80–1, 98–9
  chargeable gains *see* chargeable gains
  charitable bequests and 50
  combining CGT and IHT exemptions 76
  hold-over relief 100–5, 171, **264**
  and the home 67, 241
  indexation allowance 79, 83, 85, 86, 88–90, **264**
  on lifetime gifts 79–106, 219–20
  rates of 98–9
  reducing liability to 66, 79, 167–71
  retirement relief 102
  scope of 66–9

taper relief 79, 80, 81, 82, 84–5, 92, 95, 96, 97, 100–1, 102, 103, 104, 105, **260**
  tax changes 79–80
  tax-free exemptions and transactions 66–9, 76–7, 80, 167
  tax-free slice (annual exempt amount) 80, 95, 96, 124, 128, 168, 169, 244
  and trusts 68–9, 149, 151–2, 153, 154, 156, 159, 162, 163
  UK residence and 169–71
  when payable 105
Capital Taxes Office 122, 213
capital transfer tax (CTT) 13–15, 108
  see also inheritance tax
cash gifts 221
chargeable gains
  allowable losses 96–8
  assets acquired before April 1982 86–8
  assets acquired between March 1982 and 1 April 1998 83–6, 93–5
  assets acquired on or after 1 April 1998 81–3, 92–3
  calculation 81, 82–3, 84–5, 86–8
  holdover relief and 100–1
  net chargeable gain 81, 82
  notifying the tax office 105–6
chargeable gifts *see* chargeable transfers
chargeable transfers 100, 108, 116, 171, **260**
  death rate 108, 109, 113
  fall-in-value relief 117
  and gifts with reservation 119–20
  giver dies within seven years 113–14, 195
  lifetime rate 108, 109, 113
  notifying the tax office 122
  reassessment 116–17, 195
  running (cumulative) total 108, 113, 115, 122, 196

taxation of 108–12, 195
trust gifts as 153, 156
charitable trusts 52–5, 138, 148, **260**
setting up 53–4
tax treatment 52–3, 54, 55
temporary charitable trust 54–5
charities
administration costs 29
annual accounts 28, 29
business rates relief 31
categories 22–3
charitable status 24–5
checking out 26–8, 29–30
choosing 21–30
community amateur sports clubs
23–4, 32, 33, 71
definition and scope 21–4
giving to 8, 11–12, 21–61, 76,
123, 198, 221
assets, gifts of 45–8, 49
CAF Charity Account 44,
50–2
charitable bequests 49–50
charitable trusts 52–5, 148, **260**
donation cards 60–1, **262**
door-to-door and street
collections 26–7, 29–30
gifts from businesses 55–7
tax-efficient schemes 8, 11–12,
33–45, 50–1, 52–3, 55–7
via community development
finance institutions (CDFIs)
57
via discretionary trusts 52
via National Lottery 12, 57–60
incomes 25–6
money spent by 28–9
political activities 24
registered charities 22, 25–6, 28,
267
tax status 22, 25, 31–2, 69, 71
telephone appeals 21, 27
total amounts given to 11, 34, 44,
58
VAT liability 31–2
will-writing services 188

Charities Aid Foundation (CAF) 11,
28, 44, 53–4, **260**
and charitable trusts 53–4
Charity Account 44, 50–2
Give As You Earn (GAYE)
scheme 44
Charity Commission 24, 25, 27, 28,
53, **260–1**
chattels 66, 77, **261**
CGT liability 85
surviving spouse's entitlement to
177
cheques, gifts by 222
child tax credit 38, 40, 248, **261**
child trust fund scheme 243, 248,
261
investment 248
non-government additions 248
children
adopted children and stepchildren
179, 190, 193
definition 73, 179, **261**
estate of a child 177
gifts to 128, 129, 171, 243–57
arranging your gift 246–8
from friends and relatives 246
investing for capital gain not
income 245
parental 128, 129, 244–5, 246
via trusts 132, 135, 142–3, 144,
146, 147, 246, 247
guardians 176, 190
illegitimate children 179, 193
inheritance under intestacy laws
179–81, 183
investments for 245, 247, 249–57
maintenance payments to 73–4
personal tax allowance 244
tax-free income 245
children, investments for
bank and building society
accounts 247, 249, 250
cash-ISAs 245, 249, 251
friendly society plans 245, 247,
249–50, 253
investment trusts 255–6

NS&I Children's Bonus Bonds
245, 249, 252
NS&I Premium Bonds 252–3
open-ended investment
companies (OEICs) 254
stakeholder pension schemes 73,
245, 249, 250, 256–7
unit trusts 245, 249, 250, 254–5
Christmas presents 75
codicils 191, **261**
community amateur sports clubs
23–4, 32, 33, 71
community development finance
institutions (CDFIs) 57
Community Fund 58, 59, 60
community investment tax relief
57
companies
gifts from 56, 107, 109
gifts to 75, 107
qualifying companies 102–3
unlisted companies 103
compensation
investment losses 251
for wrongs suffered in war 216
covenants 11, 33, 42–3, 56–7, 68,
261
deed of covenant 56, 72
gross covenant 43, **263**
net covenant 43, **266**
old covenant tax rules 42–3
under gift aid rules 42–3
credit card/charity link-ups 60–1
Crown, estate passes to 182
currency, CGT liability and 66, 68

death
alteration of will after 232–4
gifts on 13, 70, 216, 231–2
tax payable on 195–213
decorations and awards, CGT
liability and 66
decreasing term insurance 223, 225
deed of covenant 56, 72
deeds of variation 222, 232–3, 234,
268

demonstrative legacies 192, **261**
disabled trusts 148, **261**
disclaimers 222, 232, 233, **262**
discounted gift plans 228–9
discretionary trusts 52, 101, 107,
108, 141, 145–6, 165, 171, 218,
219, 222, **262**
charitable gifts via 52
exit charge 157, 159
gifts and loan plans 222, 226–7
gifts with reservation to 119–20
tax treatment 52, 110–12, 145,
156–62, 171, 218, 219
see also accumulation and
maintenance trusts
domicile 71, 74, 75, **262**
donatio mortis causa 231–2
donation cards 60–1, **262**

employee share schemes 80
endowment policy 224, **262**
Enterprise Investment Scheme (EIS)
68, **226**
estate **262**
claims against 177, 183, 193–4
excepted estate 212
free estate 196
freezing 222
power of appropriation 192
'proving' and 'distributing' 175
reducing size of 49–50, 54, 70,
219, 224–5
tax on see inheritance tax
valuation of 196
estate duty 13, 14
see also inheritance tax
exit charge 157, 159

fall-in-value relief 117
family business see businesses
family provision claim 183, 193–4,
263
family wealth trusts 230
farms 105, 121, 211
fixed interest trusts see interest-in-
possession trusts

flexible power of appointment trusts 136
flexible trusts 136, 230
foreign currency and CGT liability 68
forms (Inland Revenue)
  chargeable transfers (form IHT100) 122
  jointly owned assets (form 17) 126, 127
free estate 196
free-of-tax gifts 197, 200–7, 218
  gifts under your will 197, 200–7
  grossing up 200–1, 202
  mixed with taxable gifts 202–7
friendly society plans **263**
  children's savings 245, 247, 249–50, 253

gardens, CGT liability and 67, 241
generation-skipping 222
gift aid 11, 33–42, 51, **263**
  and age allowance 36–8
  benefits as result of gift 41, 42
  carrying back donations 39–40
  declaration 34, 35, 36
  donations via charitable trusts 53
  gifts from companies 56
  higher-rate taxpayers and 34, 54
  millennium gift aid **266**
  non-taxpayers 39, 40
  and tax credits 38–9
  tax refunds, donation to charity 41–2
  tax relief 33–4, 36
gifts
  to charities 8, 11–12, 21–61, 69, 71
  to family and friends 12–17, 65–171
  see also gifts with reservation; gifts under your will; lifetime gifts; specific gifts
gifts with reservation 108, 118–21, 196, 220, 221–2, 239, 240–1, **263**
  circumstances 118–19

and gifts between husband and wife 120–1
and IHT planning 220
trusts and 119–20, 164, 230
gifts under your will 17, 190–3, 197–207, 216
  free-of-tax gifts 197, 200–7
  legacies 192
  residuary gifts 192–3
  specific gifts 190–1, 197
  tax-bearing gifts 197, 199–200, 218
  tax-free gifts 196, 197, 198
gilts 68, **263**
Give As You Earn (GAYE) scheme 44
gross covenants 43, **263**
gross gifts 109, 197
  calculation of IHT on 110, 112
grossing up 200–1, 202, 203, **263–4**

Heritage Lottery Fund 59, 60
higher-rate taxpayers
  and charity donations 34, 54
  and investment income 127, 247
  and trust income 152, 155, 159, 162
hold-over relief 100–5, 171, **264**
home 237–41
  business use 67
  CGT liability 67, 241
  giving the freehold to charity 45
  IHT liability 7, 15
  and inheritance 183
  joint tenancy 237–8
  main home, nominating 67
  making a gift of 119, 239–41
  tenancy in common 238, 239
  a will, importance of 238–9
home income plans 241
home reversion schemes 241
housing associations, gifts to 72, 198
husband/wife
  entitlement under intestacy laws 177–9, 183

family provision claim 183, 193–4, **263**

gifts between 69, 71, 74, 75, 81, 99, 120–1, 123–8, 169, 198, 230

independent taxation 123–4, **264**

jointly owned assets 125–8

maintenance agreements 74

married couple's allowance 127–8

income tax **264**

and gifts 123–9

and trust income 149–50, 152–3, 158–9, 161

independent taxation 123–4, **264**

indexation allowance (CGT) 79, 83, 85, 86, **264**

calculation 88–90

Individual Savings Accounts (ISAs) **264**

'bed-and-ISA' shares 168

cash ISAs, children and 245, 249, 251

mini-cash ISAs 245, 251

tax treatment 68

inflation

capital gains due to 83, 86

see also indexation allowance

inheritance 173–234

inheritance planning 16, 215–34

aims 215

anti-avoidance rules 128–9, 147, 220–1, 243, 244, 245

associated operations 220–1, 228, 240

associated operations rules 220–1, 228, 240

complex planning tools 8, 225–30

donatio mortis causa (gifts from the deathbed) 231–2

gifts under your will 17, 190–3, 197–207, 216

insurance 222–31

lifetime gifts 219–22

long-term care insurance 230–1, 241, **265**

trusts see trusts

will see will

Inheritance (Provision for Family and Dependants) Act (1975) 182, 193, 239

inheritance tax (IHT) 15, 70–6, 100, 101, 124, 176, 184, 195–213, **264–5**

chargeable transfers see chargeable transfers

charitable bequests and 49–50

combining CGT and IHT exemptions 76

conditional exemptions 71

delivering an account 211–12

'effective rate' 199

excepted estate rules 212

excluded property **262**

expenditure-out-of-income exemption 72–3, 119, 221, 223

fall-in-value relief 117, 118

'final estate rate' 202, 207

and gifts of business or agricultural property 121

and gifts with reservation 118–21

and gifts under your will 197–207

on gross gifts 109, 110, 112

heritage property in lieu of 213

Inland Revenue leaflets 213

on lifetime gifts 15, 107–22

on net gifts 109, 111

'notional rate' 205, 207

payment

by instalments 211, 212

by whom payable 109, 116, 212

insurance policy to cover 225

loan to pay 212

when payable 122, 212

potentially exempt transfers see potentially exempt transfers

quick succession relief 208–9

rates of 7, 15, 108–9, 113, 195

reducing liability for 7, 54, 215–34

scope of 70, 108

seven-year rule 15, 76, 108,
113–14, 119, 195
small gift exemption 75
and taper relief 115, 196, **268**
tax-free gifts 15, 70–6, 76, 167,
171, 196, 197
tax-free slice 7, 74–5, 108, 109,
113–14, 115, 196, 216–17,
221, 238
carrying forward 74–5
threshold 7, 15
and trusts 149, 151, 153–4, 155,
156–7, 162, 163, 164, 218–19
interest in possession 218, **265**
interest-in-possession trusts 141,
143–4, 165, 218, 228, **265**
beneficiaries 135
life interest 135
protective trust 148
reversionary interest 135, 143,
153, 154, 155, 218, 228, **267**
tax treatment 144, 151–5
intestacy 16, 176–85, 238–9
estate of a child 177
meaning of term 176, **265**
in Northern Ireland 183, 185
partial intestacy 182
problems caused by 16, 175–6,
182–3
in Scotland 183, 184–5
survival by children 179–81, 183,
238
survival by no near relatives
181–2
survival by spouse/partner 177–9,
182–3, 238–9
survivorship provision 177
tax and 184
and unmarried partners 177,
182–3, 238–9
investment trusts 249, 250, 255–6,
265
split-capital investment trusts 245
investments
capital risk 251
and CGT liability 68

for children 245, 247, 249–57
compensation limits 251
gifts of to charities 45, 46–7, 51,
56
with-profits investments 254

joint tenancy 125–6, 177, 237–8,
265
severance of 125–6, 188, 189

Kink test 87

land and buildings, gifts of to charity
48
leases 239
lease carve-out 120
legacies 192
demonstrative legacy 192, **261**
pecuniary legacy 192, **266**
life insurance 222–30
back-to-back plans 227–8
capital withdrawal 133, 225, 226,
229
decreasing term insurance 223,
225
endowment policy 224, 228, 247,
262
inheritance planning tool
222–30
investment-type life insurance
226, 228, 229, 247
non-qualifying policies 226
payment of IHT via 225
PETs and 118, 222, 223–4
policy proceeds and CGT 68
premiums as tax-free gifts 72,
223, 224
protection from IHT using 118,
222–5
qualifying policies 226
single premium life insurance
bonds 73, 229, **267**
term insurance 118, 223, 224
trusts and 133
whole life policy 224, 225,
227–8, **268**

writing a policy in trust 134, 216, 223, 225, 247
life interest 179, **265**
life interest trusts *see* interest-in-possession trusts
lifetime gifts 219–22
    CGT on 79–106, 219–20
    CGT-free gifts 65, 66–9
    to charities 8, 11–12, 21–61, 69, 71
    to family and friends 12–17, 65–171
    home, making a gift of 119, 239–41
    IHT liability 107–22, 219–22
    IHT-free gifts 65, 72–6, 221
    notifying the tax office 122
    planning 167–71
limited companies, gifts from 55, 56
living wills 188, 189
loans
    interest-free 222
    to trusts 226–7
long-term care insurance 230–1, 241, **265**
lotteries
    syndicates 74
    tax and 74
    see also National Lottery

maintenance payments 73–4
marriage settlements 76
mentally incapacitated persons, trusts and 148, 261
Millennium Commission 59, 60
millennium gift aid **266**
mirror wills 186, 188
money, CGT liability and 66, 68
motor vehicles, CGT liability and 67–8
museums and art galleries, gifts to 69, 71, 76

National Council for Voluntary Organisations (NCVO) 11, 22, 51, 58

National Endowment for Science, Technology and the Arts (NESTA) 59
national heritage property
    gifts of 69, 71–2, 76, 100
    in lieu of IHT 213
National Lottery 12, 57–60
    capital grants 59
    charities, amounts given to 58, 59
    effect on charitable donations 58
    funding programmes 59, 60
    good causes 58–9
    public attitudes towards 58
National Lottery Charities Board *see* Community Fund
National Savings & Investments 247, **266**
    CGT and 68
    Children's Bonus Bonds 245, 249, 252
    Premium Bonds 68, 249, 252–3
National Trust 69, 71
net covenants 43, **266**
net gifts
    calculation of IHT on 109, 111
    meaning of term 109
New Opportunities Fund 59, 60
Non-taxpayers
    and charity donations 39, 40, 51
    and investment income 127
Northern Ireland
    charities 26
    IHT payments 211
    intestacy laws in 183, 185
number plates, personalised 68

open-ended investment companies (OEICs) 245, 249, 253

partial intestacy 182
partnerships, gifts from 56
payroll deduction *see* payroll giving schemes
payroll giving schemes 11, 33, 43–5, 51, **266**

approved agencies 43–5
charity accounts 44
elective schemes 44
government bonus 43
size of donations 43
staff charity funds 44
stopping donations 45
see also Charities Aid Foundation
    (CAF)
pecuniary legacy 192, **266**
pension schemes
    lump sum payments 216
    stakeholder pension schemes 73,
        224–5, 225, 245, 249, 250,
        256–7
periodic charge 156
Personal Equity Plans (PEPs) **266**
    tax treatment 68
political parties, gifts to 72, 100,
    198
potentially exempt transfers (PETs)
    69, 70, 72, 76, 77, 100, 101, 107,
    108, 114–15, 167, 220, 229, 230,
    239, **266–7**
    fall-in-value relief 118
    and gifts with reservation 119
    and insurance to pay IHT bill
        118, 222, 223–4
    reassessment 113, 114, 115, 116,
        122, 196
    seven-year rule 195, 225
    and taper relief 115
    taxation of 114–15, 122, 195
    trust gifts as 151, 153, 162
    see also chargeable transfers
Premium Bonds 68, 249, 252–3
prisoners of war, ex-gratia payments
    to 216
Probate Registry 211
protective trusts 148
public benefit gifts 69, 71–2, 76,
    100, 198
purchased life annuity 73, **267**

qualifying companies 102–3
quick succession relief 208–9

relatives
    dependent relatives 74
    entitlement under intestacy laws
        181–2
    gifts to children 246
remainderman 135
residence 70, 101, 169–71, **267**
    'resident' and 'ordinarily resident'
        169, 170
residuary gifts 192–3, 197, **267**
residue 192–3, 197, 218, **267**
Retail Prices Index (RPI) 83, 90,
    91, **267**
retained interest trusts 229–30
retirement relief 102
reversionary interest 143, 153, 154,
    155, 218, 222, 228, **267**
rising-value gifts 221

Scotland
    charities 26
    IHT payments 211
    inheritance rights 176, 183, 194
    intestacy laws 183, 184–5
    joint assets in 128
    trusts 132, 135
Scottish Charities Office 26
self-assessment 105
self-employed persons and charitable
    donations 56
settlements 128, 131
    see also trusts
settlor-interested trusts 134–5,
    163–4, 230
seven-year rule
    IHT 15, 76, 108, 113–14, 119,
        195
    potentially exempt transfers
        (PETs) 195, 225
shares
    bed and breakfasting 79, 92,
        168–9
    'bed-and-ISA' 168
    business property relief on 210
    CGT liability 68, 90–5
    employee share schemes 80

gifts of to charities 33, 45, 46–7, 51, 56
last-in-first-out (LIFO) basis 92
share-pooling 79, 92–4, 95
single premium life insurance bonds 73, **267**
small gifts 75
Society of Trust and Estate Practitioners (STEP) 186
solicitors 185, 186–7, 188–9
sovereigns 66
specific gifts 190–1, 197, **267**
split-capital investment trusts 245
Sports Councils 58, 60
stakeholder pension schemes 257
contributions for someone else 73, 225, 245, 249, 250
survivorship destination 128, **268**
survivorship provision 177

taper relief
CGT 79, 80, 81, 82, 84–5, 92, 95, 96, 97, 100–1, 102, 103, 104, 105, **260**
IHT 115, 196, **268**
tax
anti-avoidance rules 128–9, 147, 220–1, 243, 244, 245
intestacy and 184
refunds, donation to charity 41–2
see also capital gains tax (CGT); income tax; inheritance tax (IHT)
tax credits
child tax credit 38, 40, 248
and gift aid 38–9
trust income and 152, 161
working tax credit 38
tax-bearing gifts 197, 199–200
tax-free gifts
gifts under your will 196, 197, 198
IHT reduced by using 221
to charities 221
to family and friends 65–77, 223

tenancy in common 125, 126, 127, 238, 239, **268**
term insurance 118, 223, 224
traded options 168–9
Trustee Act 2000 137, 139, 141, 183
Trustee Investments Act 1961 139
trustees 132, 134, 136–41, **268**
accounts 140
appointment 137
beneficiaries as 136–7
challenging the actions of 136
conflicts of interest 136, 139
delegation 138
duty to act jointly 141
duty to take reasonable care 138, 139–40
expenses 138
investment decisions 138–9, 140
maximum number 136
new trustees 139
powers and duties 137–41
professional trustees 138, 140, 141
removal 136, 137
trusts 16, 103, 131–65, 176, 218–19, **268**
accounts 140
appropriate circumstances for using 132–3
beneficiaries 132, 133, 134, 135–6, **260**
consulting 141
fairness between 140
with life interest 135, 136
multiple beneficiaries 135
payments to 134, 137, 150, 152–3, 159, 162–3
with reversionary interest 135
as trustees 136–7
CGT liability 68–9, 149, 151–2, 153, 154, 156, 159, 162, 163
creating a trust 131–2, 133–4
defined 131
flexible trusts 136, 230

gift with reservation rules 164
IHT liability 149, 151, 153–4,
    155, 156–7, 162, 163, 164,
    218–19
investment criteria 138–9
legal requirements 133, 134
lifetime gifts to 151, 156, 162,
    171, 221–2
maximum lifetime 134
periodic charge 156
purposes of 131
retained interest rules 163
set up under a will 54, 55, 144,
    218–19
settlor 132, 135–3, **267**
tax-efficiency 131, 133
tax treatment 133, 141, 142,
    149–65
trust deeds 53, 132, 133, 134,
    136, 137
trustees see trustees
types of 141–8
writing an insurance policy in
    trust 134, 216, 223, 225, 247
see also accumulation-and-
    maintenance trusts; bare trusts;
    charitable trusts; disabled trusts;
    discretionary trusts; family
    wealth trusts; interest-in
    possession trusts; retained
    interest trusts; settlor-interested
    trusts; will trusts

unit trusts
    CGT liability and 90
    gifts of to charities 33, 46, 56
    investments for children 245, 249,
        250
    share-based trusts 254–5
unmarried partners 177, 182–3, 193,
    238–9

Venture Capital Trusts (VCTs) 68,
    268
vintage and classic cars 67

wealth
    distribution in UK 13, 14
    taxation of transfer 13–16
    see also inheritance tax
wealth taxes 13
wedding gifts 75–6, 77
whole-life policy 224, 225, 227–8,
    268
will 175–94, 238–9
    administrator 176, **259**
    alteration after death 232–4
    beneficiaries 176, **260**
    charitable bequests 49–50, 54
    claims against the estate 177, 183,
        193–4
    codicils 191, **261**
    drawing up 185–9
    dying without see intestacy
    exclusion of dependants 193
        194
    executors 176, 188, 189–90,
        262
    gifts under 17, 190–3, 197–207,
        216
    legacies 192, **261**
    living wills 188, 189
    meaning of term 175, **268**
    mirror wills 186, 188
    personal representative 176, 177,
        192, 212, **266**
    residuary gifts 192–3, 197, **267**
    revising 190–1
    revoking 190, 191
    separation/divorce/remarriage
        and 190
    solicitors and 185, 186–7, 188–9
    specific gifts 190–1, 197, **267**
    storage 188–9
    testator/testatrix 176, **268**
    variation 232–4, **268**
    witnesses 186
    writing your own will 185–6
    see also estate
will trusts 54, 55, 144, 218–19
will-writing firms 187–8
working tax credit 38